IN THE MAGIC LAND OF PEYOTE

THE TEXAS PAN AMERICAN SERIES

In the Magic

UNIVERSITY OF TEXAS PRESS • AUSTIN AND LONDON

Land of Peyote

by Fernando Benítez *1911-*

Introduction by Peter T. Furst
Translated by John Upton

The Texas Pan American Series is published with the assistance of a revolving publication fund established by the Pan American Sulphur Company.

Library of Congress Cataloging in Publication Data

Benítez, Fernando, 1911–
  In the magic land of peyote.

  (Texas pan-American series)
  Translation of En la tierra mágica del peyote, first published as part of v. 2 of the author's Los indios de México.
  Includes bibliographical references and index.
  1. Huichol Indians. 2. Peyotism—Mexico. I. Title.
F1221.H9B413   970.3   74-23171

ISBN 0-292-73806-4

CONTENTS

ILLUSTRATIONS

INTRODUCTION

Seventy-five years have elapsed between the publication in 1900 of the first description of a Huichol peyote pilgrimage by Carl Lumholtz, the Norwegian pioneer ethnographer of northwest Mexican Indians, and the appearance in English of Mexican author Fernando Benítez's personal story of this most authentically pre-Columbian of Indian rituals surviving in modern Mexico. In these seventy-five years the Huicholes, of whom some eight to ten thousand—many still monolingual—live in the rugged Sierra Madre Occidental at altitudes ranging from five to seven thousand feet, have experienced their most intensive acculturative pressures. Also during this time, great technological changes have been superimposed upon their traditional lifeway as subsistence slash-and-burn *milpa* farmers.

And yet, reading Benítez's sensitive and insightful chronicle, and thinking back over my own experiences on two such pilgrimages, I am impressed by how little substantive change has occurred in the content of the sacred journey from the time of Lumholtz to the present. The sequence of events may vary a bit, some things may be left out and others added, but the basic structure is intact. Nor should the variances bother us. Within a generally uniform cosmology and world view, a degree of ideological idiosyncrasy is almost built into the Huichol system: some beliefs and ceremonies have different values in one *comunidad* than in another, the ranking of different deities in the crowded pantheon may vary from one area to the next, myths considered of great importance by one shaman (Huichol: *mara'akame*) may be slighted by another, and so on.

That no two Huichol shamans agree completely on every detail of the sacred stories was already noted by the German ethnographer Konrad Theodor Preuss (d. 1938), who spent many months among the Huicholes and Coras a decade after Lumholtz, recording Huichol myths and making an intensive study of the religion of the Coras, their immediate neighbors as well as closest linguistic and cultural cousins. In addition, the Huicholes admire creativity in their shaman-singers (provided they remain within the generally accepted norms and perform the crucial rituals in the proper manner), and that makes some artistic license acceptable. Finally, we must remember that what we see as Huichol religion today almost certainly includes a synthesis of several distinct, though ultimately related, pre-Hispanic traditions. Some of these must have come into the sierra from the Pacific coastal plains to the west, some from the north-central desert where a major component of Huichol culture is ultimately rooted, and some even from central Mexico, mediated, apparently, by Tlaxcalan Indians whom the colonial Spaniards of the sixteenth century placed as buffers on the Huichol frontier. (Although there was some Spanish presence in the sierra as early as the mid–sixteen hundreds, the Huichol country, and that of the Coras, was not formally brought under colonial control until 1722, two centuries after the conquest of Mexico as a whole.)

In the peyote pilgrimage itself, there are also the inevitable modifications of tradition that result from the gradual adoption of wheeled transport by parties of peyote seekers for at least a portion of the three-hundred-mile distance separating their ranchos from Wirikuta, the sacred land of the peyote cactus (*Lophophora williamsii*, Huichol: *hikuli* or *hikuri*) in the north-central Mexican desert in the state of San Luis Potosí. Although, as in Lumholtz's day, some pilgrims (*hikuritámete*) still insist on walking the whole way—usually in fulfillment of a vow made to the gods in exchange for a divine favor, such as the curing of an illness—it is by no means unusual nowadays to encounter *peyoteros* aboard trucks, buses, wagons, or even the train, either on their way to or returning from Wirikuta.

This whole question of walking versus riding on so sacred and traditional an enterprise as the peyote pilgrimage (actually a hunt in the literal sense, since *hikuri* is perceived as qualitatively "the same" as the divine Deer and must be "stalked" and ritually "slain" as such before it will allow itself to be harvested) again underscores the remarkable flexibility of Huichol intellectual culture. It is generally agreed among the Indians that riding to the peyote country is all right as long as all the sacred places established on the primordial peyote pilgrimage of the ancestral deities are visited or at least ritually acknowledged, and as long as one does not violate the actual abode of the Deer-Peyote with modern vehicles but alights from them at some distance. There is nonetheless a certain nostalgia for the old ways. Asked whether they preferred the comfort and relative speed of our vehicles to walking across mountains and desert for two or three weeks on near-empty stomachs, our Huichol companions replied that "walking is more beautiful." On our 1968 pilgrimage they overcame the conflict to some degree by insisting, with typical Huichol humor, that they were not really riding in cars at all but going on foot. Before starting out from Nayarit they asked the gods to make their sandals strong for the long and arduous *walk*, and they also composed a song about the cars: "This machine, this machine in which we ride," they sang amid gales of laughter, "is so good for walking, so good for walking, to the land of our ancestors, to the land of the brilliant-colored flower [peyote]."

Actually, even in the time of Lumholtz's visit in the last decade of the nineteenth century, mules or, more often, burros—both Spanish introductions—were frequently employed on the pilgrimage as beasts of burden, to carry the heavy baskets filled with peyote on the final leg of the long journey from San Luis Potosí in the east (where Wirikuta roughly coincides with the old colonial Spanish mining district of Real de Catorce), across Zacatecas, and back to the safety of the rugged sierra. Here the Huicholes live to this day not in villages or even hamlets, but in widely dispersed, semiautonomous extended family ranchos. Each of these has its headman or elder, who is usually also the residential kin group's shaman. Also, each rancho has its *xiriki*, a small thatched hut where the sacred paraphernalia are kept and that serves as the house of the *urukame* (from *uru* = arrow), a deceased shaman who has returned to dwell among his kin as a household god or guardian spirit in the form of a rock crystal tied to a composite wooden-pointed hunting arrow.

Beyond the rancho with its family oratory is the *calihuey* (from the Aztec *huey* = big, *calli* = house) district, centered on the large circular native temple, which in Huichol is called *tuki* or *tukipa*. Of these *tukis*, there are several for each of the five territorial *comunidades* that together comprise the Huichol homeland as a whole. The membership of a peyote pilgrimage may consist of a few people from the same residential kin group only, or it may, as it usually is, be made up from representatives of several related or unrelated ranchos in a *calihuey* district. Much of the rich traditional ceremonial life takes place at home, in the different ranchos, or in the forests, caves, and other sacred places, while the ceremonial centers, the domain of the elected indigenous civil-religious hierarchy headed by a *tatuan* or *gobernador*, stand virtually empty for most of the year. Only on certain ceremonial occasions that involve the entire *comunidad*—for the most part Spanish-Catholic observances, such as Holy Week or the annual changing of the civil-religious hierarchy, that have become heavily Indianized since their introduction in the early eighteenth century—do they become crowded with celebrants from near and distant ranchos and the larger *rancherías*. It is a pattern that is familiar from other parts of Mesoamerica as well, particularly the Maya country. The difference—and it is a crucial one—is in the absence of permanent population groups larger than the extended family, and the fact that for many of these small kin groups, which rarely exceed fifteen or twenty souls, a visit to their closest neighbors may involve hours of difficult walking.

It is, in fact, the characteristic Huichol settlement pattern of scattered small-scale kin groups enjoying a high degree of autonomy that helps explain the remarkable integrity of the autochthonous intellectual culture four and a half centuries after the fall of the Aztecs. Try as they might, even after 1722 the Spaniards were never able to force the Huicholes off their ranchos and into larger pueblos, where they might have been subjected to sustained instruction in the Catholic faith and where the influence of their shamans might have been more successfully uprooted. Instead, as anthropologist

Evon Vogt has noted, the typical response of the Huicholes when acculturative pressures became too great was to abandon their ranchos and cultivated fields and retreat into even less accessible reaches of the sierra.

There is still some of that isolation, but the situation is rapidly changing. Airstrips have existed on several mesas for some years, and, even as this is being written, the first roads in history are being constructed, virtually by hand, to link the interior of the Huichol sierra with the larger world outside. While this will facilitate exploitation of natural resources—particularly the forestlands—and the movement of cattle, and presumably will be of some immediate economic benefit to *some* of the Indians, one cannot help but be uneasy about the ultimate consequences of increasing modernization. Certainly some Huicholes are.

In Lumholtz's time, of course, there was no way to get into and out of, or around, the Huichol country except on foot. One senses something of the incredible hardships of his extended fieldwork as a collector of ritual art and ethnographic data for the American Museum of Natural History when he tells us that there were times of such total exhaustion that only the stimulating effects of a fresh peyote cactus eaten whole enabled him to go on. That is an interesting point: the whole Huichol universe is magical and sacred, without any sharp divisions between what is "sacred" and what is "secular," in our sense of those terms, but what is sacrosanct and even divine in one context can, like peyote, be treated simply as an efficacious medicine in another. Lumholtz certainly understood the essential meaning of *hikuri* in the Huichol world view. He recognized the pilgrimage as crucial to the very survival of the indigenous lifeway: the little *hikuri* cactus, he wrote, is to the Indians the very "plant of life," and only by following in the footsteps of the divine ancestral *peyoteros* would one have the vision of the meaning of being Huichol. And that has never changed.

Lumholtz himself was not able to accompany a peyote pilgrimage—an opportunity that was not to present itself to even the most sympathetic stranger until decades later—but he managed to obtain from his informants a good description of it, and also some of the mythology that provides the charter for the pilgrimage. This he published first in his scholarly American Museum monograph, *Symbolism of the Huichol Indians* (1900), a classic of its kind, and subsequently in *Unknown Mexico* (1902), the fascinating two-volume chronicle of his travels and explorations among the Huicholes, Tepehuanos, Coras, Tarascans, and other indigenous Mesoamerican peoples.

That Lumholtz's account of the *hikuri* quest, however unique, evoked no great response among students of culture in his day is surprising only from our vantage point. There was not then a particular interest in "hallucinogens" and the ecstatic experience as a phenomenon of American Indian cultures, and, furthermore, with the publication of Matilda Coxe Stevenson's massive Zuñi Report (1901–1902) by the Bureau of American Ethnology and similar studies of traditional North American Indian cultures, there did not then seem to be anything especially remarkable about a Mexican Indian population whose aboriginal ceremonial had managed to survive relatively intact into modern times. Furthermore, the Huicholes lived in virtual isolation from the outside world in extremely difficult country, not to mention the fact that for decades after the revolution of 1910 the Huichol sierra was the haven of contending armies, including that of Pancho Villa. Even the bloody Cristero revolt did not leave the Huicholes untouched. Conditions in the Huichol country, then, were hardly propitious for scholarly fieldwork in the years from before World War I to at least the 1930s.

In any event, there was no rush to follow up on Lumholtz's secondary description by studying the peyote rites firsthand. In fact, not just before the 1930s, but even by the 1960s, barely a handful of ethnologists had ever visited the Huicholes, much less attempted to carry out in-depth studies of their culture. Even keeping in mind the limitations mentioned above, this is not quite so easily explained, considering that after Lumholtz there could be no doubt that Huichol religion was at the very least far less modified by Spanish Catholicism than any other in Mexico and therefore offered unique opportunities for a better understanding of pre-Hispanic religion, and also that in North America a new, syncretistic pan-Indian religion with peyote as its sacramental focus had already by the end of the nineteenth century begun to spread northward through the plains from the Mexican border, raising questions of origins that are still not wholly resolved. Furthermore, as the linguist Joseph E. Grimes, who spent most of the 1950s and 1960s studying Huichol (a member of the Aztecoidan branch of the Uto-Aztecan language family), has noted in his *Huichol Syntax* (1964), even the Huichol language had "come through white contact relatively unscathed," meaning that it retains, like the world view, a basically aboriginal pattern. So there should have been much to attract scholars from the outside world.

Apart from Lumholtz, however, before World War II only two ethnographers, the German Preuss and the American Robert M. Zingg, made extensive collections of Huichol mythology and oral traditions, the former a decade after Lumholtz, the latter in the 1930s. Neither went on a peyote quest. Zingg published abstracts of many myths in his book *The Huicholes: Primitive Artists* (1938), but for the *hikuri* hunt itself he had to content himself with confirming and augmenting Lumholtz's account through his own informants. Preuss published an important book on the religion of the Coras (1912), but apart from brief articles on Huichol belief and ritual, which appeared in print before his death in 1938, his unpublished collection of over sixty Huichol narratives, presumably including peyote traditions, was destroyed in bombing raids during World War II. Ironically, his publisher in Leipzig was about ready to go to press with the edited Huichol manuscript when the bombs fell; the only other copy in the late scholar's home was lost, along with his field notes and other effects, in an Allied air raid on Berlin in March 1944.

The picture has changed considerably since the early 1960s. Indeed, the mere trickle of visitors of former decades has at times threatened to turn into a flood—not always, one fears, to the benefit of the Indians. Many Huicholes are fine artists, and their colorful yarn paintings, especially, have found a ready market. Inevitably there has been exploitation (low prices to the Indians, high prices in U.S. galleries), as well as copying of published Huichol art, resulting in loss of originality and quality. Also, apart from serious students of Huichol language and culture, there has been a veritable pilgrimage to Huichol-land of alienated middle-class romantics, who, though ignorant of the meaning of "being Huichol," come in search of gurus comparable to Carlos Castaneda's don Juan and of instant religious revelation via the peyote trip. I suppose all that was inevitable. Anthropologists, other than those in the applied or action fields, like to count themselves among those whose impact on traditional cultures is minimal and whose appearance on the indigenous scene results in the least amount of disruption and change. Whether or not such self-congratulation is justified, in the case of societies that, like the Huicholes, focus on some botanical hallucinogen for sacred purposes, we must plead guilty at the very least to having helped inspire with our published work the minor plague of would-be mystics that have of late imposed themselves on the Huicholes and other Indians.

Fernando Benítez is not an anthropologist, at least not in the sense of formal academic training. He is a well-known Mexican journalist-historian, editor, and social critic and, above all, a sensitive and informed *aficionado* of the surviving Indian cultures of his native Mexico, the subject of his most recent four-volume work, *Los indios de México* (1970–1974). To U.S. readers he is perhaps best known for two of his books that have appeared in English, *In the Footsteps of Cortés* (1952) and, more recently, *The Century after Cortés* (1965), a brilliant historical study of the formation of Mexico's ruling class, the Creoles, children of the *conquistadores* and of the first Spanish immigrants born in Mexico, and of the despotic sixteenth- and seventeenth-century colonialism, which he thinks inevitably left its mark on the historic and contemporary Mexican national character. The present book should thus not be read as an anthropological work, but as the personal observations of a well-informed, humanistic, and erudite chronicler who brings to his craft substantial insights drawn from anthropology, along with a great respect not only for his country's Indian past but also for the validity of living cultural systems different from the dominant society.

Something needs to be said about how this book came to be. It is actually excerpted from his *magnum opus* about Mexico's Indians and came to be published separately in Spanish in 1968 because of the special circumstances then surrounding Huichol studies. As Benítez notes in his Prologue, he had long been disturbed at the imbalance in anthropological research among the native peoples of Mexico, who always seemed to draw greater interest from foreign scholars than from Mexicans. Mexicans, he felt, should be at least as eager as their foreign colleagues to chronicle every aspect of the living Indian component of their own self-professed Spanish-Indian national culture, and the necessary resources should be made available to accomplish this. Since Benítez voiced these feelings the situation has improved considerably for Mexican anthropology, but the essential validity of his argument is evident even now when one looks for anthropological works in Spanish about the Indians of Mesoamerica. The majority, including those published by the Instituto Nacional Indigenista, are authored by non-Mexicans; in INI's list of hard-cover monographs there is only one—a very good one— on an indigenous religion, that of the Totonacs of the Sierra Madre Oriental, and it is by a French anthropologist, Alain Ichon.

In any event, in 1968, when Benítez was preparing the second volume of his four-volume work, which was to deal largely with the Huicholes, he learned that, while he had evidently been the first non-Indian to have gone on a peyote hunt, the pilgrimage had finally also been experienced by anthropologists who, alas, were non-Mexicans. Accordingly, he decided to publish the chapters on his own peyote pilgrimage at once as a separate book, under the title *En la tierra mágica del peyote.*

It so happens that the foreign anthropologists who in December of 1966 had accompanied a group of *peyoteros* to the sacred land of the *hikuri* were Barbara G. Myerhoff, whose own book, *The Peyote Hunt,* an affectionate anthropological exploration of the rich symbolic world of the Huicholes, appeared in 1974, and myself (I did not then know Benítez). In December 1968, my wife, Dee, and I were able to experience a second peyote hunt. As in 1966, the pilgrimage was led by the late Ramón Medina, an extraordinarily gifted and charismatic artist who was in the process of becoming a *mara'akame*, and who permitted us to make a 16-mm documentary film record of the sacred journey—his fifth and, hence, the crucial time of his "completion" as a shaman. Benítez knew him, too, and at least some of his perceptions stem from that association, although it was another, and very famous, shaman, Hilario by name, who led his particular pilgrimage. Ramón's death in the summer of 1971 was a great loss, to us as well as to his people.

One goes on the peyote hunt, say the Huicholes, "to find one's life." The shamans tell stories of how it all began, "in the time of our grandfathers." According to one version, related by Ramón, one night long ago, Tatewarí, Our Grandfather, the Great Mara'akame who is the divine fire, called the ancient ones to assemble in the *tuki*. Those old ones, those who are now gods, arrived and seated themselves in a circle around their shaman. But they were ill—one with a pounding in his head, another with cramps in his stomach, a third with an ache in his shoulders. "Cure us, Tatewarí, cure us, Our Grandfather," they implored the great shaman, who had put the world in order, who had set up the trees of the four cardinal points and the sacred center that hold up the sky, "tell us why we are weak and in pain." And Tatewarí told them they were not well because they had not gone to Wirikuta, to hunt the divine peyote who was Deer, as their ancestors had done and as it is proper for Huicholes to do. "Let us walk together to Wirikuta, there in the east, there where is the Burned Hill, there where is the Deer," he told them, "and you will find your life."

So the ancient ones prepared themselves in the proper manner, purifying themselves, abstaining from their wives and from salt. Those of their families who remained behind laid a fire with the wood that is the favorite food of Tatewarí. The fire had to burn day and night, never being allowed to die so long as the *peyoteros* were gone. As they headed east, walking in single file, each in his proper place behind Tatewarí, the principal log of the fire pointed east, as it would point west during the journey home. At their head walked Tatewarí himself, playing his bowstring with his arrow as he went.

Behind him walked his first assistant, Tatutsí (Great-grandfather), and Tamats Maxa Kwaxí (pron. Masha Kwashí), Elder Brother Deer Tail, and all the others who were animals and people at the same time.

The journey was hard, very hard, beset by dangers and many difficulties. Some were not strong enough: Rabbit Person saw a cactus thicket and chose it for his home, preferring to remain there for all his life. The others sang a song about him and Tatewarí named the place "In the Cactus." However far they traveled, in the same manner he named all the different places where they camped, where they assembled in council, where they cooked their tortillas. When they came to where the *uxa* bush grows, they cut its branches and from them ground the yellow face paint with which *peyoteros* decorate themselves. That is why that place is called "Where They Ground Their Face Paint." When they arrived at "Where the Clouds Clash Together," where one must pass through to that other world, Tatewarí asked Deer to hold the dangerous clouds back with his antlers, so that all could pass safely to the other side.

Again they walked until, more dead than alive, they arrived at Tatei Matinieri, "Where Our Mothers Live." There some Huichol women, all dressed in their finest clothes, awaited them. And from these women, who are Our Mothers (the female deities of springs, water holes, rain, and fertility), the ancient ones received their first water. The Mothers gave them water to drink, water with which to wash their hair in the proper ritual manner, and water to take back to their ranchos for the ceremonies. That is why on the peyote hunt one goes to Tatei Matinieri, for those who travel to Wirikuta are like the ancient gods, those who were the first to make that journey.

From the place of Our Mothers they could already see the distant mountains of Wirikuta, where Deer was waiting. Refreshed and filled with gratitude, for without the life-giving water of Our Mothers they would surely have perished in the desert, they left prayer arrows, flowers, and other offerings. Then, "as they were all happy and of one heart," the Mothers accompanied the men, and when on the next day, or the next, they arrived in Wirikuta and at last, perceiving the Deer that was the divine *hikuri*, pursued and killed him with their arrows, they ate his flesh and learned "how one goes about being Huichol."

Fernando Benítez, too, came to understand some of that, and through his eyes and his heart so may we.

Peter T. Furst

The Huichol Indians are great travelers. Every year they set out on journeys to the coast of Nayarit where Haramara, the goddess of the sea, lives; to Teakata, the region of the caves in the heart of the sierra where Tatewarí, Grandfather Fire, was born; to the Nayar Mesa where the Cora Indians worship their god Tsakaimuka; to Xapawiyemetá, a mysterious place on Lake Chapala where stands Xapa (*Ficus* spp.), the Tree That Rains, also known as the Goddess of Paper; and to Catorce, the far desert in the state of San Luis Potosí, the home of Tamats Kauyumari, Elder Brother Deer Tail, where the peyote grows and which the Huicholes call Wirikuta, and also Parítsika.

This last, a region known to the Huicholes as the Middle World, is a vast holy land. It was there that the gods performed their deeds of creation at the beginning of time. There is hardly a rock, spring, pool, plant, cave, ravine, or hill that is not bound up with some mythic event or complex ritual. Like Cézanne, the Huicholes have re-created the landscape; and, though their purpose was religious rather than aesthetic, they have done so with equal profundity and beauty. What we see as a commonplace object may be for them a *kakauyari*, a supernatural being who failed to withstand the rigors of creation and with the birth of the sun was transformed into a stone or a bush.

Sometimes a rock bears the imprint of a god's hand or foot; a scorched hollow high on a mountain is the crater left when the new-born sun shot up; a certain yellow root is the sacred ingredient of the symbolic face paint worn by those who have made the journey to Wirikuta.

Not all divine matters are marked by tangible manifestations. During the pilgrimage to Catorce the shamans open invisible doors with their eagle-feather scepters (*muwieris*); and they ascend the heights of Reunar, the Burned Hill, by way of an ethereal shamanic stairway furnished with five blue altars.

The principal features of this landscape have been translated into religious codes, some of which are extraordinarily complex. Among these is that of the sacred cactus, which is at the same time peyote, deer, and corn. The intimate association of a deity proper to a gathering culture—the peyote—with that of hunters—the deer—and another representing agricultural peoples—the corn—not only rules the Huicholes' lives, but also presents the culmination of a mythic and religious symbology that has been only superficially investigated.

As the Norwegian explorer and anthropologist Carl Lumholtz pointed out, the most important of all the Huichol pilgrimages is that dedicated to the peyote. Although he never left the sierra and was unable to make the trip himself, Lumholtz devoted five pages of his *Unknown Mexico* to a cursory description of the journey.

Forty years later the second great student of Huichol culture, Robert Mowry Zingg, reproduced his predecessor's account in an annotated form. In Zingg's opinion, Lumholtz's "dramatization of the peyote myth" had been recorded with such care, penetration, and detail that it must be considered an unequalled contribution to the literature of anthropology.[1]

Lumholtz's work is, in fact, that of a pioneer. In spite of the conditions at the time, when it was all but impossible to make such a journey—the Huicholes refusing to take any stranger with them, even a Mexican—the famous explorer was able to trace its broad outlines and to observe that the route "was marked by religious associations from beginning to end." In order to learn what these associations were, however, and relate them to the mythology, or even to list the ritual ceremonies performed during the long and arduous trip, it would have been absolutely necessary to observe their practices *in situ.*

Although the Indians' attitude of wariness and suspicion has changed little since Lumholtz's day, a series of lucky circumstances finally made it possible for me to accompany the pilgrims when they set out from a little village hidden in the mountains. I visited the key sites along the way and was present at the most important ceremonies. Later, thanks to the testimony of several shamans, I was able to fill in the most obvious gaps and establish the itinerary. Even so, I was not entirely satisfied. Tribal troubles, together with the prevailing hostility in the sierra, kept me from completing an accurate picture of what may well be considered the best-preserved body of archaic myth and ritual in Middle America.

Although I intend to present the bulk of my investigations in another volume, I have decided to publish this account of my trip—a complete book in itself—in view of the not at all remote possibility that some foreigner may have the honor of being the first (as usually happens) to bring out a study on these vital aspects of our society today.[2]

Perhaps it is needless to say that I am not nationalistic, and that I have no objection to foreigners working in our fields; it is to them that we owe fundamental studies, and their competition should serve as a stimulant. What I do deplore is the underdeveloped state of Mexican ethnography. The valuable work done by Pozas, Aguirre Beltrán, and Pablo González Casanova (the culmination of the impetus given to ethnography by Gamio) only points to the mediocrity of current field studies. It is not that we lack ethnologists, but that they are not encouraged or given adequate funds. Our people are condemned to vegetate while composing little monographs or working as assistants to foreign anthropologists. Thus ends a sorry tale: nearly always it was the foreigners who began the basic research, and it is they who seem destined to document the death throes and final extinction of our surviving cultures.

Paradoxically, our decadence coincides with the revolution and unprecedented increase in ethnographic studies throughout the world. Thus there is an urgent need for us to put new life into this branch of anthropology, to set up ambitious programs for our young people and provide them with proper funds.

In a recent work by Jean Cazeneuve, where the author presents a sketch showing the geographical distribution of primitive groups, the map of Mexico appears as a blank. Cazeneuve observes: "We shall not concern ourselves here with the ancient Toltecs and Mayas, nor with the Aztec empire, the study of which belongs more to archaeology and history than to ethnography. These cultures were wiped out completely by the Spanish conquest, and today nothing remains but ruins or ancient customs more or less driven underground by evangelization and Western civilization. All the ethnographer can find to study there is an occasional survival from an illustrious past."[3]

Cazeneuve's statement stems not only from the paucity of ethnographic literature but also from ignorance of the facts about Mexico. We know as much as Cazeneuve about the Chochos, the Amusgos, the Itzáes, the Tojolabales, and the Mames—which is to say little or nothing. More than eighty languages, with their dialects, are spoken in Mexico today; and many isolated groups in the mountains and jungles still cling to their myths, their religions, and their primitive customs. We are essentially ignorant concerning many of these cultures. No one has taken the trouble to make a map of Indian mythologies—indispensable if we are to comprehend such societies— or to examine the changes, vicissitudes, and incredible adventures undergone since the conquest by the large Aztec, Mixtec, Mayan, and Totonac groups. Here can be found every variety of religion, from animism to Catholicism; every cultural stage, from the Neolithic to twentieth-century industrial society; and every aspect of the painful and instructive process of decolonization. An Aztec from Mexico City is not the same as an Aztec from Chiapas, Oaxaca, or the slopes of Popocatépetl, any more than a Mixtec from the city of Oaxaca is the same as a Triqui or an inhabitant of Tilantongo or Tututepec.

Material for the ethnologist is inexhaustible. We cannot even complain too much about the lack of money; huge sums, undreamed of by Gamio at Teotihuacán, Caso at Monte Albán, or Alberto Ruz at

Palenque, are now granted for certain projects. A very small part of this money could be dedicated to some worthwhile studies of indigenous groups that have not as yet been the objects of serious research, thus giving our young people the opportunity of enriching a social science that is today in total decline in this country.

We are living in the era of structuralism, that revolution and reaction against a series of concepts reigning until quite recently in philosophy, language, and ethnography. It is an imperialism in that it is a scientific method in search of the hidden structure in apparent organization, ordering and classifying observed elements according to their relationships and, especially, their differences. It has thus replaced the psychological system as a means of explaining anomalisms. After all, as Jean-François Kahn has pointed out in a particularly lucid résumé, "This antihumanism has not yet rejected Sartre's quite simple observation that perhaps man is what structures have made of him; but the problem is to discover what man, in turn, makes of what they have made of him."

This, then, is structuralistic imperialism. It seems to be our destiny to be unable to elude some form of imperialism; but this one, at least, does not tie us hand and foot or imprison us. Rather it opens new perspectives for the study of the human condition, allowing us to investigate what lies hidden within those structures as well as the ways in which the ancient and the modern Mexican have reacted to them.

IN THE MAGIC LAND OF PEYOTE

Why Do We Study Indians?

The little two-engine plane ran the length of the runway and abruptly took to the air, heading for the Sierra Madre Occidental across the hot, luminous valleys of Tepic. I could not help reflecting that the Coras and perhaps some ancestral Huicholes once lived in these valleys, so rich in tobacco, sugar cane, and corn. The conquest, of course, had driven them out of their paradise, their sea teeming with fish, their ceremonial centers, and they had retreated into the lonely mountains to the northwest—then, as now, a kind of holy land.

The plane gained altitude and entered the mountain range. The landscape was lovely. Small extinct volcanoes came into view, clothed in green velvet like precious objects in Nature's boudoir. Dark rivulets of lava reached to the cultivated plains that were turning gold with the approach of autumn. The cool, blue-green vegetation on the hillsides and the round white clouds clustered above the mountain peaks were reminders of the recent rains.

Then that open, geometric, civilized landscape vanished, and in its place appeared another that has not changed in five thousand years. That is to say, we moved, with no transition, from the Tepic of the nineteenth century—we cannot say it has ever really lived in the twentieth—into the neolithic. From this solitude, this realm of eagles, we could see a stormy surf of stone rising below us. Nearly every word the Spanish language has for mountains and their never-ending variety of formations was represented here: *abismo, altos, barranco, cadena, cantil, ceja, cerro, cordillera, cresta, desbarranca-dero, despeñadero, espigón, farallón, laja, loma, mesa, mogote, monte, peña, peñasco, peñolería, peñón, picacho, pico, puerto, re-ventazón, serranía,* and *tablón.*[1]

The words buried in the dictionary came to life, taking on color, nuance, sharpness, depth, and drama. Victor Hugo's romantic image of "an arrested tempest" came to mind again and again, for every-thing in the Sierra Madre Occidental, seen from above, seemed strangely motionless. The forests and ravines were dark stains and fissures; the hills and passes displayed the texture of straw; the rivers at the bottom of the canyons stood still. Beyond this world of boul-ders, this labyrinth of stone, hung the pearly tints, the transparent blues, and the liquid violets of the distant mountains.

From time to time a tiny hut with its corn patch appeared on a mountain side and then was lost to view; this trace of man afforded a truer measure of the infinite loneliness of the sierra than any im-pressive geographical feature.

After flying for an hour and a half, our bimotor dropped suddenly toward a forest of oaks and pines, grazed the treetops, and came down on the San Andrés landing strip. All I can remember is a row of Huichol Indians standing at the edge of the field in a flaming sea of purple and yellow sunflowers, and the sense of surprise that in-variably accompanies these first encounters. It was like landing in Tarahumara or Mixtec country, or in the highlands of Chiapas. There they were—Tarahumaras, Mixtecs, Tzeltales, or Huicholes—standing in their native landscape, speaking a different language, and living lives I knew nothing of. They had not come looking for me; it was I who had searched them out. I looked into their eyes, and they returned my gaze with the same curiosity. "Who are you?" they seemed to be asking. "What is it you want?" I couldn't give them any answer, or even communicate with them. I was a strange being, and they seemed just as exotic to me.

Claude Lévi-Strauss has wondered how the ethnologist is to escape the contradiction arising from circumstances he himself has created. "He has a society at his disposal, right before his eyes: his own. Why does he choose instead to examine some other culture—chosen from among the most distant and dissimilar ones—with a patience and a devotion he denies to his fellow countrymen?"[2]

A man from Paris who travels seven thousand miles in order to study the customs of a handful of Indians has the right, no doubt, to ask himself that question. Can a Mexican who flies from his own capital to investigate Huichol culture do the same? These human beings, just as strange to us as the Nambikwara or the Bororo are to Lévi-Strauss, are nonetheless our fellow citizens; they may speak a different tongue, paint their faces, and have a religion and a manner of dress that seem to us exotic, but they are Mexicans in their own right.

These circumstances produce serious misunderstandings. The ethnologist soon discovers that being an Indian means being treated as an inferior, being depreciated and steadily exploited by the society of which the investigator is a member. Aware that this intruder represents that other culture, the Indians regard him with suspicion; they believe that he has come to steal their land or to do them harm in some way. The ethnologist, if he is an honest man, ends by becoming their defender; thus he not only loses the objectivity indispensable to his work, but he also turns his back on his own society without being able to become part of the one he is studying and defending. He can no longer calmly take notes on some religious ritual or symbolic art, knowing that that ritual and that art are objects of widespread exploitation. The problem is further complicated by the fact that the alienation of such a large segment of our population is detrimental to the economy and progress of the entire nation.

These were some of my feelings and thoughts as I began my investigation.

I had with me Carl Lumholtz's *Unknown Mexico*, illustrated with photographs of the Huicholes taken by the author with a camera that was then—in 1895—the last word in such equipment. It was at once evident that Lumholtz's Huicholes were not appreciably different from those standing along the airstrip at San Andrés. Their appearance had not changed in seventy years. The Norwegian explorer's camera, however, had somehow robbed the Indians of their beauty, reducing them to mere ghosts of themselves; the photographs were mummified documents, very much like the pictures found in morgue and prison files. The Huicholes I saw on the landing strip, on the other hand—though they had the same long hair and richly embroidered sashes and shoulder bags that Lumholtz's camera had recorded—were filled with life and beauty.

Two Ghost Towns

After a quarter of an hour in San Andrés, we took off for Mexquitic, one of the two principal *cabeceras municipales* (seats of local government) in the area. The other is Bolaños, which I had visited seven years earlier on my first trip to the sierra.

Bolaños is a ghost town. It was founded, with all the vigor and elegance of the eighteenth century, upon the wealth of its mines; but the wars of independence brought the industry to a standstill, and Bolaños—situated "at the tail-end of the world," according to its alcalde—never became a second Taxco. There are still a few mansions with fresco paintings, as ruined as the proud baroque churches that stand half-finished among the stones the masons were cutting on the eve of the revolution.

Mexquitic had no mines, but it, too, enjoyed a certain prosperity due to farming and cattle raising. There are no mansions here, nor was there ever any attempt to erect a sumptuous baroque church; but the eighteenth century left its mark on the doorways and carved stone work of some of the larger houses. The two towns are equally decayed and miserable today. The collapse of the mining industry, the exhausted soil, the lack of money for upgrading the livestock, isolation, and abandonment have made them twin villages. Although they lie at the entrance to the sierra and enjoy the position of governmental centers for the Huicholes, their poverty and the independent nature of the Indians have kept them from becoming white metropolises like Tlaxiaco and San Cristóbal de las Casas in southern Mexico.

The Huicholes visit the *cabeceras municipales* only when they install new authorities, have some judicial matter to settle, need supplies or certain items for their festivals, or bring cattle and objects of art to sell. The white world of Mexquitic and Bolaños, with its imperious alcaldes and town clerks, and the world of the Huicholes who live in their scattered mountain settlements are so dissimilar that, for better or worse, there can be no permanent contact between them.

Surprisingly enough, these tumble-down hamlets, these veritable skeletons of stone, are populated by some aristocratically handsome and vigorous Creole families. The women are matronly, the men are well built, and they have numerous children. Since there is not much to do in villages where the rains are meager and capricious, the young men tend to move away. They sign up as braceros—the only industry that survives today—or they become bus drivers, brick masons, priests, carpenters, and hired hands. Many end up in Mexico City or Guadalajara; some are lucky enough to remain as laborers in the United States. Those who have a little money stay at home to run their stores and cultivate their eroded parcels of land, sighing for the good old days that neither their fathers nor their grandfathers knew. They live without electricity, without running water, and without hope, much as minor noblemen of Castile might have lived fifty years ago as they watched the inevitable crumbling of their houses.

A Piece of Good Luck

In Mexquitic, what had begun as an exploratory trip with no well-defined objective suddenly turned into a mystic pilgrimage. The *gobernador* of Las Guayabas, a tiny Huichol village a short distance from San Andrés, had asked Professor Salvatierra, director of the Cora-Huichol Center, to provide him and his party with a bus for their annual journey to Wirikuta, the far land where the peyote grows. Eager to make friends among the Huicholes and break down their traditional mistrust of outsiders, Salvatierra had granted the *gobernador*'s request; moreover, he had been able to persuade him to let me go with them.

The pilgrims had departed from the *calihuey* at Las Guayabas two days earlier; now, together with the *gobernador* and two of his aides, we were to catch up with them at Valparaíso, a village in the state of Zacatecas near the sierra. From there we would all proceed to Fresnillo to meet the bus that would take us to Catorce, an old mining town in San Luis Potosí.

When I set out on the trip, all I knew about it was what I had read in the five pages Lumholtz had given to the subject in *Unknown Mexico*. I was not familiar with the classic itinerary, which according to the Norwegian explorer was rich in religious and mystic associations; I had no idea whether the route to be taken by the bus coincided with that traditionally followed by the Huicholes; and I did not even know if it was possible to reach the town of Catorce by means of modern transportation. None of these unknowns worried me, however. I was sure that an expedition that had begun in such an auspicious fashion would end successfully, and that Tamats Kauyumari, Elder Brother Deer Tail, the principal deity of the magic land of peyote, would look kindly upon me all the while.

I believe now that my ignorance only enhanced the mysterious fascination of that journey. The language, the ceremonies, the landscape, the enigmatic symbolism, and the shutting out of the profane world transported me into a kind of dream where I lived at the beginning of time, when the gods were engaged in their feats of creation.

Hilario, the Great "Mara'akame"

A few hours after my arrival in Mexquitic, Hilario Carrillo appeared with two religious functionaries. In his broad humanity— at first I saw him as Bernal Díaz del Castillo's "Fat Chief"—Hilario incorporated every office and honor a Huichol can hope for: *mara-'akame* or *cantador*,[3] medicine man, headman, and *gobernador* of Las Guayabas. He was stout, but still nimble at sixty or sixty-five. His hair, worn long in the medieval fashion and nearly always disheveled, was hardly touched with gray. Solidly built, he carried a paunch to match his broad shoulders, sturdy legs, and powerful hands.

In the days to come Hilario was to reveal himself as an extraordinary shaman and actor. His face, with its thick lips, slightly sagging jowls, and dark, gentle, intelligent eyes, was extremely expressive and pleasant. Calm, always self-possessed, he was a kind of Indian Gargantua.

In a shoulder bag Hilario carried his scepters of command, partially wrapped in red flags. These symbols of authority were gods that must be constantly revered and nourished, and he was never without them. The ends of the scepters rose behind his head, giving him the appearance of one of those Aztec warriors or princes whose complicated insignia seemed to be part of his body.

The Beginning of the Trip

We set out on Saturday, October 3. The back of the jeep was occupied by the *gobernador* Hilario with his two companions, the Italian photographer Marino Benzi, and Jerónimo, a young Huichol who represented the Indian Center. In front, next to the driver, rode Benzi's bizarre girl friend, Nicole, and myself.

This time I would be traveling away from the sierra toward the deserts of Zacatecas and not, as on previous occasions, into the states of Nayarit and Jalisco.

The first obstacle was the Mexquitic River. Cattle were slowly walking through the stream; pigs were swimming across, snorting and splashing as if their lives were in peril; some women, more inhibited than the animals and unwilling to show their legs in our presence, were wading through water up to their thighs without lifting their skirts, indifferent and dignified.

The jeep reached the farther side easily, raising waves and a wake that added to the confusion, and took the dirt track used only by a fleet of battered buses during the dry season. The road climbed uphill and down, over boulders and along creek beds, across corn patches, and through little clumps of mesquite and thorn bushes. On the horizon high mountain tops crowned with flat, almost horizontal mesas lent a kind of order to the baroque labyrinth of the sierra.

Farther on, the mountains gave way to small valleys covered with cornfields and a rich carpet of summer flowers. Often our vehicle was lost in an ocean of yellow and white blossoms and damp grasses that bent under the weight of their spikes.

We came out onto the plains of Zacatecas. The naked mineral hills flattened; the ravines, rocky cliffs, and mesas receded into the distance to become the far blue backdrop of the northern deserts. Everything was softened and still.

On the outskirts of Valparaíso stood a grove of silvery poplars; there were green fields, acacias, and broom brilliant with yellow flowers.

Valparaíso is a tumble-down village that naturally does not live up to its name. We took five rooms at an inn; but not until a fair's juke boxes and the movie theater's loud speakers were good enough to fall silent were we able to get to sleep.

We Find the Pilgrims

Sunday in Valparaíso was like Sunday in any village. As in the time of Goethe, the new day was announced by children's voices and the sound of sweeping. In the market old women toiled over their charcoal braziers and steaming kettles. It was a town of adobe houses with worn stone thresholds and Dutch doors; by opening only the upper half, light could be admitted to windowless rooms without letting in the street dogs.

Since this was the day we were to meet the peyote pilgrims, I decided to go out and look for them instead of waiting all morning with nothing to do. On the edge of the village I hired three horses; we left Hilario sitting under a tree and rode out of town with Jerónimo and the horses' owner as guide.

Little groups of farmers were coming into Valparaíso along the road lined by stone walls, cactuses, and mesquite bushes. The women, in their Sunday best, were riding burros. Some of the men were mounted on skinny nags, while others walked behind animals loaded with fruit or sugar cane.

"Have you seen any Huicholes?" the horses' owner asked them.

"No, excuse us, we haven't," they replied, with a kind of politeness that has disappeared from the world.

At the end of two hours we made a halt, and Jerónimo and our guide knocked down some prickly pears for us. They were bright red, tender, and very sweet.

When we had been resting for half an hour, a passing farmer told us that some Huicholes were approaching. We mounted, forded a small stream, and soon saw the travelers.

Although I had lived among the Huicholes, these pilgrims seemed like beings from another planet. After five days of traveling, their embroidered clothing was dirty and torn. They carried curved machetes, blade upward, and heavy baskets at their backs, suspended from a band across the chest. I did not know, of course, that the ten Indians represented and bore the name of a god and marched in accordance with a carefully established ritual. Even so, their slender figures, their bowed heads, their folded arms, and their faces—half-hidden beneath their hat brims—expressed a spirituality and an inner withdrawal so deep that they were in some way sanctified, as the desert landscape itself was sanctified by their presence.

We who live in cities, surrounded by crowds, are no longer aware of the beauty and meaning in the face of man. Thousands pass before us in a monotonous stream: pale, listless, inexpressive shapes with which we cannot communicate.

Hardly half a century ago the European or North American who visited those countries that have come to be known as the Third World was complaining that he could not tell one Chinaman from another, one Negro from another, or one Indian from another Indian. As it was impossible for the traveler (usually a man with a large nose and skin the color of a turnip or a carrot, clad in a bush jacket, pith helmet, boots, and an exaggerated notion of his own importance) to see how he himself looked in the midst of these dark people in turbans, silk robes, or loincloths, he failed to notice that it was he who was exotic. Today the roles have been reversed. The sight of Orientals and Africans in New York, Rome, Paris, and Moscow makes us realize how indistinguishable the citizens of these great capitals of the Western world have become. Our sameness, our uniformity would be unbearable if it were not for the fact that young people, with their long hair, their horror of asepsis, their wholesomely outlandish attire, and their contempt for convention, have introduced a regenerative element into the crushing dominion of mass media. These champions of individuality are as yet too few in number, however, to change the whole picture.

Hence the madness evoked by the "sacred monsters"—certain rulers, artists, and movie stars—that ranges from demanding autographs, standing in line in a futile attempt to get into the Grand Palais to see Picasso's paintings (800,000 admissions in one month), nudist weddings, and the compulsion to strip the last shred of clothing from some goddess of the screen to the assassination of President Kennedy. It also explains why we try to recover the beauty and originality we have sold so cheaply, by going to savage, primitive peoples—that is, to the men we once were and no longer are because of our stubborn determination to become "civilized." The surfeit of civilization is driving us toward what we had always thought of as the opposite pole: not exactly to freedom and the savage state, but to a different way of life with different relationships, where everything tends toward sanctification in the midst of a world that is being desanctified. The Huichol pilgrims typify the primitive peoples we are drawn to.

When Marino saw the Indians approaching, he threw himself from his horse, camera in hand, crouched, and performed all kinds of pirouettes and contortions. The pilgrims went on their way without even seeing him. They were going to a place peopled by gods and were making every effort to remain withdrawn. We were among the malevolent beings to be encountered along the way, this time in human form, and the Huicholes were determined to avoid any intercourse with us. Eyes lowered, they seemed not to notice Marino's maneuvers. They closed ranks and moved forward with the same light, almost ghostly tread, in spite of the slabs of automobile tire that served them as sandals and all the baskets, shoulder bags, bottles, and gourds with which they were loaded down.

Tatewarí, Grandfather Fire

Hilario sat on the bank of a dry creek and listened gravely to an account of the trip given him by his son Eusebio, the tall, one-eyed shaman who had led the expedition from Las Guayabas. The rest of the pilgrims were seated on the ground in the Huichol fashion: knees up and legs wide apart. Not far above us were the outlying houses of Valparaíso, and we could hear the faint sound of church bells.

Since the ceremonies were not to begin until late that afternoon, we left the Indians to their own affairs and went back to the village for lunch. When we returned at five, the *gobernador* was drinking beer in front of a little store at the side of the road. Some of the farmers we had seen earlier were returning home with their purchases of kerosene, sour apples, cloth, meat, and lard.

Hilario smoked incessantly. He drank each beer straight down without a pause, then belched noisily. Sitting with his back against a tree, he kept up a steady monologue that made his companions laugh. Because of ritual regulations he had not eaten a mouthful all day, and the beer was beginning to take effect; but never at any moment did he lose the dignity or the eloquence tinged with humor that were to distinguish him throughout the entire trip.

Like all remarkable men, the *gobernador* had his weakness: he could not resist turkey feathers. In the course of the conversation his eye happened to fall upon a magnificent bird; he dropped his beer bottle and, beside himself, made Benzi understand by signs and a few broken words that he must have the feathers. Not knowing at the time that these played a significant part in the pilgrimage, I attributed this mania to a survival of the ancient Indians' love for any kind of feathers.

The woman who owned the fowl did not like the idea of seeing her turkey stripped of his plumage—after all, he was the king of her chicken yard; but Benzi, in his eagerness to please the *gobernador*, began pulling out feathers right and left. When the poor bird began to bleed terribly, the owner finally resigned herself and brought out a pair of scissors. Thus, in a moment the huge turkey lost his tail and both wings. When Hilario had three dozen feathers in his sash, he favored us for the first time with a friendly smile.

We moved to the creek bed, where the pilgrims had set down their baskets around a bonfire. Here they would perform the rites of confession and purification, an essential part of the mystic journey of the peyote. When I inadvertently walked across the magic circle, the *gobernador* took my arm without a word and led me around the fire. This was Tatewarí, Grandfather Fire, a living god; anyone who failed to pay him the proper respect not only compromised himself but also jeopardized the outcome of the religious pilgrimage to Wirikuta.

The Huicholes sat around the fire and busied themselves with preparations for the ceremony. Eusebio, Hilario's son, set to work stringing together the turkey feathers with a needle and a thread of *ixtle*, so that they could be fastened around the crown of his hat. Others, who had bought pieces of automobile tire and leather straps in Valparaíso, made new huaraches; their old ones were nearly in shreds after the long walk. Eusebio gave his father an account of the vicissitudes of their journey, to which the *gobernador* responded with a long, uninterrupted groan, spitting from time to time without always missing his blouse.

Although I had paid for several cases of beer and the invaluable turkey feathers, we did not exist as far as the pilgrims were concerned; or, what was worse, we existed only as intolerable intruders whose company was the price they had to pay (and too high, at that) in order to gratify the fantastic whim of traveling in a bus. Aside from Hilario, no one spoke a word to us or even glanced in our direction. Jerónimo had forgotten his Spanish and ignored my questions; as a result I had to be satisfied with making notes on ceremonies whose meaning I did not understand.

The bonfire had been lighted two hours earlier by Eusebio, the guardian and double of the fire, whose name he proudly bore. It was Tatewarí Mara'akame, also called the Man with the Arrows, who led the procession, setting the pace; who carried the gourds containing the *macuche* tobacco—the Heart of the Fire; who in ancient times had been entrusted with the flint and tinder—today the matches and slivers of pitch pine—for kindling the flame. Only he and his two assistants could perform this sacred act.

As the fire caught, the *mara'akame* said: "Tatewarí, Grandfather Fire, be with us tonight. We are traveling eastward, toward the Land of Wirikuta."

The peyote pilgrims cast their branches on the flames, with the tips pointing to the east.

"The time has come to cleanse ourselves of sin," the *mara'akame* went on. "This was done by the gods, and by the old ones; this we, too, shall do."

Night had fallen. In the firelight the men's figures stood out vividly against the darkness behind them. The expression on their handsome, ancient faces was one of deep withdrawal. They brushed their legs, heads, and clothing with fresh mesquite branches, tossed them on the fire, and stood for a long while watching them as they burned.

The ceremonies beginning with this rite of purification normally took place on the evening of the fifth day of the march, at Xurawemuieka, the Hill of the Star, which lies a day's journey from Valparaíso; but the change in the itinerary had obliged the Indians to perform them in a locale devoid of magical significance. Nevertheless, they made a mental effort to think of the creek bed as the sacred Xurawemuieka, where, according to the myth, the Star Goddess had descended with Eakatewari, the God of the Wind, and the two deities had agreed to remit the sins of the supernatural beings who made the pilgrimage when the world began. Thus Eusebio announced: "We have reached the Hill of the Star, the sacred spot where we shall confess our sins and be cleansed. We must all confess. He who conceals even one of his sins will be punished by the gods. But first we must appoint the authorities."

Even though Jerónimo was interpreting unwillingly and very sketchily, there could be no doubt that the appointment of authorities had been mentioned. But who were these authorities? Actually, these rites—which I was watching as though in a dream and which only later, on my return to the sierra, would I come to understand clearly—had one fundamental purpose: to make possible the transition from the profane to the sacred without danger. The chain of purifications was not enough. In addition, it was necessary to upset the order of everyday affairs, to alter the normal rhythm of the world, to set up different authorities, and to give things new names.

The pilgrims who expected to be named to some office in this symbolic government hid themselves behind rocks and trees, while the *topiles* (constables) pretended to engage in a fruitless search for them. There were some amusing incidents. One of the constables cried out that a fugitive had tried to kill him. The *gobernador* ordered the aggressor to be bound and brought before him; the culprit then offered him a bottle of water, very seriously, and said: "Here is a bottle of *sotol*; it's a gift in honor of your being named *gobernador.*"

"Hey, Semaría [José María]," called out another peyote pilgrim. "Come to the party. You've been appointed alcalde."

"Just a minute," the other answered. "I haven't finished sewing up my shirt."

This sally provoked a great deal of laughter, because of an old folk tale. The Indians say that, while the armadillo was busy sewing his shirt, someone invited him to a party; in his haste he finished the job very badly. As a result, even today you can see the ragged seam in his shell.

When the fun was over, they chose a *gobernador*, an alcalde, a bailiff, a *mayordomo*, and two constables. The constables had only one duty: collecting fines from the pilgrims who could not remember the new names for things.

Next came the ritual of purification. Tatewarí, with his two assistants, Parítsika and Kewimuka, turned to Jerónimo. "Now that we are following the tradition of Tatewarí, Tatutsí, Tamats Maxa Kwaxí (Elder Brother Deer Tail), and Parítsika, and now that the day of confession has arrived, you shall tell us your sins."

"Well, if that is the custom," Jerónimo replied, "I will reveal my sins."

Parítsika bound him with the *kaunari* cord they had prepared, and warned him: "If you leave out any of your sins, you will fall ill in Wirikuta; you will go mad, and you will find no peyote."

Sex and Its Excesses

Tatewarí, loaded down with gourds and shoulder bags, sat down under the trees. With his feather-bedecked hat hiding his face, he listened attentively as Jerónimo, head bowed, recited his sins in a low voice.

Jerónimo, who had been given a brief training course in Mexquitic and was here on an "official mission," had become one of the pilgrims and had assumed, naturally and easily, all the obligations of a neophyte—a *matewame*, "one who does not know and is going to learn," a person making the peyote pilgrimage for the first time.

"Confess your sins," Parítsika commanded, striking him gently with his sash. "Confess every one of your sins."

With each sin, Tatewarí tied a knot in the cord and asked, "Is that all?"

"Yes," the *matewame* said at last. "That is all. I have done as you asked. Only the Fire knows if I have told the truth."

When every pilgrim had made his confession, they stood before the bonfire, each holding the cord that recorded his sins, and intoned aloud a new general confession. Then they threw the cords into the flames, so that the Grandfather might conclude the rite of purification.

Among the Huicholes, pride, avarice, gluttony, wrath, envy, and sloth are not capital transgressions. Their sins are reduced to one alone: that of the flesh, with all its implications. Some of their cords had fifteen or twenty knots, which marked not only acts committed—a great many, in most cases—but also a much broader gamut of intentions: desires, accidental contacts, glances, chance encounters.

When Mautiwaki, one of their mythological personages, was a neophyte, or *matewame*, he broke his vows of chastity and allowed himself to be seduced by the prostitute Irumari, the woman who ruins men. Tamats Kauyumari, the master of shamanic arts, appeared to him in a dream and gored him with his sharp horns and kicked him with his glittering hoofs. The next morning when Mautiwaki got up he cried out: "Oh, God, how my side hurts! Oh, God, how my foot hurts! Oh, God, I'm dying!"

Gradually one of his eyes dried up, one of his legs shriveled, and his body became numb and paralyzed; he was left crippled on one side, but healthy on the other. From that day on he was known as The Palsied One, The Cripple, The Chastened One.

Nuipaxikuri, "he who blinds, dazzles, and intoxicates women," was the protagonist of another typical episode.

Tatei Nakawé, Mother of the Gods, once caused Nuipaxikuri's penis to grow until it was three hundred feet long, at the same time exacting from him a solemn vow of chastity. This was too much for Nuipaxikuri. Although he walked about with his organ wrapped around his waist, there was still a long section left over that he had to carry in a basket on his back. He did not suffer so much from the weight of the monstrous increment as from the vow that kept him from enjoying it. He was a kind of sexual Midas, dying of the torments of unsatisfied desire. One day he saw in the distance a beautiful woman lying asleep; he forgot his vow of chastity and succumbed to temptation. The serpent he carried with him stood erect, rushed upon its victim, and entered her. At that moment the woman turned into a high, rocky cliff, and Nuipaxikuri found himself hanging over an abyss, howling with terror. That would have been the end of him if the friendly vulture, the inveterate savior of divine personages, had not severed the member from which he hung and lowered him safe and sound to the bottom of the canyon.

The Huicholes, who have endowed Nuipaxikuri with their own vices and virtues, are aware of their sensual nature and try to mitigate it by subjecting themselves to repeated vows of continence. They are obsessed by carnal desire, their only sin, and by its antithesis, ritual purity. Men begin this struggle against the flesh when they are very young, trying to maintain their chastity by fasting and avoiding contact with their wives. Since, like Mautiwaki, they are defeated by their inability to resist temptation and are subject to punishment for their transgressions, the pilgrimage to Wirikuta is for them the one great opportunity to lay down the burden of their sins.

We ourselves are, in fact, just as sensual as the Huicholes. Satisfying our sexual desires often means infidelity, along with the obligation of keeping such behavior secret for the sake of our good name and that of others. Thus any extramarital sexual activity calls for deception and a series of precautions designed to minimize its effect on our society and to help us elude retribution.

The Huicholes, too, engage in surreptitious love play, with the difference that while we continue to conceal it they are obliged to confess it publicly. At the moment when the pilgrim is told "Confess your sins, *every one* of your sins," he knows the price—sometimes a very stiff one—he must pay to attain ritual cleanliness and to be worthy of communion with the Luminous Divinity. His entire existence and that of his family depend upon this courageous act, this sacrifice that is demanded of him. A knot in the *kaunari* cord may mean a glance, a chance touch, or a fleeting urge, or it may mark an act with fatal consequences. The man who is confessing may very well have slept with the wife of the Man with the Arrows, or with that of one of his two assistants, and must say so. Faced with the dilemma of incurring the wrath of the divine Peyote or the anger of the offended husband, the sinner does not hesitate. It may be extremely painful for him to expose himself and the wife of his friend or neighbor, and yet he must. The husband will do nothing about it at the moment when his dishonor is revealed, nor at any time during the trip. He is helpless, tied hand and foot, forbidden to take vengeance. The sacramental rite embraces both the offender and the offended and obliges them to rise above their differences; during this magical interlude life's everyday occurrences have no validity. For both parties it is merely another step in the slow process of sanctification. Later, perhaps during some fiesta after they have returned to the profane world and the evidences of their mystic pilgrimage have been consumed in the fire, the husband may give vent to his fury by stabbing the offender or attacking him with a bottle. Even so, his vengeance will not seem to be a direct result of the confession, but rather the outcome of a simple drunken quarrel.

The Sacred and the Profane

As the pilgrims threw their knotted cords upon the flames, they declared: "We have burned our sins. We are cleansed."

At that moment the citizens of Valparaíso began shooting off fireworks for the fiesta of San Francisco. Bengal lights and the multicolored pinwheels of the *castillo* lit up the sky above the village, and we could hear the church bells ringing. The manifestations of another, different religion came and went without the slightest effect on the Huicholes immersed in their archaic ceremonies.

From the beginning I had been astonished at the ease with which the Indians moved from intense religious devotion to gaiety and mundane humor.

This occurred even during the confessions. When it was Hilario's turn, Parítsika said to him in a joking way: "Now it is time for you to confess. Since you're an old man, you must have a lot of sins."

"No," Hilario replied in the same humorous vein. "When I was young and made the trip for the first time, I was a terrible sinner. But now I have very few sins."

Tatewarí—in Las Guayabas he is also called Tatari—asked each pilgrim for his right huarache. "Bring me your sandals," he said. "I will cleanse them so that they may carry you safely, so that they may show you the way and help you avoid the scorpions, snakes, and demons along the road, so that they may lead you quickly and easily to the Land of Wirikuta. Thus it was done at the beginning of the world, and thus it was done by our fathers; this I, too, shall do, according to the tradition of our Elder Brother Deer Tail."

As Tatewarí brushed the huaraches with his *muwieris*, he sang the song of the coyote Tsamurawi. According to Eusebio, this was because "the coyote runs swiftly through the night, and nothing bad happens to him." The song began:

> We are brothers of the coyote Tsamurawi,
> And we travel with Tatutsí,
> Parítsika, Haramara, and Maxa Kwaxí.
> With us are Tatei Nariwame,
> Tatewarí, Auxatemai, Wirikuta,
> And the Kakauyari Muyewe.

He returned the huaraches and said: "Now you can wear them. I have cleansed them. Nothing bad will happen to you on the way."

I was reminded of the incantation the Indians in Guerrero addressed to their sandals when they went out to hunt for beehives in the seventeenth century: "Ea, come hither, ye who are beaten against the ground, for we must walk and take up our journey; ea, come hither, *chichimeco vermejo* [the axe used to cut down the tree where the beehive hung], for we must go now and walk. Come hither, too, guardian spirit, Seven Jaguars, fruit and flower of the earth, or flower of the wine. Ea, bring that which was placed and stored within thee, the green spirit, the green genius, for I must take thee where there are woods and thick groves of trees and grass. We are going to look for our uncles, the spirits, for those who are as gods or superior beings among the spirits, many living together, who are yellow and have yellow wings, people who dwell in gardens and live in a company in the air."[4]

My translation has undoubtedly lost the beauty and rhythm of the incantation, but I have preserved the sense. Those "who are beaten against the ground" would carry the Huicholes to the land of Elder Brother Deer Tail, to the mountains where the Black Deer, the White Deer, and the Blue Deer "live in a company in the air," where the peyote buttons, transformed to flowers, form garlands on the peak of Reunar, the Burned Hill.[5]

In the Beginning Was the Word

Tatewarí Mara'akame then asked for the gourds of tobacco and purified them. When he had returned them he lit a cigarette and went through the motions of writing something on a scrap of newspaper. He turned to the first pilgrim. "Play with this ball," he said, and then pretended to read what he had written: "*Tintamakanititiutautua.*" ("Here is some ink so you can write to Cuba. Let's see what answer you get.")[6]

They gathered again by the bonfire, and Tatewarí threw a cupful of water on the flames. "Grandfather Fire, you must be thirsty. Drink first, then we shall drink."

When each had drunk, they took their places around the fire in the original marching order and began the really formidable task of assigning new names to people and things. Hilario was called Tutúmukanoatuwa (The Flower Descends) and, because of the scarf he wore around his head, Ocaratsimauyutinama (The Old Lady Tied Up in Rags). Eusebio, perhaps because of his high position, received two conventional names: Huriwakonsika (The Hills Appear) and Tutúmekonoaxa (The Flowers Were Returned). The *mara'akame* Antonio Vicente Bautista, Hilario's younger brother, was named Tutúmatahane, and his wife Tutúkuayari (The Flowers That Are Eaten). As one can see, most of the names began with the prefix *tutú*, flower; this is because the peyote, in its most common syncretism, is identified with a flower, sometimes being called Rosa, Rosita, Santa Rosa, or Rosa María. Jerónimo, like those of us who were not peyote pilgrims, was given a different kind of name. Because he was the only person wearing shoes, he was called Ayetsiomaka (literally, He Who Stands on a Turtle). Young Gregorio, the *gobernador's* grandson, was named Waweme (Big Tree). Nicole was christened Cochinera (Cocinera, or Cook) and Tenatsí (a kind of female sacristan who burns copal incense in the church); since she had done nothing to merit either appellation, the intent may have been humorous. Marino, who was always running about and shouting, was named Matahawarka (He Who Blows the Whistle) and Keixariene (The One Who Keeps Falling Down). Both were very fitting for a photographer. I was given the name of my sleeping bag.

When everyone had been renamed, Tatewarí took the hand of the pilgrim he had chosen as his traveling companion, walked him around the fire, lifted him in his arms, and shook him vigorously over the flames "so that his old name would be burned, and so that Grandfather Fire would protect them both." His companion did the same with him. They sat down again and lit cigarettes, which, after a few puffs, they exchanged; thus they sealed a friendship that would continue after the journey was over.

This ceremony, a glorification and consecration of friendship, was aimed at warding off the dangerous consequences of confession and at binding the members of the group more closely together.

The lad Gregorio chose Jerónimo as his companion; the boy's

efforts to lift him and shake him over the fire, as well as the solemn way in which they lit and exchanged cigarettes, were an endless source of laughter and comment.

It was a particularly gay evening. The "companions" danced; even Antonio Vicente's wife, always in the background, danced alone and a little apart, covering her face delicately with her hand as though apologizing for her inferiority and for the obvious fact that in spite of her recent purification she represented a source of contamination.

Two Indian Personalities

Hilario, as we have seen, was a Rabelaisian figure, a man of un-limited vitality. Although he played a secondary religious role in the pilgrimage, as a human being he was vastly superior to Eusebio. He worried about the men, reassured them, and made them forget their weariness. They brought him their problems, and he kept them cheerful and fascinated with his stories and outrageous jokes. He was wizard, medicine man, storyteller, and prestidigitator; he could embroider, make an arrow, or prepare a votive tablet. Like the brothers in the *Popol Vuh*, he was able to confront and confound wicked sorcerers, change the course of rivers, play with mountains, and raise the dead. Wielder of the god-canes and eagle-feather scep-ters—the *muwieris*—and invested with the civil and religious au-thority they conferred, he was in a position to exercise considerable magical power; and we must say he used it generously and with visible satisfaction throughout the journey.

He ate and drank—when the rites permitted—almost as much as the rest of the pilgrims together; and his gaiety, his inexhaustible talents as an actor, storyteller, and shaman placed him always at the center of the stage, where everyone could enjoy his histrionics. Whenever we met by chance he would roll his eyes, slap his belly, and confide in a rueful tone, to give me an idea of his self-denial and tribulations: "Huichol customs, hard work, much hard work."

His sister-in-law, on the other hand, did her best to pass un-noticed. She never spoke, never asked for anything, never com-plained. Because of ritual regulations she remained at a distance, where the warmth of the fire, Tatewarí, did not reach; this must have meant additional suffering, since the desert nights are freezing. Although she was very young—surely no more than twenty-two—she marched behind her husband, Antonio, carrying two shoulder bags that must have weighed as much as the men's baskets. She was a slender woman with high cheek bones, and her intelligent face revealed a religious devotion that accentuated the modesty and solemnity of her bearing. She kept up with the rest, cut firewood, cooked the meals, took care of her husband, and never spared herself. She was enveloped in an aura of mysticism. By the end of the trip, with all her silence and withdrawal, she had made her presence felt as strongly as Hilario's. During the hunting of the deer that concluded the pilgrimage to Wirikuta, it was not she but Antonio who came down with pneumonia on the banks of the Chapalangana. After traveling on foot for four or five weeks through the mountains, living the life of a hunter or a food-collecting nomad, she returned to the *calihuey* at Las Guayabas the same silent, almost wraithlike woman—in spite of her spiritual regeneration, the white turkey feathers in her hair, and the large suns painted on her cheeks.

Jokes and Archaic Gods

Now, for the first time that day, they were permitted to eat; they lined up their gourd bowls before the fire and filled them with *tostadas*, bread, cheese, crackers, and chocolate. The bonfire was the center of attention. The Mara'akame Tatewarí and his two assistants thrust three forked sticks into the coals: one was Grandfather Fire's cane, another was his scepter, or *kupieri*, and the third was his pillow, or *muritari*.[7] Eusebio then picked up a bowl and fed the fire with *tostadas* and *pinole* that had been set aside for the purpose, saying: "We have waited for you to have supper with us. First, eat your *tostadas* and *pinole*; then we shall have ours, as is the custom. Thank you, Tatewarí, Grandfather Fire, for having watched over us along the way, for having kept away the scorpion and the mountain lion. Sleep now, and rest well."

When supper was over they renamed the women who had been left behind in Las Guayabas. Hilario's wife was christened Xukuritirixi (Little Gourd Bowls), Eusebio's woman was called Tutúmekiwekie (Rosebuds), and Tatutsí's wife was given the name Subiri-tirixi (Little Cactuses). Apart from some additional purification rites, nearly the entire evening was devoted to inventing new names for things. Children were called "sacks to carry things in," huaraches were "bicycles," stones were "frogs," trees became "fish," violins were "victrolas," deer were "lambs," paper money was "playing cards," the peyote was named Tutúmutienixu, and Marino's disquieting Rolleiflex, with its twin lenses, was dubbed "the eyes that look at you and there you are forever."

The assigning of names turned out to be another inexhaustible source of fun. The Indians were delighted whenever they were able to base these names on some amusing similarity. The fact that they had called Hilario "The Old Lady Tied Up in Rags," or Jerónimo "Turtle Feet," the mistakes everyone made when trying to remember this new vocabulary, and the ensuing fines collected by the "constables" who had been appointed for this express purpose provoked gales of laughter and many funny comments.

Mundane Considerations

Bars and pool halls open early in Valparaíso. This might point to the triumph of vice, if it were not for the fact that the church opens its doors early, too—thus establishing a kind of moral and religious compensation. Even so, the church was still empty that morning, while the taverns could boast several dozen worshippers, who suspended their games and libations to admire Nicole as she passed by in her tight purple slacks.

At nine o'clock we climbed into the broken-down bus that was leaving for Fresnillo. This part of Zacatecas is still one of the bleakest and most sparsely populated regions in Mexico: bare plains, canyons, a few meager cornfields, little clumps of thorn bushes and mesquite.

In Fresnillo, which is on the main highway and thus better supplied, we bought coffee, canned goods, and bread. Then we descended upon the vehicle the bus company had provided for us. The heavy coach was transformed into a rolling stage set for a hunting scene from archaic times. Hilario's god-canes, the votive arrows, the richly decorated hats and costumes, the stuffed deer heads, the Indians' long locks and handsome faces illuminated with an ancient passion, all seemed much more exotic and bizarre in the carpeted and comfortable interior of the bus.

The desert that these people had made holy down to the smallest detail was—for those of us who did not hold the mythic key—merely an interminable succession of adobe hamlets and desolate plains. As we approached Zacatecas, once a mining center where soldiers, adventurers, outlaws, wild Indians, bonanzas, and miracles created a way of life that has long been forgotten, the reddish slopes and barrancas of La Bufa appeared before us. Beyond Zacatecas the landscape was one of vivid colors: gilded silos, red churches, fields of sunflowers and tiny yellow blossoms, hills the color of blood, ocher plains, an aquamarine sky, and distant ranges that were not mountains but transparent and luminous patches of blue.

We were passing through the kingdom of the *Opuntia*. Just as the mountains had been transformed into pure color, so the nopal cactuses, laden with their pearlike fruit, had turned into the most astonishing pieces of modern sculpture. Here were the handsome, flat, fleshy leaves—with good reason called *Platyopuntia* by the botanists—each growing out of the last in a series of superpositions, their volumes balanced by the empty spaces between the stalks and branches. This play of mass and space penetrated the atmosphere and was penetrated by it in turn. Their color—that of malachite— their smooth texture, the glitter of their long spines, and the ornament of their fruit were the complementary adornments of a desert creature so strange that it could be taken—as is the case with many cactuses—as the perfect model for abstract sculpture.

From the kingdom of the *Opuntia* we moved into that of the *Yucca carnerosana*. With the characteristic grandeur of the desert, the sky took on a scarlet hue that slowly deepened until it seemed to be in flames. It was a massive, smokeless, almost tangible conflagration, against which the grotesque heads and tortured arms of the yucca stood out in black silhouette.

Hilario looked gloomy. For the first time, he had nothing to say, and his uneasiness communicated itself to the entire company. The terrain was totally unfamiliar to him; there was no mountain, land-mark, or geographical feature by which he could orient himself. The Huicholes sat watching the yuccas go by, with their outstretched, impotent arms, and they, too, felt impotent.

It was almost nightfall when signs began to appear along the international highway, advertising the hotels in Matehuala. Many of the brightly lit enticements, designed to attract weary American tourists, were in English: Air Conditioned, Mexican Hospitality, Desert Food, Swimming Pool. But this neon oasis, these indications and blandishments of civilization, left them unimpressed. They had no point of reference that would have enabled them to understand the purpose of this pyrotechnic display. The signs blinked on and off, in a futile effort to drive back the desert night.

Beyond the bright excrescence of Matehuala lay unfamiliar coun-try. We could have gone directly from Salinas to Catorce, following the traditional peyote route, but we were not certain of our bearings; in any case, the bus would not have been able to strike out across the high plain. We were, in fact, making a long detour. Real de Catorce was far from Matehuala, at the opposite end of a chain of mountains that the Huicholes usually approached in a direct line from Salinas. So we would have to spend the night in Cedral, at the end of a local paved road, and set off the next day across another desert that was, in a manner of speaking, the back yard of Wirikuta. Beyond lay the land where the Divine and Luminous Peyote grew.

We stayed at a small hotel and at dawn the following morning set out on the last stage of the journey, along a narrow, dusty track lined with mesquite bushes. The bus climbed out of one pothole only to drop into a deeper one, while the thorns scratched its new paint. Four kilometers from Cedral, after we had been stuck twice, the driver refused to go any farther. We found ourselves, with all our baskets and bags, standing beside the vehicle. Its shiny bulk, stranded in the middle of the arid waste, was as splendid as it was useless.

Luckily, it was the fifth of October, the last day of the San Fran-cisco fair held in Real; trucks were still going back and forth carry-ing merchandise and visitors. Within half an hour an empty truck came by and, although the owner was a little surprised to see such an outlandish party of fairgoers, he took us aboard. After we had arranged for the bus to meet us in Cedral in three days' time, we were on our way.

Scenes of the Desert

We were now in a desert in every sense of the word. The diminutive forests of thorn and mesquite that at the beginning of our journey had seemed to be the distinguishing characteristics of the northern desert had been left behind; not even the towering candelabra or the silver-maned organ-pipe cactus, which elsewhere had mitigated the terrible desolation of the hills and canyons, grew here.[1]

The blackened, nearly leafless trunks of the yuccas rose like columns of burned temples from the low, grayish, ragged underbrush that only partially concealed the coarse, bleached earth. One had the impression that these plants suffered intensely, and that their torment was part of a vast world where time had ceased to exist. The immobility and silence of the desert itself were oppressive, and the naked mountains in the distance, with their smooth mineral folds, added their own silence, immobility, and feeling of absolute timelessness.

Among the ashy vegetation there was only the occasional glitter of the profuse spines, covered with transparent sheaths, with which the *clavellina* (*Opuntia tunicata*) defends its green and fleshy stalks, or, more rarely, the needles that form a reddish halo around the cactus known as *Echinocactus grandis*.

The latter, like its near relative *Echinocactus ingens*, grows from a tiny black seed into a gigantic bubble that lifts its cupola above the vegetation of the high plains. The Aztecs called this cactus *comitl*, a pot, which it actually is, or, if you like, *teocomitl*, divine pot, because of its shape and the great quantity of water contained in its tissues. With the passing of the years the *Echinocactus grandis* loses its spherical shape and shoots upward, often to a height of six feet. Then the protruding ribs surrounding the cupola bend under the weight of the water and bulge outward, making one think of a monstrous twisted Romanesque column afflicted with elephantiasis.

Every year the buds, or areolas, at the center of its crown, which are protected by a very delicate skin, send out stalks and silky yellow flowers; when the blossoms have been fertilized and the plant releases its seeds—sometimes it is the ants who distribute them—they grow spines and shift to the side. Thus the botanist has only to count the areolas to know the age of the cactus.

The name "pot" given them by the Indians is not simply a metaphor. Of all plants it is the Cactaceae—the principal denizens of the American deserts—that hold the greatest quantity of water. True medusas of the vegetable world, they are like cisterns standing among the calcareous rocks, basalt, porphyry, and gravel of the mountains. But in order to bring about this paradox they have had to undergo a change so radical, departing in such a remarkable way from European plants, that the first Spaniards in the Indies must have seen them as an unmistakable sign that they were indeed in a New World. The candelabra, with their tall columns standing on the rocky mountain sides, reminded them of the organs in their churches or made them think of enormous candles set out by the devil for the celebration of some bloody rite.

It is certainly not easy to get used to being surrounded by these vegetable creatures, much less realize that their presence in the middle of the desert means "the triumph of life over the dead aridity of the mineral world."[2]

It was a hard-won victory. In order to obtain the necessary water, the cactus had to develop a thicker root or reach out beneath the rocks with a complex, shallow system that could take advantage of the last drop from the occasional rains. At the same time important changes took place in the rest of its tissues. The leaves, through which plants breathe, were eliminated and replaced by spines. The stem, enveloped in a thick cuticle, took on the shape of a column or became globular like a water jar. Large or small, thick or thin, scattered or clumped, the Cactaceae were now ready to conquer the desert.

Almost all cactuses are hidden under a crown of thorns. Some spines are long and flexible, others are stiff and sharp; some are shaped like stars, or hooks, or are broad and curved like sabers; some are slender and erect, while others are like bristles, or horsehair, or thick white locks. The last are known among the natives as "little old men." On the other hand, some are round balls set with thick spikes, like a medieval warrior's mace.

Thorns and bristles may be placed in a haphazard way or in the most rigorous order. At one extreme are the "little old men" and the agave cactus—*Leuchtenbergia principis*—with their long, tangled hair; at the other are the *Mammillaria microhelia*, with its delicate geometric tracery, and the *Mammillaria ortiz-rubiona*, whose white stars are like a glittering display of ice crystals.

Spearheads, grilles, shutters designed to protect the cactus's succulent flesh, these spines may be naked or clad in marvelous tunics, soft or as hard as steel, poisonous or innocuous; they may be ruby red, ocher, green, or blue. Some envelop the plant in a splendid cloak, as in the case of the *clavellina*; others make the tiniest and most vulnerable cactus all but invisible among the rocks and sand.

As in any society, it is the giants, the "sacred monsters," that attract the most attention. Who notices a tiny cactus hidden among the rocks when a sixty-foot cereus stands nearby? And yet it is not these Briareos who have conquered the high desert, but the host of little Amadíses and Tirants, known to botanists by the equally exotic names of *Ferocactus*, *Echinocactus*, and *Thelocactus*.

In the desert this multitude is hidden beneath the grayish mantle of the creosote and tar bushes, the *lechuguilla* agaves, and the sotol.

Their stubby stalks and green globes shrink during the dry season like the humps of emaciated camels, until they all but disappear into the ground. But as soon as the first rains fall their roots and greedy tissues absorb every drop of water within reach, and their flesh recovers its former plumpness. By the time the rains are over, their roots have broken up the rocks and gravel; their fruit and seeds drop upon this new soil, building the humus so necessary not only to them but also to the less sturdy plants that follow in the footsteps of these rugged colonists. The parable of the seed that fell upon stony ground is meaningless among the Cactaceae.

Exploits of the Prickly Pear

The truck approached the mountains we had seen in the distance. The blue and violet hues had faded away, and we saw the hills as they really were: brown and mottled, with patches of coarse grass and white streaks that were like bleached bones showing through their torn flanks.

At the foot of the mountains lay Potrero, an old mining town of the eighteenth century: a dozen whitewashed houses, some empty corrals, and ruined buildings taken over by nopal cactuses. Those we had seen creeping along or erecting their vegetable architecture in the Zacatecas and San Luis Potosí deserts had joined here in an organized siege in accordance with all the rules of the military art—a siege that must have lasted for over a hundred years. They had entered the ruins through windows, doorways, and collapsing roofs and taken possession of the miners' parlors and bedrooms.

All those foremen who had descended the mine shafts in chairs lashed to the backs of "ponies"—as they called those human beasts of burden—all those inspectors who had performed their "indecent searches" on the squatting peons, looking for the gold they might have hidden within their bodies,[3] all now were in their graves, turned to dust. Today their proud houses were inhabited not by their great-grandchildren, but by these green, bristly, aggressive creatures. One is tempted to see it as a kind of vegetable revenge; but, since that is a theme that really lies within the domain of science fiction, we shall merely point out that the nopal is quite capable of even more ruthless warfare and colonization tactics, as will be shown later.

Theoretically, this cactus can grow indefinitely. New leaves usually sprout from the edges of the old ones, and, if one is blown off by the wind or drops during an extreme dry spell, the areolas facing upward produce stalks and those underneath produce roots. They are adapted to survive under the most difficult conditions. *Opuntia stenopetala*, the creeping nopal that laboriously lifts its dusty leaves in the desert solitudes, is a real outcast, doomed, like the Wandering Jew, to travel forever without rest. Botanists have revealed the secret of its eternal peregrination: its leaf at first stands erect and then as it grows larger bends to the ground and takes root. From that point another leaf grows. Thus it can creep along for miles and for centuries, plowing and cultivating the terrain it traverses.

The *Opuntia* have another weapon for conquering the desert: their prodigious fecundity, common to all cactuses. While their trunks and roots do not send out shoots like the agaves, the yuccas, or the bisnagas, a piece of the leaf has only to fall to the ground to reproduce itself. In addition, twice a year they are covered with thousands and thousands of white, yellow, and red prickly pears. This mad profligacy means the survival of the nopal, as well as that of millions of Mexicans. The invaded feed on the invaders. This vitality explains their conquest of the ruins of Potrero and Catorce and at the same time resolves the paradox of their prevalence. On the one hand, they have made many men's lives an anachronism by imposing upon them the ways of a food-collecting culture; on the other, the conquered can literally feed on the flesh of their conquerors and even nourish their hungry cattle.

Some of these natives of Mexico—it is in our country that plants from the extreme north and the extreme south meet—are not very different from what we think of as the conventional tree. They have a woody trunk, but their numerous branches produce not leaves but stems, bristling with spines. *Opuntia imbricata*—which gives us the sour Indian fig known as *xoconostli*—has dispensed with the luxuriant branches seen in the *Opuntia versicolor* in order to devote its energies to tall trunks fancifully crowned with long, hanging stems.

Some *Opuntia*, armed with enormous spines, are nothing more than a long stalk with arms, twisted like a rope; others, like *Nopalea karwinskiana*, grow side by side in tight clumps. Their fleshy branches swell and round out to herald the traditional cactus stem, although they do not take on the flattened shape characteristic of *Nopalea cochenillifera*, their near relative that is world famous not so much for its own sake as for the parasitic cochineal insect—*Coccus cacti*—that feeds on its red sap. The Aztecs named it *tlalnopal* (the dye cactus), since from the insect they obtained the dye for their princes' robes. For them, this scarlet was the color of authority, as was purple for the Romans. During colonial times the production of this dye was Oaxaca's principal industry; it was replaced by the German aniline dyes, and today it is no more than a zoological curiosity.

Another peculiarity of the nopal is its resistance to disease and insects. Although the same cochineal parasite attacks and weakens some of the other *Opuntia*, on the whole most cactuses, after many centuries of adaptation to their surroundings, have developed adequate immunity to local pests. In Australia, where there were no harmful insects or blights, the nopal imported from America multiplied so rapidly that it became necessary to bring in parasites from Mexico to check the advance of these aggressive immigrants.

It must be said in their favor that the nopals' behavior abroad has seldom reached such reprehensible excesses. Introduced into the Mediterranean countries in the sixteenth century to become neighbors and companions of the umbrella pine and the sensual laurel, they have not only added an exotic New World element to the classical landscape, but also benefited the poor peasant of southern Italy. Their tenacious roots have broken up the lava beds surrounding Mount Vesuvius and built the soil, enriched by broom and esparto grass, that has been so excellent for vineyards. "The lava desert has been conquered," an enthusiastic Italian botanist has observed. "All that the lava had destroyed and buried in its fiery path has been reconstructed through the slow, patient, tireless labor of these succulents."[4]

Today, as a result of the triumph of these colonizing plants, men in the ruins of Pompeii and Catorce drink their sunny wine and dine on the prickly pears and tender leaves of the nopal.

The desert flora—and this is another of its paradoxes—is in some ways reminiscent of submarine life. The coral forests, or madrepores, with their luxuriant branches and motionless, fleshy shoots, the round sponges, the seaweed, the fanciful limestone formations, bring to mind the close-set stalks of *Myrtillocactus geometrizans*, the embroidered serpents of *Aporocactus flagelliformis*, and the textures and shapes of the *Opuntia*. The contrast between the glossy, bluish cuticle and numerous buds protected by the yellow hairs we call *ahuates* to be found in the *Opuntia microdasys* or the *Opuntia fulgida* with their branches crowned with blossoms and thorns makes us think more of the work of calcium—as though they were stony creatures of the submarine depths—than that of chlorophyll.

Real de Catorce

Catorce, which lies hidden at the bottom of a small valley, appeared before us rather theatrically as we emerged from a long, narrow, dusty tunnel. The truck left us on an esplanade in front of the colonial granary, a massive two-story structure overlooking a ravine. The windowless upper floor had been used to store grain for the miners and their animals; the ground floor, once occupied by offices, now housed a few improvised stores, restaurants, and candle shops beneath its lofty ceilings.

The fiesta of San Francisco was just ending, and many of the visitors were beginning to leave. Some were boarding trucks, but most of them were setting out on foot for the railway station, twelve kilometers away. Those who had come from Cedral were heading back through the tunnel.

A dark-skinned man wearing a crown of thorns stood nearby; his face was covered with a handkerchief, and a large blade of cactus hung from his neck like a scapular. While this type of religious fanatic certainly spares himself no suffering, he does not neglect to extract the greatest possible spiritual and material benefits from it. In one hand he held a plate for alms, and in the other a branch of thorns. His motionless attitude, his spiny torment, his veiled face went to make up a living symbol not only of the beautiful desert but also of the religious fervor of the servant girls, the peasant women with their gaunt, angular faces, the workingmen, and the sick children wearing their *cordón de San Francisco*.

With the arrival of the Huicholes, the man with the crown of thorns was forgotten. The mestizos had rarely seen such strangely attired pilgrims. Even though they themselves were extremely picturesque, they crowded around the Indians, filled with wonder, wanting to know who they were and where they came from.

An old man with a cane hobbled up to the *gobernador* and handed him a peso. Hilario accepted the alms with humility, taking off his hat as a sign of gratitude. The old man's gesture had immediate repercussions. A servant woman from Monterrey tried to take up a collection. "Help these poor people!" she cried, filled with zeal. "Help these poor Indians who have come so far to see our Padre San Francisco!"

The Huicholes stood there, arms folded, still loaded down with their baskets, indifferent to the curiosity they had aroused. The church bells were clanging, but the sound meant nothing to them. Their only thought was that within an hour they would be in Reunar, the dwelling of Tamats Kauyumari, the holiest stopping place of all in their pilgrimage to Wirikuta.

Hilario had had enough. This was his chance to get rid of us. "Well, we'll leave you here," he told me.

Suddenly I felt that the entire trip had been a fiasco. My efforts to gain Hilario's confidence had come to nothing. Here I was on the point of accomplishing what no other anthropologist had ever been able to do, and yet now that the Huicholes were in control of the situation they were going to abandon me in Real de Catorce.

I called Jerónimo, He Who Stands on a Turtle, the only one who knew a few words of Spanish, and begged him to talk to the *gobernador*. "Hilario must wait for us," I said. "Only for an hour, while I find some mules to take us to the Burned Hill. I have kept my promises, and Hilario must keep his."

After a long discussion, Jerónimo succeeded in persuading Hilario to delay their departure for an hour. Meanwhile they would shop for candles, chocolate, and kerchiefs. Colorful handkerchiefs hold an irresistible fascination for the Huicholes, and it was the prospect of buying one at the fair that finally convinced the *gobernador*. I found a boy to take me to the house of a mule driver, where I contracted for four of the animals.

But my troubles were not over. The mules were in a pasture some distance away, and it would take a good two hours to round them up and saddle them. However, the sight of some money and the intimation that I might be a rich man looking for an abandoned mine to buy seemed to work a miracle; the mule driver's suspicious reluctance turned into a remarkable briskness. With the energy of a crusader, he leaped onto his horse and flew to the pasture where the mules were grazing, all unaware of the high destiny reserved for them by the gods of the Burned Hill.

The Worlds of Mexico

It took 150 years for this mining town to be stripped of its flesh and become nothing more than a skeleton of stone. Count Masa's palace, with its wrought-iron balconies, its cornices, and its baroque niches, had been abandoned long ago. The houses in town, built along the narrow, steep, winding streets, were slowly crumbling, half-hidden now behind the white sun shades that had been tacked up for the fair. The rest—houses, walls, outlying streets, little churches—had already been taken over by the conquering cactus. The desert, held back for a time, had retaken its ancient domain. Catorce looked like a razed village, with the blackened walls of its houses and reduction plants overgrown with the fleshy, bristling leaves of the gigantic nopal.

Real's only treasure is Saint Francis, a carved saint dressed in a red velvet tunic hung with tiny silver votive tokens. The image stood on a side altar, illuminated by hundreds of candles, resplendent in the otherwise dark and deserted church. No one prayed to the other saints or even glanced at them. The few remaining pilgrims were entering on their knees, murmuring and carrying handfuls of lighted candles. They gathered before the altar. Some wiped the dust from the floor and rubbed it on their faces as others, eyes closed, begged for some favor. Suddenly a tight, shrill cry rose above the drone of voices; every head turned toward a fat, pallid woman who was having a kind of fit, head thrown back, mouth agape and flecked with foam. Her companions tried to hold her erect, but she slipped from their arms and fell to the floor. Her skirt slid up, revealing obese thighs with a network of blue veins and a round, protruding belly. As her body twitched convulsively, terrified children burst into tears while the women nearby hastened to cover her with their shawls and *rebozos*.

Outside, a blind man was playing an ancient harp and singing revolutionary *corridos* in a high, thin voice. Hawkers were crying their wares: religious pictures, purple ribbons, stuffed humming-birds, and amulets against the evil eye. Among the booths that were about to close, a vendor was knocking down his merchandise to the highest bidder. He gestured toward an old man with a withered face who sat peering out from among the scarves, bolts of cotton cloth, looking glasses, and portraits of saints. "This old fellow just got married, and he's anxious to take his bride back to Saltillo."

Since no one else seemed inclined to help the old gentleman resume his interrupted honeymoon, I bought a couple of straw hats and two plastic canteens—one blue, the other yellow—that I thought might come in handy in the desert.

Hilario showed up an hour and a half later, wearing the print neckerchief he was not to take off for the next six months. A few minutes later the mules' owner made his appearance, followed by a miner friend in a yellow helmet and four wretched animals. As soon as our luggage was securely in place we were ready to resume the pilgrimage.

The Huicholes, as usual, walked in Indian file with folded arms and bowed heads. Little Gregorio, with his small, sturdy legs, took the lead, carrying three shoulder bags and wearing a faded bandanna tied over his eyes. We moved out silently, like a parade of ghosts, past the blackened walls and ruined mansions of Real. Our departure was contemplated by other phantoms: the mestizo pilgrims from faraway places who had come to pay homage to Saint Francis.

Three worlds met here. The first, the most ancient and mysterious, was that of the Huicholes. In some way that we do not understand they had made this part of the far desert a sacred place and for two thousand years had come here as pilgrims in search of the Divine. Neither the Spanish Conquest, nor the persecutions of the Inquisition, nor the passing of time had been able to make any essential change in the spiritual significance of their journey.

The second world was that of the descendants of the miners who had raised an eighteenth-century city in these vast solitudes, who now lived—or survived, rather—by clinging to the past. When the miraculous silver strike had come and gone, it had been succeeded by the miracle of San Francisco. Most of Real had been taken over by the cactus; and, as always happens in a society where the conquered live side by side with the conquerors, each was able to live and tolerate the other at the price of a certain restraint. The inhabitants lived in a few ruined houses; their respect for the established social order would not allow them to occupy the abandoned palaces. They lacked the boldness of their forebears. Today, nearly two hundred years after Catorce's zenith, it is touching to talk with the great- and great-great-grandchildren of those administrators and overseers.

Pedro, the mule driver's friend who had decided to come with us, was a blond lad with the face of a child. He had this to say: "With God's help, we're able to get by. We do some mining, but sometimes we go for a week without finding anything. Our real trade is raising maguey: *lechuguilla, palma, guapilla*. It gives us *aguamiel*; we roast the flowering stalk—the *quiote*—over the fire; and we cook the leaves—the *chacuaco*—in the oven. We eat young nopal leaves and prickly pears, too. You might say we live on nopal and maguey. It's all a lot of hard work. We're *ejido* members, but all three hundred of us together make only thirteen hundred pesos a month. Some people think about nothing but money, and it's always the farmer who gets the short end of it. We can't do the things we should because we don't have enough education."

This young man thought of his existence on earth as a gift he had done nothing to deserve. He knew that the men who bought his silver and *ixtle* were robbing him; but he did nothing to defend himself and was ready to accept his fate. There was no tension between the exploited and their exploiters, and no class struggle. The peasants showed absolutely no sign of rebellion. With the collapse of the mining industry they had found themselves trapped in the desert. They put all their hope in divine providence. "God will provide," he kept saying. "Our lives are in San Francisco's hands—if the Virgin grants it—if it is God's will."

The third world in evidence here was that of the mestizos who had come to pay homage to Saint Francis. They were a precise representation of the double heritage of the Indians and the Creole inhabitants of the old Spanish mining towns. Between them and the Huicholes there were undeniable similarities. Both undertook long journeys to holy places, both subjected themselves to terrible physical suffering, and both sought tangible and immediate rewards.

During their pilgrimages the mestizos saw children killed by witches who sucked their blood, and balls of fire leaping across the mountain tops. They implored the saints to "show them some way to make a little money," and found relief from their sorrows and troubles as they kneeled before their statues in the shrines. In return for this sympathy and attention they left "a tiny heart made of silver, some candles, and a few centavos in alms."[5] The Indians saw apparitions and natural phenomena that filled them with terror. They begged their gods for health, rain, and good luck in the hunt, and in exchange they offered money, candles, blood, and precious oblations of arrows and gourd bowls.

But there was a difference. The mestizos belonged to a culture of transition: they were no longer Indians from the hills, but neither had they become assimilated into the world of the cities. They were halfway along the road to a painful transformation. Their poverty, their ignorance, and the misery and isolation of their lives were such that, of the two opposing cultures, they had inherited from the one only superstitions and vestiges of magic, and from the other only the detritus of an industrial civilization: radio, television, and comic books.

The Huicholes had the hope and expectation of salvation, knew that they were reenacting the feats their gods had performed at the time when the world was created, and were familiar with every detail of the ritual. The mestizo pilgrims, on the other hand, not only knew nothing of the life of Saint Francis, but also had notions that were diametrically opposed to everything he stood for in the realm of the spirit. For them he was a miraculous idol, a deity invested with supernatural powers, very much like the Virgin of Guadalupe or Our Blessed Lord of Chalma. They bought his picture and his *cordón* and had them blessed. At the same time they purchased charms to assure success in their love affairs, got savagely drunk, fought among themselves, and left, as a souvenir of their visit, an enormous amount of excrement in the streets near the church.

The mestizos crowded about the Huicholes, plaguing them with questions. They wanted to know why they wore feathers in their hats, and why little Gregorio was blindfolded. The embroidered costumes, the deer heads, and the scepters were to them totally exotic, just as the mestizos' chromos of San Francisco, their songs from the time of the revolution, their patched clothing, their insolence, and their senseless excitement seemed exotic to the Indians.

The mestizos spoke Spanish, while the Huicholes had retained their original tongue. Their interests, their customs, their racial backgrounds, and their attitudes seemed to display nothing in common, although in the overall picture of Mexican culture they represented the two extremes of a slow evolution. It was an evolution that moved from the Huicholes, with one of the best-preserved cultures, marked by a religious passion embracing every aspect of their lives, toward these mestizos only recently absorbed by an urban world where two heritages were struggling, where magic had been reduced to sharply limited dimensions without freeing it completely from its original matrix.

As for the palaces, the abandoned mine shafts, the houses clogged with cactuses—all that remained of the Colonial period—they, too, could be included among the factors in that evolution. For it was not by mere chance that the old mining towns that had produced the fabulous wealth of New Spain were now the most poverty-stricken areas in the Republic.

Reunar

The road to Reunar, the goal of the Huichol pilgrimage, was a
gradual ascent. Not all the Indians came as far as the Burned Hill, or
even reached the mesa of Wirikuta, five hours away. Most of them
remained at Tsinurita, on the plain below; there, too, the peyote was
plentiful. Every Huichol, however, feels obligated at least once in
his life to leave his offerings in the dwelling place of Tamats Kauyumari.

Catorce lay behind us, a cluster of white houses surrounding the
church. The older settlements on the outskirts were a vague, dark
stain on the bleached mountainside. The rutted, stony road glittered
white in the sun. On our right, on the opposite side of the barranca,
we could see the portals, ruined roofs, and massive walls of an abandoned mining operation.

As we moved on and left the works of man behind us, the landscape began to take on a hallowed aspect. For the Huicholes, accustomed to their green granitic mountains carpeted with oaks, where
rivers glide through grassy ravines, this bare, waterless land would
have seemed a particularly magical place even if the Divine and
Luminous had not grown here.

In the scenes of heaven pictured in the *Codex Vindobonensis*
there is an area rich in colorful precious stones; men, too, are made
of stone, as is Quetzalcóatl himself, the god who symbolizes the cultural exploits of the neolithic. Catorce reminded me of this celestial
vision. The mountains were covered with stone the color of dried
blood, lying in strata veined with green, blue, and yellow, like rivers
of turquoises, opals, and aquamarines. The soft, golden outlines of
the hills topped with coarse grass stood out against rounded lunar
peaks in the distance.

After two hours we reached the high, broad saddle that leads to
the summit of the Burned Hill. The desert usually traversed by the
peyote pilgrims, with its blue mountains in the background, lay at
our feet. Hilario removed the blindfolds from the two *matewames*,
and for the first time they saw the country their ancestors had
crossed for centuries. Once again the Indians dropped their baskets

in a semicircle and sat down, gazing out over the broad desert. Their pilgrimage had begun where it should have ended.

Now that the hole burned by the sun was within reach, the Indians began to feel uneasy; perhaps we might contaminate this especially sacred spot with our presence. Hilario begged me to leave them. We could not accompany them to the Burned Hill. They had decided to make the return trip on foot and thanked me for bringing them. Perhaps we could meet later, when they got back to Las Guayabas.

I understood and sympathized with Hilario's desire to rid himself of a source of defilement, but, naturally, I was loath to give up the trip. I launched into a defense of what I called "my rights." Hilario had chosen a bad time, for he was in a state of religious exaltation and could not allow himself to become angry or lose precious moments in arguments. So he bowed to the irremediable. His face took on the resigned expression of a stoic about to pass through the gates of hell.

When the mule driver learned that our trip was not to end at the Burned Hill, he said he was returning to Catorce. Then he agreed to go on if we paid him a staggering sum for the additional use of his animals. At last, since he could not believe that I had taken so much trouble just to watch some Indians collecting peyote, he settled for a somewhat more reasonable amount.

With these difficulties out of the way, we began the ascent to Reunar. At the summit, amid *lechuguillas* with their slender central stalks and underbrush thick with yellow flowers, yawned the opening from which the new-born sun had sprung.

It is quite possible that no one but the Indians and an occasional shepherd had ever visited Reunar. The two mestizos, Antonio's wife, little Gregorio, and another Huichol had remained below with the mules and the baskets. For the first time, intruders were beholding —and, what was worse, photographing—the evidences of a cosmic event of which only the Huicholes had kept the memory.

They formed the prescribed circle around the pit and stood gazing out across the desert. The cold wind of the highlands ruffled their long, heavy locks, but they seemed not to notice. Hilario took the bundle of god-canes and passed them over his companions' heads, invoking the assistance of the gods.

Their offerings—arrows, corn flowers, candles, a stuffed deer's head—were tossed into the hole. Then Eusebio, the one-eyed *mara-'akame*, sprinkled the blood and *tesgüino* on the ground and chanted a prayer. At the conclusion of the ceremony Hilario brushed away their fatigue, sins, and illnesses with his *muwieris*.

The Intoxication of the Infinite

We went down a winding path along a ravine to the mesa where the peyote grew. We were dwarfed by desolate mountains that towered above us like temples. Erosion and aridity had rounded their outlines, carving the limestone cliffs into gigantic truncated pyramids, altars, and pillars that glittered white against the coarse, microphyllic vegetation. No sooner had the mind begun to grow accustomed to this motionless grandeur, these shapes carved in such a bizarre fashion, than other devastated peaks appeared behind them in the distance like a great tide of lava, presenting a new vision of the infinite. Ungaretti's line—*M'ilumino d'inmenso*—took on new meaning here in the American desert. The impressive mountain ranges of the Huichol country had not prepared me for this; by comparison, theirs was a rather conventional kind of beauty. This landscape, less spectacular, had eliminated everything superfluous until nothing but the pure and naked image of the essential desert remained. Here one could not even recall the forests, rivers, meadows, and mists of the Sierra Madre Occidental. The sunlight that fell upon this monotonous waste had a material of marvelous plastic possibilities to work with, and it certainly made the most of it. With the approach of evening the rays of the setting sun washed the white altars with gold and threw the carpets of vegetation at the bottom of the valleys into shade; but the landscape remained as immobile and lifeless as before. The band of Huicholes seemed to disappear, blending into the calcareous outcrops that in a kind of mimicry had taken on shapes that were like little groups of petrified Indians. The silence was broken only by the sound of the mules' hoofs on the red schist.

We had reached a region where everything was sacred. At a turn in the path we came across a small pool; the one-eyed *mara'akame* put down his basket, dipped a flower in the water, and offered a drink to each of the pilgrims. I watched them as they approached, eyes closed, and avidly sipped the holy water. When they had filled some of their jars and bottles, we descended to the foot of the mountain along a dry creek bed filled with barite, white marble, black granite, and variegated slate.

As we emerged from the arroyo night was falling, and the *gobernador* decided to make camp in a broad, rocky clearing between two patches of brush near a little hill. I did not know then that behind that hill, less than a hundred meters away, lay the mesa where the peyote grew.

The pilgrims relieved themselves of their baskets and, showing no sign of fatigue, at once grasped their machetes and began cutting branches of *hojasé* and *gobernadora* for the ritual bonfire.

Once again I sensed the atmosphere of both relaxation and tension that preceded important ceremonies. The *gobernador* arranged the ritual objects on his *itari*, or straw mat: the feather *muwieris*, a deer's head, arrows, gourd bowls, bottles of blood, and containers filled with water from the sea, from Lake Chapala, and from the caves at Teakata. Antonio and his wife brought the firewood while the assistants of the Man with the Arrows laid the fire.

Pedro, the young miner, turned out to be the owner of a nearby cornfield and invited us to help ourselves. In a short time we had picked two or three sacks of corn and fed the mules generously on the leaves and stalks.

Suddenly darkness fell. The fire was burning briskly with a fragrant smoke; we roasted some of the corn over the coals and began to eat while the rest was boiling in a bucket on the back of Tatewarí, Grandfather Fire. The Huicholes were free to enjoy this unexpected gift without any feeling of guilt, for they had celebrated the ritual festival of the first harvest before leaving Las Guayabas.

The Divine and Luminous

We spent the night most comfortably in our sleeping bags, although we got rather well smoked by the fire. The Huicholes slept four or five hours and spent the rest of the night chatting and laughing at Hilario's stories.

They ate their *tostadas* and ears of corn in the freezing dawn and then, seated around the fire, began preparing their offerings. They heated chunks of dyed copal and "dressed" the shafts of their arrows with the wavy blue lines symbolizing water and the red bands that represented Tatewarí.

When the Indians had finished with the arrows the sun was up. Shouldering their baskets and offerings, they took the prescribed turn around the fire and marched off in single file. We went over the little hill and soon were standing on the holy ground of Wirikuta, a broad mesa lying between the foot of the mountains and the desert, with its sprinkling of white houses in the distance.

Once on the mesa, Eusebio emptied the tobacco from the gourds in which it had been carried into a calabash lined with a napkin. Then he made little packages by wrapping it in damp corn husks—*totomoxtle*—and distributed them to the pilgrims. "Take this sacred tobacco, the Heart of the Fire," he said. "It will guide us to where our Elder Brother Deer Tail lies hidden."

Each Indian took the string attached to his bundle and grasped it between his teeth, so that it hung before him. Thus the *macuche* tobacco would help them find the Deer-Peyote and at the same time protect them from the snakes, scorpions, and powerful demons hiding in the underbrush, as it had throughout the journey.

As far as I could see, Wirikuta was not very much different from the desert we had crossed on our way to Catorce. It was the same bleached, gravelly soil, with the same coarse, ragged cover of cactus and microphyllic plants. The serpentlike *clavellinas* glittered in the brilliant sunlight, and the *biznaga* cactuses made vain efforts to lift their shaggy heads above the thorny scrub. The silence seemed to spring from the deep blue of the sky, the motionless vegetation, and the smooth, rounded folds of the lunar mountains.

But where was the Divine and Luminous? It was nowhere to be seen, and, since we were not privileged to bear the magic tobacco, there was no point in our even trying to find it. The pilgrims had spied it, however. Tatewarí Mara'akame, arrow in hand, gestured five times toward a spot on the mesa; then he moved forward and planted the arrow among some rocks. He had found the first peyote.

The *mara'akame* pressed the body of a small frog against his cheek, leaving a drop of blood; he then did the same to Hilario. After leaving some of their offerings near the upright arrow, they located two more peyotes and repeated the same ritual. Fifteen minutes later they returned to the site of the first find.

Having dipped some small ears of corn in the blood of the bull that had been sacrificed during the Festival of the New Corn and Squash—the celebration of the first harvest that had begun the peyote cycle—they touched them to their offerings in consecration.

Soon the site of the first peyote took on the aspect of an altar. There were votive gourd bowls painted with tiny figures of deer, bulls, and children; another deer's head, that of the great Tamats Kauyumari, erected on a pole; a round stone carved with Tamats's image; a deer's tail; candles adorned with ribbons—a candle for each pilgrim and a ribbon for each of his bulls and cows; a larger candle that had cost five pesos, representing the dead; a piece of dried deer meat pierced by an arrow; several "eyes of god"; bottles of *tesgüino* and holy water; ears of corn; and votive arrows.

When the candles had been lighted, the *mara'akame* chanted: "May the gods make us eloquent in our singing . . . We have arrived at the holy land of Wirikuta; we have surrounded and killed our brother Watemukame, who lay hidden in the grass. Now we offer the gods their tribute, their water and their wine, their blood and their ears of corn, their bowls and their arrows. When we entered Wirikuta we made our offering to Tiskatemai, the Drunken Neighbor, who befuddled the gods with drink because they had forgotten him; we beg him not to do to us what he then did to our fathers. We are about to collect the Nierika, we are about to collect the *hikuri* [peyote]. We appeal to all of you, we implore all of you to guide us and give us luck in the hunt. O Elder Brother, who wept like a deer when we hunted you down, forgive us. The gods have spoken: if there is to be life for all of us, a deer must die."

Hilario performed his acts of purification, stroking the pilgrims'

faces and bodies with the carved stone and the feathers of his *muwieris*. He repeated the ceremony several times while Eusebio dug
up the peyote with his machete and placed it in a special gourd
bowl. Then Hilario pierced the cactus several times with an arrow,
and with the moistened point he touched the offerings and the men's
cheeks and wrists, all the while muttering an incantation. But this
was not enough. Again he sprinkled water, blood, and *tesgüino*.
Then he turned to the bowl where the peyote had been cut into
thin slices and, like a priest distributing the Hosts from the ciborium,
put a piece in the mouth of each pilgrim, throwing the rest on the
altar. Eyes closed, they slowly chewed the peyote and rubbed the
juice, mingled with saliva, on their bellies.

By nine thirty in the morning the ceremony was concluded, and
the pilgrims dispersed to search for peyote. This was hard work.
They roamed over the mesa for hours with their baskets on their
backs. The Huicholes have the sharp eyes of a people who are still
fundamentally hunters and food gatherers; thus, the members of the
group had no difficulty in spotting the little vegetable stars half-
hidden in the surrounding brush. In some places they grew pro-
fusely, and when an Indian found such a spot he summoned the
others. Most of the time, however, each hunted by himself. Sometimes they were almost concealed from view as they squatted to cut
the cactus; at other times they made one think of the Huicholes
after death, when their spirits are condemned to wander over the
Wirikuta mesa in search of Tamats Kauyumari.

Appearances Are Deceiving

Even with the help of the tobacco, peyote is hard to find. It is
among the least spectacular of the cactuses, lying hidden under the
bushes, dwarfed by its neighboring relatives, nearly indistinguishable from the surrounding rocks and caliche. During the long dry
season its tissues contract; the head literally sinks into the thick neck
of the root and almost disappears. It goes into a kind of hibernation.
When the rains begin the cactus swells again; but even then it barely rises above the surface, and it displays no showy spines. Its

white or pink blossoms go unnoticed by both wild-flower lovers and botanists.

Peyote is a member of the large genus *Mammillaria*. When the plant is young, its tubercles or nipples appear in a rather random pattern near the top; as it approaches maturity they flatten slightly and tend to line up along sharply defined ribs. It may be solitary or it may grow in clusters that are like excrescences, nodules, or malignant tumors.

The tiny nipples, the soft buttons with their curious slits, and the shifting patterns of the adult protuberances combine to give the impression of a state of metamorphosis: half-mineral, half-vegetable, prefiguring the shifting shapes of the peyote dream.

The sacred cactus is not as defenseless as it seems. It wears a coat of several layers. The exterior skin, thick and waterproof, is rich in cutin; in addition, it is covered with a sheath of blue-gray wax that lends it its characteristic color. Thus, the peyote retains nearly every drop of the water it extracts from the soil. The woody integument of its root seals it even more tightly, while the acids and salts in its tissues act to conserve liquid.

The peyote has been called a "woolly cactus." Its Aztec name, *peyotl,* and its scientific designation, *Lophophora,* seem to suggest a tufted appearance, and even Dr. Francisco Hernández has complained that it is so covered with hair he has not been able to draw it. This is an exaggeration. There are only a few scattered bristles on its areolas—never enough to be a distinguishing feature of the plant. The peyote is remarkable, in fact, for its lack of any singular characteristics. It is a small, unpretentious cactus, a plant without beauty or utility, owing its survival to its plainness and to its fame as the source of an extremely disconcerting and dangerous acid. The fact that the Indians discovered it, used it, and built a mythology and a highly complex ritual around it shows that they must have been familiar with the immense northern deserts from remote antiquity. It also indicates that they had noted and classified each and every one of the plants found there, in a truly scientific tradition. Their motives were not utilitarian or practical—although there was some of that, too: they made use of the edible cactuses and fashioned ropes and cloth from the agaves—but intellectual. They were driven by the desire for knowledge for knowledge's sake, by the natural scientist's curiosity that led them to discover and evaluate properties of the American flora that we ourselves have not discovered and evaluated until the present day.

In spite of recent advances in chemistry and medicine, it is precisely the university students, the scientists, those endowed with the greatest sensitivity—or at least those most exposed to the horrors of contemporary life—who have resorted to the "acids" and have seen in them possibilities for a new religion and a new culture.

The zeal with which the Indians had launched their study of nature ten or twelve thousand years ago was not significantly surpassed by the Spanish explorers of the sixteenth century. The Europeans collected and made drawings of plants and made some attempt to learn their properties; but their labors were not nearly as productive as those of their predecessors. In fact, both the conquered and the conquerors were able to survive only by virtue of advances made during the American neolithic: the domestication of plants that had begun in the times of the mammoth and the sabertoothed tiger. As for the use of hallucinogenic plants, the difference was that the Indians believed they were communing with the gods, while the Spaniards viewed their rituals as invocations of the devil himself. The cultural process that has been reconstructed by Lévi-Strauss took place in Mexico just as it did in other parts of the world. The scientific tradition established by preliterate man during the neolithic was broken.

With all its spectacular conquests, the sixteenth century was a period of arrest and stagnation. The knowledge of writing, with its esoteric implications, gave the crown and the clergy even greater power over the illiterate peoples of the New World. As soon as the Spanish authorities, mine owners, and *encomenderos* saw the danger in teaching Indians to read and write, they put an immediate stop to the educational efforts begun not long before by the monks. Writing came to fill the gap left by the esoteric language of the gods that had been employed by the native priests in their ceremonies.

Communion with the Divine

With the search for peyote, the Huicholes had reverted to their primitive role of food gatherers. They spent all morning and a good part of the afternoon bent over the grayish, monotonous vegetation, looking for the sacred cactus.

The deep, cloudless sky seemed almost tangible as the sun ascended majestically, its hard, yellow light accentuating the strange stillness of the landscape. The variegated mountains, with their smooth flanks and humped backs, were like a parade of mastodons and dromedaries immobilized by some supernatural force. They stood still in Wirikuta, mute. But when night fell and the Blue Deer, the teacher of ecstasy, sang them the shamanic songs, those mountains would speak; the cactuses, transformed into flowers, would begin to move in magic circles around their bald, grotesque heads.

Meanwhile, the pilgrims went on cutting peyote and tossing it into their baskets. With the magical associations of the Holy Land, they had at last become one with the landscape; they were approaching the final sanctification. Under their plumed hats, with their packages of tobacco hanging from their lips, they had left the profane world behind.

The Huicholes had become the gods whose name they bore, and they were thinking now only of the test that awaited them at nightfall. On that ordeal would depend not only the health of their children and the abundance of the coming harvest, but also something far more important: their future as individuals. Would they remain as they were—ordinary farmers and villagers of Las Guayabas—or would Tamats Kauyumari choose to elevate them to the high positions of *cantadores*, medicine men, and leaders of the community? They were hoping for grace, waiting for the miracle, as one awaits the gifts of the gods: with terror and expectation.

That afternoon they returned to camp full of spines and scratches. They emptied their baskets and sat down to peel the peyote—the husk of the root was rather like the outer shell of deer horn—and cut it into pieces. As is the custom with the flesh of their totemic animal, they strung the sections into necklaces.

Little Gregorio, who had consumed five small peyote buttons that afternoon, was intoxicated. His pupils were dilated, and he kept laughing in a silly way that amused his elders.

Everyone was at work. In the golden glow of twilight the mountains behind us seemed less solid and massive. The bleached areas were disappearing, and everything was covered with a soft radiance. The hills floated like great clouds above the stony creek bed where we were camped.

Night fell suddenly. After some difficulty—at first the *gobernadora* and *hojasé* refused to catch—the bonfire was lighted. Then, amid the fragrant smoke, the pilgrims ate their peyote and began to sink into the *hikuri* ecstasy.

Other Religions, Other Inquisitions

"It's going to be a whole new ball game, ladies and gentlemen. Man is now going to be able to make use of the electric network locked up inside his skull. The modern world had better get ready for it: our deepest convictions are going to be swept away by a tide that has been building up for two billion years. The great barrier of words is about to fall. Run for the hills or prepare to swim with the current."

The man who said that was no Huichol, certainly. It was Timothy Leary, former Catholic, professional psychologist, fired from his teaching post at Harvard, sentenced to thirty years in prison for dealing in marijuana. In 1961 he went to the Mazateca Mountains and took the sacred mushrooms—in his words, he discovered the Rosetta stone of consciousness—and ever since has been determined to found a new religion.

Leary has taken for his own a question asked by Aldous Huxley, who envisioned a future society using drugs: "Which is better? To have fun with fungi or to have idiocy with ideology?"

In the eyes of the authorities, Leary is a criminal; for the family man who believes in "the American way of life," he is a dangerous agent of corruption; for his students and followers, he is both a kind of Socrates and a high priest.

His doctrine, briefly stated, is this: man, with an image of himself and an awareness of the ontological and mythological foundations of society, is in conflict with the world, with its false conventions and mendacious morality, and is preparing to destroy it. He will inevitably destroy it because that is the law of evolution and of every historical process.

Leary has stepped through the doors of perception and will never be the same again. He has a mystical system made up of bits and pieces of oriental philosophies and tempting promises; but his followers are less interested in rituals and prayers than they are in the sacramental substance that prompted the psychedelic revolution. As in the ancient Mexican religions, what matters is not what one does or says, but the "medicine": in this case, "acid," the powerful LSD, the modern substitute for hallucinogenic mushrooms and the Divine Peyote.

Leary has won the first round, although his personal influence has declined of late. In 1967, according to conservative estimates, more than a million young people took the "cerebral vitamin." A million human beings setting out to explore their own inner space—taking "trips," as they say in Greenwich Village, headquarters for the young disciples—constitutes a revolution.

The authorities are doing everything they can to put it down—as they have always done with any revolution anywhere; but, if past experiences are any indication, we can predict that their efforts are doomed to failure. For two and a half centuries the Holy Office, whose efficiency as a police agency has never been questioned, did its utmost to extirpate the ritual use of hallucinatory drugs among the Indians. The instructive result is that today, four hundred years later, Mr. Leary had no difficulty in obtaining the sacred mushrooms.

The use of LSD cannot be controlled. It is odorless and tasteless, and one gram (1/28 ounce) is enough for ten thousand individual doses—that is, ten thousand trips to the land beyond our consciousness.

There have been some amusing incidents. One pusher spilled a small container in his suitcase, and for several months he and his friends were able to get a high merely by chewing on one of his shirts or socks.

So far the only direct casualty of "acid" has been an elephant in an Oklahoma zoo, who was accidentally given an overdose. Under the influence of the drug, animals behave in a strange way; but, since we are unable to obtain a "report from the patient," we cannot say why spiders spin more perfect webs, or carp swim on the surface of the water, or cats run from mice.

The Inevitable Dr. Hofmann

LSD was discovered by accident. On April 16, 1943, Dr. Albert Hofmann—the same man who had synthesized psilocybin from the hallucinogenic mushrooms—was working in his laboratory at the Sandoz plant in Basle, trying to purify by condensation two isomers:[1] the well-known lysergic acid, obtained from a parasitic mold occurring on rye, and isolysergic acid diethylamide. Suddenly he felt sick and decided to go home for the day.

"I lay down and sank into a not unpleasant delirium," Dr. Hofmann wrote in his notebook. "In a sort of trance with closed eyes (I found the daylight unpleasantly glaring) fantastic visions of extraordinary vividness accompanied by a kaleidoscopic play of intense coloration continuously swirled about me. After two hours this condition subsided."

Shortly thereafter Dr. Hofmann wrote: "On April 16 I had succeeded in producing a few milligrams of lysergic acid diethylamide (LSD) . . . it was inconceivable to me, however, that I could have absorbed enough of this material to produce the above described state. . . . I was determined to probe the situation and I decided to experiment upon myself." After taking a very small dose—250 micrograms—he noted "mild dizziness, inability to concentrate, visual disturbance, and uncontrollable laughter."

"I asked my laboratory assistant to escort me home, since I assumed that the situation would progress in a manner similar to last Friday. But on the way home (a four-mile trip by bicycle) the symptoms developed with a greater intensity than the first time. I had the greatest difficulty speaking coherently and my field of vision fluctuated and was distorted like the reflections in an amusement park mirror. I also had the impression that I was hardly moving; yet later my assistant told me that I was pedaling at a fast pace."

For six hours Dr. Hofmann experienced the following symptoms: dizziness, distorted vision, alternate states of the greatest excitement and nearly total prostration, a feeling of suffocation, and mental confusion relieved by periods of sharp awareness.

This is what a scientist has to tell us of his experiences. There is nothing here that could have induced any religious feeling. His exaltation had nothing to do with mysticism, and his depression was not a descent into hell. The following day Dr. Hofmann felt perfectly well, if a little tired. By ingesting acids that were being taken in the form of mushrooms by Siberian shamans fifteen thousand years ago he had rediscovered a cerebral phenomenon that was destined to bring on one of the most disturbing revolutions of our time.

It is the intellectuals, those most sensitive to the anxieties of modern civilization, who are particularly attracted to the drug. It is not laborers or farmers—at least not to the same degree as those who work with their minds. In any case, "acid" has not yet become the most popular escape; that is still alcohol, with its ruinous slavery. The conflicts between technological progress and a declining humanism—the desire of the individual to "be somebody" in the face of mass media, war, the atomic bomb, routine, and standardization —have resulted in unprecedented frustration, discord, and neuroses. In order to endure the horrors of an industrialized society, people are resorting not only to psychoanalysis but also to "uppers"— the amphetamines that provide a lift—and "downers"—the barbiturates and tranquilizers that ease tension and enable one to sleep. On these we spend 508,200,000 dollars every year.

"Each age produces what it needs," says Princeton psychiatrist Humphry Osmond. This is certainly true, at least in the realm of travel. Man invented the compass when he felt the urge to explore the world, and the rocket when he believed it imperative to control outer space. He produced LSD when the need to escape the proliferation and standardization of his society led him to cast about for a vehicle in which to travel deeper within his own consciousness.

The trouble is that, while the brain, like the earth, seems easy to explore—you have only to make a hole to look into either—they both remain inaccessible. We have no clear idea of what is happening twenty kilometers beneath our feet, or two centimeters under our skulls.

Mysteries of the Mind

The somatic disturbances caused by LSD are well known: dilation of the pupils, an increase in the electrical activity of the brain, a quickened pulse, more pronounced knee reflexes, and sometimes chills, fever, and nausea.

These changes are insignificant compared to the mental and psychological effects. In fact, when a normal dose is taken, only two-hundredths of a microgram find their way to the brain, while the rest ends up in the small intestine, the liver, and the kidneys. For a few minutes four million molecules come in contact with twelve billion brain cells, and the drug has been eliminated from the system by the time its psychological effects begin to appear.

LSD simply sets off a metabolic chain reaction, which lasts for several hours and affects only the midbrain, which "contains the limbic system, which modulates emotional responsivity; the reticular formation, which regulates awareness; and the sympathetic and parasympathetic centers."[2] Thus the drug touches a complex and formidable mechanism, and this slight contact is enough to bring about a vast cerebral revolution.

The brain has been compared to an electronic coordinator. One of its principal functions is selecting or inhibiting sensory data, thus "allowing the individual to analyze what is happening and maintain contact with immediate reality."

If LSD acts by disconnecting inhibiting mechanisms and altering the electrical current that stimulates the millions of brain cells, it is easy to see how the individual will be caught up and overwhelmed by a flood of sensations, images, and memories. There is a hidden existence, a veritable collective consciousness filled with horror and fragments of ancient "acts of experience" (Husserl's *Erlebnis*) that bursts from its watertight compartments and demands its rights of citizenship, as do outside stimuli and an uncontrollably expanded ego.

Deprived of his capacity for filtering, selecting, and classifying under the influence of the drug, a man may sink into his past, find himself obsessed by a single image endlessly repeated, go into ecstasies over a tree or a scrap of cloth, or believe himself to be a genius, an illuminate, a sinner, or a failure. There are no longer any clear distinctions between life and death, sanity and madness, waking and sleeping. Whatever evil or good that is within him, whatever is normally dominant in his nature, will take the upper hand in his delirium. A great poet may find his inner world enriched—as in the case of Henri Michaux—while a man who is filled with anxieties and frustration will only add confusion and disorder to his life. In any event, LSD reveals the incredible capacities of the human mind, its hidden power and mysterious depths.

The Polarity of the Sacred

In our secular world, LSD is not a god in itself, but it acts like a god. It has at least the polarity of the sacred. Dr. Emilio Servadio has spoken of a "pressure" on the psychic apparatus's line of defense: "If the balance of forces favors the LSD—which is always the case when the dose is large enough—the subject will discover within himself and reveal to others aspects of his personality that are generally concealed by rigid and ancient defense mechanisms." Possibly this explains the terror. The person who "takes off" feels that he is losing control of his consciousness; he witnesses the foundering and even the disintegration of his mental processes and finds himself assailed by terrifying memories and visions. Like the developer applied to a photographic negative, the acid reveals what was hidden and illicit. The buried past bursts forth in a brutal fashion; good and evil and the futility of action become evident in a way that is often unbearable. One enters a zone that is normally off-limits, where our vision of hell may alternate with a glimpse of exaltation and illumination—the ascent to an equally forbidden heaven.

It is known that LSD introduces radical changes in our concept of space-time. Space not only becomes fluid and glittering, but it also seems boundless. The "traveler" has the sensation of being part of a vast whole, of melting into it, of embracing it, of containing it. His ego disperses and blows over things like the wind, penetrating their mysterious essences. Time takes on new dimensions; there is no longer any distinction between past, present, and future. He dwells in the Never, in the horrible and delightful Land of Never.

Such possibilities may establish a myth—the myth of our time—and even a new religion, or at least a new sense of religion. There seems to be a conviction that everything will be revealed to us: the past and future, the secrets and resources of our psyche, the Truth (with a capital T) concerning our life.

But what is this truth? Where have these experiences led us? Dr. Servadio concludes: "We have no fond hopes as to the effects our observations may have on either the fans or the adversaries of LSD: we are well aware of the price we must pay if we are to modify and neutralize the deep, irrational motivations of our judgments and actions. But someone had to try to look from inside at this tremendous phenomenon of our time, to see beyond so many semblances, so much emotion, and so many illusions."

The Testimony

So, then, LSD, like peyote and the hallucinogenic mushrooms during the neolithic, has ended by creating a myth and a revolution whose consequences are still unforeseeable. Part of this revolution is brought home to us by books, pamphlets, newspapers, magazines, scientific reports, and radio and television programs.

Let us look at some of the titles: "LSD, Trip to the Heart of Delirium" (*L'Express*); "Poisons of the Spirit" (the austere *Le Monde*); "The Dangerous Magic of LSD" (*Saturday Evening Post*); "Trip to Nirvana" (*Die Weltwoche*); "I Return from the Hell of LSD" (*Gente*); "A Terrible Drug is About to Destroy the United States"

(*Epoca*); "An Atom Bomb in the Head" (*Crapouillot*); "LSD and Drugs of the Mind" (*Newsweek*); "Psychedelic Art" (*Life*); "LSD Helps Alcoholics" (*Science News*).

Dr. Roy S. Grinker exclaims in the *Journal of the American Medical Association*, "The deleterious effects of LSD are becoming more and more evident." Dr. Richard Alpert, high priest of LSD and a friend of Leary, observes with a diabolic smile: "LSD is one of the keys to wisdom. Life has seemed infinitely more satisfying since my first psychedelic experience. LSD raises more fundamental questions in both the scientific and spiritual fields than any subject I have ever dealt with."

A Harvard student describes his experiences: "I felt that *this is it, this is the moment of truth.* I knew everything had led up to this, complete harmony and ecstasy. We had arrived, we were part of the heart of being, we were transfigured—dead, and yet at the same time living with an intensity that had never been equaled. I had a feeling of initiation and participation in some great mystery; everything became known and familiar. I felt omnipotent, endowed with superhuman, divine powers."

Another student writes: "I have come back from a trip where I saw the world for the first time. . . . How beautiful it was. . . . I was drunk with ecstasy, I felt that I was exploding, losing the sensation of being myself, apart from everything else . . . no longer carried away by the confusing tide of emotions, feelings, love, and anger, of intimate union with another person."

A psychology student writes to his girl friend after having taken a normal dose of LSD:

My dear Ruth:
The strangest thing happened on the way to me this day. I met myself and found that I'm really not me after all. Or perhaps I should say that I have found out what it is like to exist. For that's all there was left that instant, at that instant when feeling, thinking, being, all were caught up into one ebbing unity; a unity which was me, but not me, too. A me-not-me which stood there nakedly and pointed back at itself in a sorrowful joy, and asked, "Why?" . . . But then the "why" didn't matter and it just *was!* . . . How can all this come out of one little capsule of LSD? Or perhaps I should ask, where was all this before now? . . . I remember saying, "It's too

much for me, it's too much." Was I afraid! I felt like a little boy, a naked, bare-faced little boy. And I pleaded, "Please stop, I don't want to see me." But it came anyway; and it overwhelmed me like the ocean washing over a little boy's sand castle despite the little dikes and moats. It washed over the little castle me and spread my sands over the ocean floor of existence and said: "Now go find yourself and live like before!" . . . I'm afraid my little ego will never be the same. It can't be; it couldn't be; it mustn't. . . . From now on I'm going to feel a little different about the kind of language we use to describe psychotics and their "little worlds." I'm going to watch a little closer and see if maybe what they are trying to describe isn't something like what I feel now and what I felt like then. I'm going to look a little closer at what the mystics are trying to tell us; at what the philosophers have to say about this. . . . Maybe today the process of twenty-two years was suddenly reversed by this little drug called LSD. . . .

I have just seen the world for the first time. About two hours ago I went out for supper, and everything was marvelous. The people in the restaurant must really have thought me queer. I watched the ice in the ice water, the water on the counter top, the reflection of the ceiling in the water, I watched the waitresses, the busboys, and above all else, I watched the cheese melt on top of my hamburger. Have you ever watched the foam on a glass of beer? What a world of delight can exist in such a common thing. . . .

All the time while I was walking around on the streets and seeing, I was thinking about when I said that all this was "too much." I remember now that I said, or felt, "It's too much for me, I'm just a kid." . . . The world looked to me like it must to a little child, all big and beautiful. And I was experiencing it without the imposed controls that we have to slap on the world in order to become adults. . . . And I loved it. . . . I think that now I notice the physical boundaries of my body coming back and the same thing is happening to my mind. But does it have to be this way? . . . Like I said, "A funny thing happened . . ."[3]

Some people are less fortunate than this young man deep in the contemplation of the cheese running over his hamburger. "There are no good or bad drugs," Dr. Sidney Cohen says, "only good or bad uses to which they are put." Actually, there are not even good or bad uses, but merely good or bad subjects for the experiments. It all depends on character, on personality. Drugs allow some people to discover the hidden splendor of the world; others find only monsters and demons crouching within their subconscious.

Says this young man, after some tests with LSD: "Over my right shoulder I could vaguely see what looked like a winged animal. It reminded me of a pterodactyl and it frightened me considerably. I was quite scared of it. We went on with the test though I still felt somewhat terrified of this thing. It seemed that instead of being in the room, it shifted outside as if I was too scared to have it inside with me and I put it outside. I felt often that it was beating its wings out there trying to get in. I could see through the window the flickering shadow of it. And once or twice I heard its wings. I was so terrified by this thing that I just couldn't move. Another peculiar reaction was that every time I heard this thing, the tester would turn a pale green color and his face would assume the consistency of cream cheese, with his eyebrows and hair being very finely etched against his pale face. It was the most frightening experience I've ever had."

A Yale graduate, age twenty-nine, describes his experience: "As I lay on the ground I looked up through the leaves, and the whole plant seemed very friendly and intimately related to me, like a human being. For a moment I was a plant, too, and felt my spinal column growing downward, through the brick pavement, sending out roots. . . . and I raised my arms, waved them in a circle like branches, and I was really a plant. But toward the end of the experiment I kept looking at Louise, and I had the impression that she was having a bad reaction to the drug. Suddenly I was frightened. I looked down, and Louise was far away, miles and miles away, as though I were looking at her through the wrong end of a telescope."

A Banquet of the Flesh, on Silver Platters

For Leary and his followers, "acid" is not only a mystical ascension and a way to regain youth, but also the new philosopher's stone, the philter sought by the alchemists. In one ten-thousandth of a gram dwells a powerful genie; to thousands of young people who have bacon and eggs for breakfast, go to the movies, dance the Jerk, and make love without pleasure, that genie—and this must be clearly understood—offers *ecstasy, revelation, illumination, and communion with nature.*

But there is something more. Leary knows very well that promises of such spiritual pleasures are too abstract. Experiences that were once the special privilege of the mystics can now be bought at cut-rate prices, as though on sale at Sears, Roebuck. What would at one time have created a real stir appeals today only to the small, irreducible group who look for salvation in Rosicrucianism, yoga, or astrology.

Thus he needs a much more concrete and convincing tourist program. Along with the religious component, he emphasizes the sensual aspect; he presents "acid" as not only a cerebral atomic bomb, but also an erotic explosion, a sexual hydrogen bomb.

In an interview in *Playboy*, Leary describes the effects of LSD on the sensory apparatus. "LSD vision is to normal vision as normal vision is to the picture on a badly tuned television set. Under LSD, it is as though you had microscopes up to your eyes, in which you see jewellike, radiant details of anything your eye falls upon. You are really seeing for the first time—not static, symbolic perception of learned things, but patterns of light bouncing off the objects around you and hurtling at the speed of light into the mosaic of rods and cones in the retina of your eye . . ."

"Is the sense of hearing similarly intensified?"

"The organ of Corti in your inner ear becomes a trembling membrane seething with tattoos of sound waves. The vibrations seem to penetrate deep inside you, swell and burst there. You hear one note of a Bach sonata, and it hangs there, glittering, pulsating, for an endless length of time. . . . You not only hear but *see* the music emerging from the speaker system—like dancing particles, like squirming curls of toothpaste. You actually *see* the sound, in multicolored patterns, while you're hearing it. At the same time you *are* the sound, you are the note, you are the string of the violin or piano. And every one of your organs is pulsing and having orgasms in rhythm with it."

"How about the sense of smell?"

"You discover that you're actually inhaling an atmosphere composed of millions of microscopic strands of olfactory ticker tape, exploding in your nostrils with ecstatic meaning. When you sit across the room from a woman during an LSD session, you're aware of thousands of penetrating chemical messages from her [coming] through the air into your sensory center: a symphony of a thousand odors that all of us exude at every moment—the shampoo she uses, her cologne, her sweat, the exhaust and discharge from her digestive system, her sexual perfume, the fragrance of her clothing—grenades of eroticism exploding in the olfactory cell."

Are these rewards not enough? Does he demand even more of the genie hidden in the miraculous microgram? Leary has not yet displayed all his treasures: "When Dr. Goddard, head of the Food and Drug Administration, announced in a Senate hearing that ten percent of our college students are taking LSD, did you ever wonder why?"

The reporter knows that Leary is about to show him the card he has up the sleeve of his wizard's robe, that he is going to dazzle him with a glimpse of his unsuspected powers. He does not answer. Leary tosses his grenade. "Sure, they're discovering God and meaning; sure, they're discovering themselves; but did you really think that sex wasn't the fundamental reason for this surging, youthful social boom? You can no more do research on LSD and leave out sexual ecstasy than you can do microscopic research on tissue and leave out cells."

The reporter feels that they have come to the heart of the matter. "Are you talking now about erotic pleasure?" he asks, thinking of the "Bunnies" baring their enormous breasts to the sun by the pool of Playboy Clubs, the twentieth-century versions of Ingres's seraglio.

"Yes. An enormous amount of energy from every fiber of your body is released under LSD—most especially including sexual energy. There is no question that LSD is the most powerful aphrodisiac ever discovered by man."

"Would you elaborate?"

"I'm saying simply that sex under LSD becomes miraculously enhanced and intensified. . . . It doesn't automatically produce a longer erection. Rather, it increases your sensitivity a thousand percent. Let me put it this way: Compared with sex under LSD, the way you've been making love—no matter how ecstatic the pleasure you think you get from it—is like making love to a department-store dummy.

In sensory and cellular communion on LSD, you may spend a half hour making love with eyeballs, another half hour making love with breath. As you spin through a thousand sensory and cellular organic changes, she does, too. Ordinarily, sexual communion involves one's own chemicals, pressure and interactions of a very localized nature—in what the psychologists call the erogenous zones. A vulgar, dirty concept, I think. When you're making love under LSD, it's as though every cell in your body—and you have trillions—is making love with every cell in her body. Your hand doesn't caress her skin but sinks down into and merges with ancient dynamos of ecstasy within her."

My God, I ask myself, who could resist a program as seductive as that? What young man, or even old man, could pretend to be indifferent to such a display of dazzling jewels? One feels like Bosch's Saint Anthony, prostrate in a fantastic landscape, surrounded by the most divine naked women, the most obscene creatures, and the most repulsive and extraordinary objects imaginable. There are the hanged man, the burning village, the gigantic bird, the nicked knife rolling on ears like a phallic tank, flying fish, sweet, mysterious faces that once seen can never be forgotten—all to be found in the delirious fabric of the mescaline dream. Leary sets himself up as a thaumaturge. He makes the blind man see, the deaf man hear, the paralytic walk. He has discovered the fountain of eternal youth and can cure the impotent and the homosexual. He holds the magic panacea for routine, mechanization, and the ankylosed structures of government, church, and the bourgeoisie.

He knows how to ingratiate himself. He addresses not the adults, but the young, the rebels. He makes use of a language calculated to inflate their pride and intensify their sense of isolation: "The generation under twenty-five today is the wisest and most honest the human race has ever known. Instead of resenting them, maligning them, and throwing them in jail, we should be supporting them, listening to what they have to say, and following their example."

We must concede that no one else speaks to young people in this way, and that no institution is in a position to offer them so much in exchange for so little. The "Establishment" has taken its revenge upon this man by sentencing him to thirty years in prison—not for his prophecies, but for the heinous crime of possession of marijuana.

Descent into Hell

Dr. Sidney Cohen warns of the dangers involved.[4] A young man of twenty-two, excessively timid, took a 450-microgram dose and developed the delusion that he was a new Messiah; he refused all food—gods have no need to eat—and had to be confined to a hospital. "When he was not howling and weeping, he lay quietly in the fetal position."

Another youth, "head of a team of magazine salesmen, became convinced under LSD that he was the Savior. He persuaded his wife, who was also drugged, that she was the reincarnation of the Virgin Mary. He gathered some other LSD apostles and made plans to retire to the wilderness. Although he harassed his employer and tried to make him see that he was Saint Peter, the man refused to take the drug. The Savior sold everything he had and gave the money away."

A third subject, on his way home from a party, stepped in front of a truck traveling at high speed, held up his hand, and yelled "Stop!" He was killed instantly.

"Sometimes," says Dr. Cohen, "it is hard to distinguish between accidental death and suicide. One student, a veteran LSD user known to be unbalanced, told a friend he was going to the beach to take 'acid.' The Pacific washed up his body several hours later. Did he think he could walk on the water, or did the difference between life and death seem trivial to him under the influence of LSD? Fixed ideas like this are very convincing in the psychedelic state.

"At times a psychosis approaching delirium will persist even after the effects of LSD have worn off. It may return days or weeks later, for no apparent reason. For example: A married student who had previously taken marijuana and small doses of LSD with very pleasant results swallowed a 300-microgram capsule. For three weeks he lived in terror; he saw tiny creatures crawling around his room, and had the frightening sensation that time had stopped. He spent the nights walking the streets with his wife, afraid to close his eyes. 'If it hadn't been for her, I'd have killed myself,' he said. He wondered 'if he'd ever be able to get out of it.' Under psychiatric treatment he finally came around."

The Daily Trip

The cases I have given here are only a few selected from a vast number involving millions of Americans and Europeans. Like the reports of eighteenth-century explorers, they tell of enchanted voyages to exotic southern islands, with hurricanes, whirlpools, and shipwrecks. They are the adventures of the luckiest and the most unfortunate of the travelers; but they do not reflect the everyday experiences of thousands and thousands of young people in Los Angeles and Paris who smoke marijuana and suck sugar cubes containing a tiny amount of LSD-25. Unlike the Huicholes, these are the children of abundance; but their long hair, their miniskirts, their tight trousers, their costume jewelry, their records, their *Playboy* magazine, and their comic books are not enough. None of it is enough. They can race along the superhighways at 120 miles an hour in their sports cars, make love, lie on the beaches, have themselves covered with tattoos, and dance frantically, half-naked, all night. But that isn't enough, either.

Jean Cau, watching some youngsters on drugs, was beside himself: "What can we offer these young people in their zoo, through the bars of their cages? Our religions, our morality, our faith? Where are they? Besides, they don't want them. Instead of our peanuts, they would rather have the sugar soaked in 'D' other 'adults' are slipping them through the wire, screaming all the while how rotten they are. They are hemmed in by demagogy, hucksterism, and money. They are isolated, drifting, knocked about, crazed, rebels without a cause; they end up questioning everything, even sex, even the path that leads to the gates of the zoo—to their own lives."[5]

What did Jean Cau see, to prompt this minor apocalypse? It was an ordinary, everyday scene in Paris, Saint-Tropez, or California: the initiation rites for a young man whom Cau calls Pierrot, a twenty-two–year–old photographer who "adored" marijuana. He was escorted by Bernard, a "D" veteran.

The host, in a black robe, served sugar cubes wrapped in tinfoil. "Candy, gentlemen?"

By nine thirty Pierrot was stretched out on a bed, beginning the slow "ascent." "A hard takeoff," the host observed. "On the first trip sometimes you have to go through hell before you get to paradise."

Pierrot complained that his jaw "weighed a ton." "You're all blue," he went on. "Completely blue, deep blue. Something out of 'op art.' I understand everything. But I can't remember what I see. Everything's in color, but not strange at all. Have I been *there* very long?"

He had "taken off." "If I just wave my hand, everything changes color."

By eleven the host was babbling: "In the Land of Fire only the initiated Wizard gets the 'charge.' Then he urinates, and the Second Initiates have the right to get their 'charge' by drinking his urine. Then they urinate and the others take their turn. . . . But the 'charge' keeps getting weaker and weaker . . . you know."

Pierrot had reached the height of his delirium. "It's terrible, I'm burning up. I'm sick. Everything is . . . I see. Everything is friendly. No. You can be your father and your mother at the same time. I'm dying. I'm an Arab. Who's buying?"

By midnight Pierrot was out of his mind. People were trying to help him "land." It was impossible. He tossed and turned among the tangled sheets and blankets. He bent double. He masturbated.

Cau: "If only that would calm him down."

The host was more pessimistic. "Just the opposite. It'll get him more excited."

Cau: "Suppose we lower the lights and go into the other room and leave him alone?"

The host looked gloomy. "He'll tear my bed to pieces."

Bernard was pacing back and forth, very upset. A friend of the host, called the Grand Initiate, came in with an American black girl who had the "profile of a proud, savage animal."

The Grand Initiate said: "The other night this guy got loaded to

An elder *mara'akame* of San Andrés presents his newborn grand-child to the Sun Father. He protects the back of the baby's head with his powerful *muwieri*, the prayer arrows with pendant hawk, eagle, and turkey feathers. Huicholes consider the head, especially the fontanel, to be the seat of the essential life force, or soul.

As they prepare the offerings for the peyote pilgrimage, the shaman-leader sings peyote songs while he decorates a composite bamboo arrow with colored yarn and paint and his wife shapes maize dough into miniature animal effigies. The load of firewood is the "proper food for Tatewarí"—fuel to keep the divine fire (Our Grandfather) burning at home for the duration of the pilgrimage.

The shaman-leader, in his role of Grandfather Fire, the first shaman and fire deity who initiated the primordial peyote quest, assists a *peyotero* in tying a knot in the sacred *ixtle* string that binds the pilgrims together with a symbolic umbilical cord. The knots, each representing a pilgrim, are tied at the beginning of the journey and untied at its conclusion.

The *kaunari*, a long string of *ixtle*, is passed from the leader of the *peyoteros* to his first assistant, *right*, and from him to the other peyote pilgrims sitting in a circle around the divine fire. The leader is playing his hunting bow, tapping out "magical" music on the taut string with the tip of his arrow. Bow music is said to attract and soothe the deer, Our Elder Brother.

On the morning of departure for Wirikuta, the small group of pilgrims, carrying lighted candles representing the divine fire, circles the dying embers before setting out in single file. They are wearing clothing specially made for the sacred journey, but their poverty is evident in the cotton flour sacking from which the pants and shirts of the two men at right were sewn by their wives.

The shaman-leader of the *peyoteros* ties knots in an *ixtle*-fiber cord for each sexual transgression "confessed" in the public purification ritual that initiates the peyote hunt. At the climax of the ritual, the cord with its accumulated knots is burned, symbolizing the return of the *peyoteros* to an original state of innocence, enabling them to enter the sacred peyote country in a state of spiritual purity.

Oblivious to evidence of the twentieth century around them, a group of *peyoteros* lines up single file by the side of a modern highway in preparation of the ceremonies of passage across an invisible, but nonetheless very real, divide "from this to the other world"—the dangerous passage through Wakurikitenie, the clashing Gate of the Clouds.

Matewames (novice *peyoteros*) are blindfolded by the shaman-leader of the pilgrimage and must make part of the journey in what the Huicholes say is total darkness. Reinforced by sitting in a simulated fetal position at certain prescribed sacred places, such as the divine maternal water holes (Tatei Matinieri), the blindfolding presumably symbolizes return to the womb, from which the novices are reborn into the company of adult peyote seekers when the blindfolds are removed. Thus, their first pilgrimage is for them tantamount to initiation.

Headwashing ceremony at Tatei Matinieri, the Place of Our Mothers, on the way to Wirikuta, the sacred peyote country in the desert of San Luis Potosí. The Huichol headwashing rites are strikingly similar in form as well as meaning to those of the Hopis and other southwestern Pueblo Indians.

Peyoteros set out single file—as the divine ancestors did on the primordial peyote hunt. The shaman-leader, *at left*, is carrying his bow and arrows with which the first peyote will be "shot." The deer antlers in his hands stand for Elder Brother Kauyumari, the Great Blue Deer who acts as divine guide and protector of the *peyoteros*. Later the pilgrims will fan out across the desert searching for the

elusive peyote. The Huicholes refer to this as "tracking" the deer, for wherever the primordial deer walked, peyotes sprang up, just as the first peyote manifested itself as a deer, transforming into his plant form when the arrows of the first *peyoteros*, the ancestral gods, reached their mark.

Hardwood bows and deerskin quivers filled with hunting arrows are stacked around a spiny cactus while the *peyoteros* search for the "tracks of the deer"—the divine little cactus *Lophophora williamsii*.

Barely projecting above ground, this clone of young peyotes was considered especially sacred because each had five sections—five being the sacred number because it signifies the four cardinal points and the sacred center and also stands for "completion."

The shaman-leader uses his knife to pry another peyote cactus from the hard ground, being careful to leave part of the long root in the earth. Roots and other trimmings from the peyote plants are carefully collected, to be redeposited in the desert. The Huicholes say these are the "bones" of the deer-peyote and must be treated with reverence, lest no peyotes appear to the pilgrims on their next journey to Wirikuta. This is reminiscent of bone rituals of hunter-gatherer societies.

With the low mountain range of Wirikuta (Real de Catorce) in the background, the *peyoteros* return single file to camp after a day of collecting peyote in the sacred land.

The wife of the shaman-leader, in her new identity as Our Mother Yurianaka, earth and corn goddess, watches intently as her husband carefully slices the first peyote for distribution in a kind of communal sacrificial meal. The first peyote is considered to be Elder Brother Watemukame, reincarnated as Parítsika, the Lord of the deer species.

The Huicholes identify peyote with the deer, and the first of the small hallucinogenic cactuses to be seen by the shaman-leader is stalked and slain with hunting arrows. Numerous offerings and petitions, including candles, yarn designs, votive gourd bowls, thread crosses, arrows, and even money, which are to be sacrificed by fire, mark the spot of the divine deer-peyote's sacrificial "death." The shaman-leader places pieces of fresh peyote in a special gourd for distribution to the pilgrims.

During and after the pilgrimage, each *peyotero* gives to every other pilgrim some of his own peyote and receives some in exchange, "so that all shall be of one heart," as the Huicholes say.

A *peyotero* displays his "harvest" of mature and young *hikuri*, as the Huicholes call the peyote. Baskets and woven bags of the sacred hallucinogenic cactuses are taken back to the Sierra Madre Occidental for use in the annual ritual cycle.

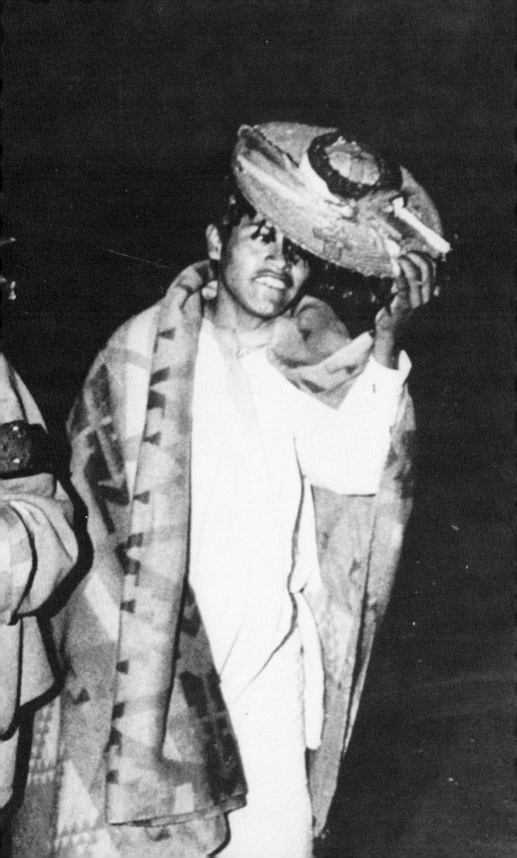

Peyoteros dancing to the music of a homemade guitar at the height of the peyote hunt; songs speak of the sacred country as the "land of beautiful, brilliant-colored flowers" and of the Huicholes themselves as the sons and daughters of the deer-peyote.

Characteristically, an experienced *peyotero* is able to come out of the peyote trance at will. Here the shaman-leader rises to fetch fresh wood for the fire—Our Grandfather, the first shaman—while his companions are deep in their peyote dreams.

The prestigious old *mara'akame* of San Andrés conducts the ritual of the parched corn, at which the peyote is consumed in liquid form.

the eyeballs and began screwing standing up, without even touching himself, with a girl nobody else could see. Finally he came like a wild stallion. It was magnificent. Out in the country, in the moonlight. Terrific."

Soon after the Grand Initiate had gone, Cau realized that Bernard had put LSD in his drink. "The Afghan music that beat in my pelvis. My incredible fascination as I watched Pierrot twisting in his delirium. The photographer who saw everything 'egg-shaped.' People in the street . . . So far I had been perfectly fine, and I mustn't lose face. But SUDDENLY: What face? Who was this person who suddenly understood the fact that he had been, that he was, that he wasn't? A blow with a hammer. Horror. I saw myself, and I knew I was drugged to the point of explosion. I must pull myself together. AT ANY PRICE."

The host gave him an antidote. "Go home, and you'll be able to sleep. You see, when you wanted to watch, I had to drug you. That's one of the rules of the game; otherwise you wouldn't have been allowed to see all this."

Jean Cau spent a miserable night, and the following day he was sick and depressed. He called a doctor and was at last able to fall asleep. "Sleep! A marvelous sleep, with no hallucinations. Black, fat, thick sleep. Health. Sleep on the far shore, and health. Three days of terrible fatigue. Unable to work. The immense fatigue of convalescence. The doctor told me to see him in a week; in the meantime I was to take my pills three times a day."

By the end of the week he had recovered. "The doctor talked to me about the terrifying ravages of LSD, about the youngsters whose shattered remains were going to end up in psychiatric hospitals. He said that when the vacation months came around again there would be an upsurge in the use of 'acid.' There was nothing like vacations to bring young people together. There would be more and more LSD users. He was very concerned. What could be done?"

"Adults, fathers, mothers, what can we do?" Jean Cau asks. "Prosperity is emptying its horn of plenty on our youth. It is a cornucopia filled with records, automobiles, miniskirts, vacations, magazines designed to bestialize their readers, thousands of luxuries, marijuana cigarettes for one franc, a shattering 'charge' of LSD for five. The drug is no longer a treat enjoyed only by homosexual antique collectors and fashionable poets. This is the day of forty-five r.p.m., paperbacks, and drugs. It is as though there were a huge electric sign high over Broadway, proclaiming: 'LSD IS A THOUSAND TIMES BETTER, AND A THOUSAND TIMES CHEAPER. DO WHAT EVERYBODY'S DOING. LSD IS GOOD FOR YOU.' "

Jean Cau's view is biased and debatable; but it is the opinion of a young writer who knows European youth and has seen how they are deceived, adulated, and made to believe that they constitute a privileged class. Abundance has made them no better than the youngsters of the previous generation. Their "trips" are truly descents into the cellar of the psyche. In an era when the word *moral* elicits a mocking smile, when no one trusts adults with their duplicity, their slogans, their religion, their law and order, their institutions, their patriotism, their sensible advice ("That way lies self-destruction, this way lies fame and fortune"), what arguments can we find to avert the disaster?

The LSD phenomenon has come with prosperity and belongs to a certain moment in history. To attack it is to attack the very foundations of our culture. The youngsters who see pterodactyls beating their wings against the window, or think they are Messiahs and Saviors, do not present, surely, a more atrocious or less edifying spectacle than that of Americans blowing Vietnamese children to bits. If the behavior of thousands of young people is irrational and absurd, the nationalistic hatred that has broken out in the Middle East or the racial discord brought about by the whites in the United States is far more irrational and absurd.

The young people in Saint-Tropez and Greenwich Village are convinced that everything must be changed and rebuilt from the bottom up. They are both rebels and pacifists; they detest the slogans mouthed by politicians, educators, and moralists, and they have devised slogans and conventions of their own to counteract them.

They have created a new language and a new experience. But in the midst of this flood of documents, descriptions of trips, warnings, alarmed and reassuring voices, this crazy mixture of hell, magic, delirium, psychosis, nirvana, mystical union, terror, indignity, and destruction, no one has turned his attention to the experiences of primitive man, who for fifteen thousand years has used "acids" and known how to utilize them as a powerful means of spiritual elevation.

Friend or Foe?

"Mescaline is not a friend of man," says one of Henri Michaux's woman friends. And, in fact, "acid" has no reason to feel friendly toward a young lady who lights the fire after dinner, lowers the blinds, makes sure that the telephone is within easy reach and that there is a good supply of oranges in the refrigerator to soothe her irritable liver, and swallows a carefully calculated dose in order to attain the ecstasy she cannot find in the movies, television, or evenings with her undemonstrative fiancé.

Peyote is not a friendly drug, and it does not lend itself to personal amusement. To move out of the human orbit into the divine is such a dangerous undertaking, an experiment so fraught with hidden and formidable meanings, that one cannot embark upon it without exposing himself to unforeseeable risks. Being God, sharing to some degree in His essence, is not comfortable. We see better, we hear better, we are more sensitive to touch; but acquiring the eyes, ears, and tactile sense of the gods does not necessarily mean a refinement or an improvement. The gods do not perceive the things of our world in a better way but perceive them in accordance with their own nature, in a way that is totally beyond our human capacities.

According to Michaux, peyote "combines the components of religious experience: the profound impression of being mysteriously linked to everything, the profound impression of the beyond, the never, the profound impression of existing outside one's body and outside of time, of participating in the Absolute, the Perfect."

A blotting out of the ego, space, time, and the laws of the world. The astronaut has emerged from his capsule and in some incomprehensible way has plunged into stellar space and become part of it. Stars streak past his eyes at incredible velocities. He is aware that he has become a luminous being and, above all, that he is no longer an air-breathing animal; he feels that he has become a part of the universal whole, that he has recovered a nobility sold too cheaply. But in order to attain the power of the gods he has had to hurl himself into the abyss, face mortal danger, and endure endless ordeals and hardships.

The Pilgrims

Upon this plunge into the abyss, this venture to the brink of madness, the Huicholes have erected an immense ritual, a code of secret signs, and a religious canon. They have ordained and sacralized madness, embodying it in a system of myths and symbols that embraces spiritual exaltation, bounteous crops, and sturdy children.

Let us return to the pilgrims where we left them, chewing their peyote around the fire in Wirikuta. What visions were they having? What did they see and hear in their rapture? Did their "trip" have anything in common with those taking place in Greenwich Village? Was it anything like that experienced by the French girl, locked in her apartment with the telephone within reach in case of the slightest sign of anything going wrong?

The time had come to listen to the singing of the Blue Deer Tamats Kauyumari:

> Wirikuta, Wirikuta,
> Who knows why
> The flowers are weeping?
> What man can say?
> What man can guess?
> Wirikuta, Wirikuta,
> Who knows why
> Flowers weep?

The three shamans—Hilario, his son Eusebio, and his brother Antonio—had heard the song; they now took it up to the accompaniment of the violin and the guitars.

> The way of the flowers
> Leads here, through Wirikuta.
> Men say that you
> Yourself are here.
> I have come to find you.
> Even though I am not as you,
> Free from sin,
> I have come for you,
> I am here.

The Blue Deer rises from the bonfire or appears in the air, since he also embodies the God of the Wind. He sings but once, and the shamans must do their utmost to learn his song by heart so they can repeat it to the other *peyoteros*. They all hope, of course, to hear Tamats's supernatural voice; but it is only the elect, the pure in heart, who are so blessed. Some must return home without having heard it. Their sorrow was expressed in Antonio Bautista's song:

> I made the journey. I was there
> Where the hills appear,
> And heard nothing.
> I went, I stood there
> Where the hills appear,
> And heard no singing.

Another chant described the astonishing appearance of everyday things under the influence of peyote. (Aldous Huxley went into ecstasies over the cloth of his trousers; the stream of automobiles along Hollywood's Sunset Boulevard seemed to be a surging Red Sea.)

The Huicholes are fascinated by Catorce's bare hills and are mystified by their inexplicable presence here in the desert:

> Who can say why
> The hills sprang up
> There in Wirikuta?
> Who can know why
> The hills speak
> There in Wirikuta?

Not every song is short and laconic. Many concern the origins of the ritual instituted by the gods when the form of the world was not yet fixed but essentially fluid, when men marveled to see all kinds of changes and metamorphoses.

The acids set in motion a twofold magical process: the recovery of the sense of the lost oneness of the world, and the perception of sacred objects that dissolve and assume new forms in a supernatural way. These phenomena occur in accordance with certain strict, established patterns, of course. In such experiences the psychological and individual reactions play hardly any part; what matters are the religious associations—which fall within the field of sociology.

Under the influence of the drug, the Huicholes invariably see the completely formed violin and the timbers of the *calihuey* springing from the living tree. Before their eyes, Elder Brother Kauyumari issues from the shaman's *itari*, or straw mat, incorporating the ever-present trinity of peyote-deer-corn that governs their lives.

These metamorphoses take place with all the rapidity of the mescaline dream. Each image rises out of the preceding one, each figure gives birth to the next, proliferating from a given element, as though an electronic brain had been set in motion by some magical punched card.

The First Song of the Peyote

> Out of the sea rose the sea,
> And after the sea
> Came all the gods.
> The gods advanced like flowers,
> In the form of flowers,
> Following the sea.

And they came to the womb,
The generating place,
The place of their birth.
Out of the womb came the cloud,
And from the cloud sprang the *xiriki*,
And from the *xiriki* was born the deer
Who became the corn,
Who became the cloud
With rain for the cornfield.
The sea spoke to the gods
Concerning the five cardinal points,
And out of the sea came the Blue Deer
With Masi, the fawn,
And all the other deerlets.
Then appeared the arrow
And the head of the Deer,
In their places on the *itari*.
The gods then knew
The secret of the arrow
That turned to cloud,
The secret of the head
That turned to rain,
And they came to the cornfield.
There in the field
They left their offerings.
"What's going on in the *coamil*?
What's going on in the breast
Of Our Mother Tatei Yurianaka?"
The gods asked each other.
"We must find out what's happening here."
They hid behind the trees
And witnessed the divine birth;
They saw the *itari* giving birth
To the grass called Wiwátsixa.
They watched the stalks spring up,
And the ears, the young and tender corn,
And the rounded squash.
Then flowered the yellow *uxa*
For the gods to pluck
And rub between the palms
Of their great hands.
With *uxa* powder

They painted three bands
On their faces.
Said the gods, "Wiwátsixa
Was the cradle of the Deer
And will be his shroud,
For they will lay him there
When they kill him in the Sierra."
Hearing this, the Blue Deer Maxayuewe
Stepped out of the blue sea
And came to stand on the *itari*;
And in the north and the south,
The east and the west,
Appeared all the Blue Deer.

The Second Song of the Peyote

Flowers are flying, flowers are wheeling,
Circling over the Burned Hill,
And out of the heart of Our Grandfather
Spring the *itari* and the Deer.
The gods are speaking,
Yes, the gods are speaking to us
And no one can understand them.
But lo! Here is the arrow
Planted in the center of the *itari*,
And the arrow knows
The language of the gods.
Now, near the arrow,
See the blue serpent, Haikayuawe,
The gods' interpreter,
Who knows the language of the arrow.
From the *itari* springs the rain,
The rain is loosed,
Sounding the message of the gods:
"Brothers, the time has come
To make the rain-arrow."
The bowstring *wikuxa* leaps
To the notch of the arrow,
And the clouds rise again,
And the gods of the four quarters
Take form.
Each speaks, and understands the others:
Wirikuta, Auxamanaka,

Tatei Nakawé, Tatei Yurianaka,
And San Andrés all agree.
All rise into the air
And circle over Reunar;
Once again on earth,
They see the arrow marking
The birthplace of the Deer.
There lies the sacred *itari*,
And on it, resting there,
Is Our Brother
Tamats Kauyumari.

The Third Song of the Peyote

There you are, *itari*, by the Fire,
Where rose the Blue Deer
That became a flower.
Or, perhaps, is the *itari*, too,
A flower?
The flower speaks; but why?
No, it is the *itari* speaking.
Or is it the heart of Nivétsika
Speaking through the *itari*?
Nivétsika says, through the flower:
"I shall paint them yellow."
Why do you paint them with *uxa*?
Because the *itari* commands it,
And Tatewarí, too.
"Ah," says Grandfather Fire,
"Since gods do not know how to eat
I shall eat for them."
We hear, we clearly hear the voice of Tai,
The voices of the *kakauyaris*:
"The time has come
To speak with the sea."
"Perhaps you can't understand us?"
Yes, I understand you.
"In Wirikuta grows a flower that speaks,
And you understand it."
Yes, I understand it,
Just as I understand Reunar, Auxamanaka,
And Xapawiyeme, too. I understand them,
I hear them clearly:

"Here is the *itari*,
Here the gods will remain
Forever."

[The *cantador* assembles the gods on the *itari* and continues:]

I saw the *coamil*. Everything was open and visible.
It filled with stalks and ears of corn,
And among the stalks
I spied the ears of Our Brother,
The Blue Deer.
Then the Blue Deer stood erect
On Mother Earth, Tatei Yurianaka.
"Why did he stand there?"
The Deer is the *itari*
Renewing itself.
He is the *itari* for all the gods,
And they will be entrusted
To bear him in the Four Directions.
The *itari* remained seated
By the fire. From the *itari*
Sprang a branch, and from the branch
Grew the arrows, the gourd bowl,
And Xuturi, the Flower of God;
And everything became a cloud.
There grew the five *iteiri*,
The five chosen trees.

[The *mara'akame* then points to the spot where the trees may be cut.]

And from the tree sprang the *calihueyes*.
Kiewimuka, Haramara,
Parítsika, and Xapawiyeme
Selected their trees.
"We have chosen. Now you must go hunting
And erect your *calihuey*. The *itari*
Will remain by the fire forever.
There goes the mountain lion. There he goes.
In the Tepari will rise the figure of the Deer,
The Deer the gods saw running in a White Land."
"O Gods," says Kauyumari, "your magic
Has always seemed strange to me:
The Deer was in the Tepari
And you saw him running in a White Land.

You have the power to do anything.
I know your candles, and I, Kauyumari,
Deliver them to you. I give you your candles."
Said the gods of the Four Directions:
"This must be our tribute.
Thus shall it be given to us always."
"Tell me, Auxatemai, tell me, Nakawé,
What shall we do to protect the children
From recurring illness?" asks Kauyumari.
"This is our answer:
Prepare an arrow, a gourd bowl, and a candle.
Then you must kill a deer.
If there is to be life for the children,
A deer must die."

The Fourth Song of the Peyote

The cloud grew like the corn in the field.
Watukari was born, grew tall, and spoke;
The corn was born, the Deer was born;
The *itari* was born, and from the *itari*
Grew the oak, and the oak
Thundered like the rain.
"I will surround the *coamil*,
I will embrace it, I will envelop it,
I will bring it to full flower."
The rain enveloped the *coamil*,
And the Blue Deer appeared,
Accompanied by Masi,
His little brother.
The oak took root
And branched out in the Four Directions;
There it stood, there it put down roots.
There was the *itari*, spread out.
The *itari* became a cloud,
And once again rained on the earth.
In the Four Directions
They set their snares,
The *hatewari* nooses,
And among the nooses
Gushed the sacred water.
The water was borne to the *coamil*
Where the gods were waiting,

Where the *kakauyaris* were gathered,
And everything was blessed.
Rain fell on them all,
And the *milpa* flourished.
The gourd bowl with corn was taken
To the *xiriki*, and there the oak was reborn
As beams for the *calihuey*,
And all the offerings were reborn.
The gods knew
That this was to be their house,
And they spoke thus:
"It will rain in Tukipa,
And there will appear the head
Of Our Brother, Tamats."
Then, from the good earth,
The earth of Hapuka,
The gods were born:
Tsakaimuka, God of the Coras;
Tukaimuka, God of the Spiders;
Reutari, the Line of Shadow;
Kayawarika, God of the Tuxpan River;
And Atuxame, God of the Lerma.
Each went his way;
They scattered throughout the sierra.
They took their places.[1]

Nicolás's Experience

Religious considerations aside, the Huicholes personally dislike the effects of the acid. Nicolás, a shaman and medicine man from San Andrés, confessed to me that he had taken as many as ten large peyote buttons. "I heard guitars and violins playing, a red thing came out of my head, and I saw something like a drizzling rain falling. The trees seemed to be talking to each other; I heard voices somewhere over my head, but I couldn't see anybody. It scared me."

Nicolás was not only one of the most intelligent Huicholes I had ever met, but also one of the outstanding religious and civic personages in San Andrés. He had made the pilgrimage to Wirikuta thirty-two times; he had been the guardian of the bowl of Tatei Utuanaka, the Fish Goddess, for six years, and of the bowl of Parítsika, patron saint of the hunt, for another six. He had been *gobernador* and a leading member of the Council of Headmen. As the guardian of Utuanaka and Parítsika, it had been his duty to carry their bowls, decorated with figures of fish and deer, to Wirikuta and to see that the hunters and fishermen fulfilled their religious obligations.

Of all the Huicholes, Nicolás was naturally the least capable of disregarding the context of religious associations that had ruled his life since childhood. This is how he described his first experience: "I was twenty, and the *peyoteros* had just returned from Wirikuta to the *calihuey* in San Andrés. Not realizing that the buttons were intoxicating, I ate several of the large ones and went off to cut firewood with some friends. When we reached the woods I climbed a tree and tried repeatedly to cut off a branch; I refused to give up until I had broken my machete. They told me about it later. I didn't remember a thing from the time we left at seven in the morning until five in the afternoon, when I came down from the tree. Then I heard a sound like a train going by, and a lot of people singing.

"Then a 'señor' told me I would be a medicine man and *mara-'akame*, and that I must learn the song they were singing in order to use it to cure sick people. This 'señor' looked like a deer, with four legs and horns, but he talked like a person."

Nicolás's by no means enjoyable intoxication, in which the well-known disturbances of hearing and vision were mingled with terror, culminated with the appearance of the deer and the revelation of his shamanic powers; for when the Indians take peyote they always expect—consciously or otherwise—some communication from the divinity who dwells in the sacred cactus.

Hilario's Experience

In a society where there are a great many shamans, the neophyte is naturally eager to know whether the gods have destined him to be a good one or an evil one. In Wirikuta today, as it was at the beginning of time, there are two *tukipas*: one ruled by the great *cantador* Elder Brother Deer Tail, the other governed by the infernal *mara-'akames* who practice black magic. The shaman knows that some of the disasters and diseases suffered by the Huicholes are caused by sorcerers, and that in order to combat them effectively he must have a thorough knowledge of the mechanism of witchcraft.

The shaman Hilario's first experience, when he was a mere apprentice *mara'akame*, is significant in this regard. As his son, José Carrillo, tells it, Hilario consumed a great number of peyote buttons while at Wirikuta to see "what the gods had to say to him." He began at noon, and by seven o'clock he heard the voices of all the gods. One of them said: "Since you want to be a *cantador*, I am going to show you the difference between good and evil. There are things that can cause great evil, and you must learn to recognize them. Come with me, and I'll show you." Hilario followed obediently, and the god spoke again: "There have been many *cantadores* who have been more interested in doing bad things than in protecting their own people. Do you want to see them? They are farther on. Come with me." When they had gone a long way the god spoke to him a third time: "Watch what those people are doing."

According to José, his father saw a *mara'akame* holding enchanted *muwieris* made of owl feathers, and many men chanting and discussing matters of witchcraft. "Look at them carefully," the god told him. "Come closer."

The god led him farther, and spoke for the fifth time. "Look at that man. He is performing black magic; he is destroying people. You must act in the right way: you must be a good *mara'akame*, even if they try to bribe you with cattle and money to practice sorcery. Have you seen everything clearly? All right, let's go on."

The god spoke for the sixth time, and said: "This is where sorcerers are punished. Open your eyes, and don't miss anything."

Two men were heating an iron spear in the flames, while two *topiles* were bringing in a sorcerer. They bound him hand and foot, and then they drove the red-hot spear through his anus until it came out of his mouth. They put him over the fire and roasted him, turning him on his spit; they leaped and danced around him, crying out that they were going to eat him.

José Carrillo's father was too frightened to speak. Then the god said: "Turn and face the east, where the sun comes up. We, too, have our struggles and hardships. Look at those three iguanas: the yellow one belongs to the rising sun and is found in the east; the red one belongs to the setting sun and lives in the west; the green one belongs to the regions under the earth and stands in the center."

The three iguanas were engaged in battle on top of a huge boulder; they were shooting arrows at each other and flinging stones that glittered like *urukames*, each trying to cast a spell. The yellow one said, "I have only one arrow left," and shot it at the green one. The green iguana was wounded and fell from the boulder, and all the iguanas that were watching the battle began to die. "Don't look at me, or we'll all die," said the yellow one. Then he crawled into a hole in the stone.

"Remember carefully what you have seen," the god told José's father. "These iguanas are friends of the evil *mara'akames*, who use them to shoot enchanted arrows at anyone they wish to harm. Come with me; I want to show you something else."

A little farther on they came to a huge yellow scorpion in the east and a black river snake in the west. They were firing arrows at each other.

"The scorpion always defeats the snake," the god said, "because he belongs to the sun and is defending it against the serpents that are trying to cast a spell over it. Sorcerers are like the snakes: because they cannot be companions of the sun they-try to cast an evil spell over it, and over us. They work against everybody, like the green iguanas and the black serpents. It is your job to defend the sun and those who have been bewitched."

José Carrillo's father came to his senses in the early morning. He would never forget what he learned that day in Wirikuta when he ate the flower—the peyote.

Panchito's Experience

Panchito is one of the most loved and respected citizens of Ocota. This tiny village of adobe houses high on a mountain side could be called the antipodes of San Andrés. Its only shaman is my old friend Panchito Chibarras; it has no important *calihuey*, although most of the families have their private *xirikis*; and its inhabitants are remarkable for their honesty and hospitality. Because there is no priestly

class, Ocota is more open to outside influences. The men wear print-
ed cotton shirts and baseball or chauffeur's caps, which gives them
an incongruous appearance. Panchito Chibarras himself, the guardian and depository of the ancient wisdom, surprised me one evening
while he was seated in his ceremonial chair in his faded serape by
emitting the sound of a jazz band. The grand old shaman had a tran-
sistor radio under his blanket.

Panchito is not averse to such innovations. The strictest dictates of
tradition are reflected in the red tassels on his hat, his earrings, his
bracelets, his long hair, and his richly embroidered attire; but his
red cape is adorned with figures of cats, a radical departure from
traditional motifs. His aged, handsome wife is the only woman in
the village who wears glasses when doing embroidery. I used to see
her sitting on the ground by her front door, spectacles perched on
her tiny nose, absorbed in her work.

Like all Huichol men, Panchito aspires to be a *mara'akame*; but,
even though he has been an assistant *cantador* for five years, he is
still far short of his goal. This may be because he lacks the necessary
boldness and self-confidence, for he is a shy and kindly man. His
peyote experience has been bound up with his obsessive ambition
to become a shaman of the first rank.

"I went to Tsinurita [a mesa near Catorce where the sacred cactus
grows abundantly] seven times before I heard the deer. The eighth
time I was in the trance, about midnight a black water snake six
feet long, called Aik, came up to me and kept me company for a
while. Then he went away, and Watemukame, the Little Deer, appeared and talked to me like a father: 'Come back to Tsinurita and
take peyote again, and you will find me here. I will give you something precious, something that will make it possible for you to become a *cantador*.' A little later the Great Deer Ixikuikame came to
me and said: 'When you get home, eat no salt with your meals, and
do not sleep with your wife. Sleep alone, near the fire, so that Our
Grandfather Tatewarí can watch over you.' He plucked a peyote
with his horns. 'Take this peyote and eat it. It is my gift. Listen to
the sun: it is rising and knocking four times inside the earth. Did

you hear it? Did you hear the four knocks?' 'Yes, I heard them,' I answered. As he left, Ixikuikame said: 'When the sun comes up, look for me on that hill over there. Come alone. You'll find me there.'

"When I awoke at dawn I tried to orient myself. Both deer seemed to be telling me that on a certain hill I would find peyote: a large one with three small buttons on top, a *nierika* [the face of god]. 'Don't eat the big one,' they warned me, 'only the three little ones . . .' I went to the hill. There were the peyotes. I put the big one in my handkerchief and ate the little ones, and when I returned to my friends I was drunk. I sat down by the fire, and in a little while I recovered. When I got home I planted the peyote; since then I sleep alone and eat no salt. I must return to Tsinurita twice more, because Ixikuikame told me that on the tenth trip he would give me permission to go to Reunar, the Burned Hill. The three small peyotes I ate taught me three songs, and I kept them in my heart. But only Tamats Kauyumari will teach me to sing on the Burned Hill. The *mara'akames* know ten songs; I know only the three the peyotes sang to me."

I asked him to repeat them for me, but he refused. "No, I must not. Only my wife has heard them. I am not a *cantador*. I can sing for two hours at home, but during the festivals I follow the *mara-'akame*. He is the only one who knows the songs of Tamats, and he lets me sing just a little.

"When I went out deer hunting during the last dry season, I got drunk and saw Watemukame standing close to me. This is what he said: 'I am the one who spoke to you at Tsinurita. I am he. I am Watemukame. Why do you want to kill me?' When I came to, the Deer was gone. My friend asked, 'Why didn't you shoot? The deer was right there in front of you.' I had to keep my secret. I said, 'My rifle jammed.' "

The Secret of the Sphinx

When interrogated, the Sphinx may reveal to us a hidden aspect of our ego, but she says nothing as to how we are to make use of that revelation. The users of LSD, unlike the Huicholes, have no "prospect of salvation." While the youngsters in Greenwich Village and Saint-Tropez hope to find a kind of sexual Golden Fleece in the acid, the Indians make their pilgrimage to the far land of Wirikuta in an attempt to reenact the magical hunting of the Deer that took place at the beginning of time.

Their journey means self-sacrifice and demands immaculacy. For them the only sin is that of the flesh; it is the most persistent trace of the profane world, the most indelible stain. If they are to be worthy of communion with the Divine and Luminous, their sins must be washed away by means of a general confession and a series of scrupulous and obsessive ritual cleansings. It is here we first see the striking contrast between unbridled sensualism and asceticism, between the glorification of the senses and a rite dedicated precisely to their repression and ultimate nullification.

Where does the trip lead? What is the itinerary? The LSD traveler, according to the tourist literature, will take a journey to the center of his brain. Once his discriminatory defenses have fallen and his mental processes have been altered, he will be a helpless witness to the dispersion and fragmentation of his own ego. There will be no antidote for his terror, and the confused visions of his tiny hell and of the futility of his life will often throw him into a state of depression for which no momentary ecstasy can possibly compensate him.

The Huichol journey, on the other hand, follows a fixed itinerary: a route through the mountains and across the desert, laid out by the gods. Each of its stages is associated with some supernatural event. After leaving Tatei Matinieri the pilgrims enter Xirikitá, a splendid natural temple whose magical doors are guarded by deer; at the end of the trip they ascend a shamanic stairway with five blue altars leading to the summit of Reunar, where the new-born sun shot up.

As they move through this enchanted landscape, the pilgrims make sacrifices and present offerings to the gods who point the way. It is a way of partaking of their divinity, for the Indians already bear their names, are their doubles, and represent them. Within this process of consecration, personal reactions play no part. Psychology has hardly any role: what matters is not the individual, but collective concepts.

For a Huichol under the influence of peyote, dispersion of the ego is actually translated into communion with the whole. His fear announces the presence of divinity; he "hears" the singing of the gods, the trees, the rocks, with their mysterious and resonant messages; he "sees" Tamats rising from the fire and taking the form of garlands of strange and luminous flowers that crown the head of Reunar. He sees the same flowers again transformed into blue deer, and the blue deer into clouds, and the clouds into rain falling on his cornfield. This is the moment of creation, of virginal time, of the first days ruled by the Makers seated on the water, surrounded by blue and green feathers. The Huichol has won back to that time, and the Divine and Luminous has raised him to godhood.

In the Beginning
Was the Deer

We are in the presence of an aggregate of myths associated with an extremely complex form of worship; and, as usual, anthropologists are faced with the eternal problems. Where and when did this body of myths originate? How did the deer-peyote-corn trinity that governs the Huicholes' religious life take shape? At what moment did the religious cult become linked with that mythology, so permeated with re-creational elements?

"According to their mythology," writes Lumholtz, "the corn plant was originally a deer; this idea has its origin in the fact that deer were the tribe's principal source of food in primitive times." Lumholtz's reasoning does not reach the heart of the problem, but he has at least established a priority based on myths. The fact is that among the Huicholes the deer is Elder Brother Deer Tail, who predates one of the most ancient deities known as the Old God of Fire (now called Grandfather Fire) and is even older than Father Sun. This priority fits well into the Middle American religious context, where the creator-gods, the Makers, man and woman, bear the calendrical names One Deer and One Deer—as they are designated in the *Codex Vindobonensis*—representing the creative principle of duality in unity.

The deer was part of the natural world in America before corn; or, rather, it was present before the beginning of the domestication of the corn plant, a process that lasted ten or twelve thousand years, as recent investigations in Tehuacán have shown.

The deer is a godlike figure, personifying the special communication between primitive hunters and animals that is manifested in the well-known demigod called the Lord of the Animals, or Lord of the Hunt. The Eskimos of Labrador believe in a Lord of the Reindeer, a gigantic animal who protects the herds and leads them to his magic house. Once they have passed between his colossal legs and are safe inside, the Lord of the Reindeer remains on guard, lying before the door.

The deity who protects the reindeer is also the one who delivers them to the hunters and to their death; it is he who establishes the rules and limits of the hunt. Without his intercession the hunter cannot hope to take even one piece of game. "What is important here," says Jensen, "is limiting the slaughter of the animals. This is assured by a set of precepts whose violation offends the religious sense."[1]

The idea of a Lord of the Animals is seen again in the Huicholes' concept of the deer, their totemic animal and until recently one of their principal sources of food. Tamats Kauyumari, the Great Blue Deer, is Lord of the Deer, a distinction he shares with his brothers Ixikuikame and Watemukame, who are sometimes distinguished by the colors white and black. Tamats lives in Reunar, a particularly holy place inhabited by the souls of the dead; it is he who has the final decision as to whether they are worthy to enter the region of Tatei Werika Uimari (the sky eagle) or must endure the torments of the underworld ruled by the terrible demon Tukákame. Although Tamats did not create the world, he performed his feats at the beginning of time. He lifted the new-born sun in his horns, thus making life possible on earth, and came to be regarded as a solar deity; he is also the shaman who chants during the peyote rapture. Tamats saved his brother Watemukame from death at the conclusion of the magical hunt; it is he who founded the religion and who made the peyote sprout from his brother's horns.

Tamats Kauyumari is sometimes called Elder Brother Deer Tail (when deer are running in tall grass they show only the lifted flag of their tail); but in actuality he is often identified with his brothers. This agrees with the ubiquitous nature of beings who date from an essentially fluid age, when no entity had yet assumed a definite personality, when the most surprising changes were still taking place.[2] In any case, all three come from the beginning of time and may appear as deer, men, or whirlwinds.

The Lord of the Hunt

Tamats Kauyumari's elder brother, the deer Watemukame whose sacrifice created the present order of the world, is in one of his incarnations Parítsika or Paríkata, the Lord of the Hunt, who decrees and makes possible the killing of his own kind. The Huichol makes a sharp distinction between the deer-gods and the ordinary deer he hunts, although the latter partake of the divine nature. With his finger on the trigger, the Indian often hears the deer say, "Why do you want to kill me? I am Watemukame. It was I who talked with you and taught you the songs of the peyote." The neophyte recognizes his teacher and lets him go unharmed, to the astonishment of his companions, who see the animal only as a piece of game.

At other times the deer are protected by a *kakauyari*, a supernatural being who failed to survive the ordeal of the creation of the world and now lives in a stone, a pool, or a plant. He will authorize killing of the animals only in exchange for offerings and ritual sacrifices. The plant known as *kieri*, inhabited by the *kakauyaris*, is employed in a ceremony involving the hunter (Lumholtz observed that being in love incapacitates the Huichol for hunting), his snares, and his rifle.

Watemukame-Parítsika-Paríkata is the proprietary deity of bows and arrows, snares, and the modern rifle. Even today when a son is born the father goes to the temple with a votive arrow to which are tied a tiny bow and snare, so that Parítsika may know the boy and make him a good hunter.

The most precious part of the dead deer is not the utilitarian meat but the blood, indispensable for the ceremony of consecration. As soon as the animal falls the shaman opens the heart with his knife and collects the blood; it will be used later to fecundate the earth of the cornfield.

The Deer-Corn-Peyote Trinity

According to a myth recorded by Zingg in the San Sebastián region, Paríkata was the husband of the goddess Keamukame, Mistress of the Corn; with the blood of his first-killed deer he made it possible for the sacred grain to grow. Thus was established a relationship so intimate that today a deer must be killed before a field can be planted.

Another myth concerning the origin of corn, which I collected in Ocota, tells of the union between the deer Paríkata and Yoame, the Corn-Girl. Her mother-in-law, Yurianaka, Goddess of the Earth, made her leave her dwelling place in a gourd bowl on the altar and forced her to grind the sacred grain. Since Yoame was herself the corn, she lacerated her hands grinding herself; her blood, mixed with the tortilla dough, became the corn of today and the symbol of the arduous toil of the farmer.

The parallels between deer and corn are obvious: both date from the beginning of time; both can change themselves into plants or human beings; both engage in their own ritual death; and, from their bloody sacrifice, their acts of creation, derive "that which exists," the "order of being" and of life, and the present world, which was created at the end of primeval time.[3] We are dealing, then, with three typical deme deities: the deer, god of a hunting people; the corn, god of an agricultural people; and, in a mystical association, the peyote, god of a food-gathering people.

As for the Divine and Luminous, the myth of the sacred hunt of the deer Watemukame tells us that it sprang from the enchanted *muwieris* borne by the mythical animals of Tukipa; during Watemukame's journey the *muwieris* continued to grow until they had become the great horns of the adult deer.

The Huicholes make no distinction between the deer and the

peyote: when they first find the cactus in Wirikuta they see it as a deer, surrounding it and killing it with an arrow. When it is dead they bleed it (its juice is nearly as powerful for purposes of consecration as is the deer's blood), skin it (the root is peeled), and cut up its flesh and allow it to dry in the form of necklaces (as is done with venison). At the end of the pilgrimage it is taken to the cornfield to fecundate the earth, like the blood and flesh of the deer killed in the hunt.

The mechanism of the deme deity governs not only an animal and two totally dissimilar plants, but also a great number of ancient religious figures who performed their creative feats at the beginning of time, and whose immolation made possible the order of the world. The blood sacrifice links the deer, and by extension the corn and the peyote, with Xipe Totec, Our Flayed Lord, god of spring and of jewelers. Xipe Totec puts on the skin of a human sacrificial victim, just as spring clothes the earth and the jeweler pours liquid gold into the mold. In the peyote dance, too, some of the participants cover themselves with a deer skin, and the stuffed head appears in the dance and in all the ritual acts.

But there are even more extraordinary resemblances. One of the most dramatic landscapes and one of the most sacred regions in the Sierra Madre Occidental begins at Teakata, the cave where Tatewarí, or Grandfather Fire, was born, not far from Santa Catarina. The Huichol is a great artist but a wretched architect—perhaps because he realizes that nothing can surpass the natural grandeur of Catorce, of the sea, or of Lake Chapala. At Teakata there is a series of narrow mountain passes overlooking abysses, rock cliffs, river beds, dark gorges, and gigantic, ruined caves. At the bottom of a hidden canyon, near the streams that pour from the temple-caves, lies the cemetery of the deer. It is a kind of *tsompantli*, with piles of antlers that gleam like yellowed ivory.

Below, in the dense forest along the river, one can hear the roar of mountain lions, and eagles wheel overhead (the shamans use their feathers to make their magic *muwieris*). Often an extraordinary pair of birds flies by: the raven and the macaw. The companionship of the raven, the dark and mysterious bird of the romantic poets, and the macaw, one of the most luxuriant and richly caparisoned birds of the subtropics, tempts us to digress into some inopportune considerations concerning the ugly but intelligent creature who seeks out the company of the gorgeous fool. However, the recollection that their feathers—black, green, and red—were mingled in Quetzalcóatl's plume reminds us that every feature of this landscape has a mystical meaning, and that everything here speaks of the doings of the gods.

In Search of a Lost Time

For the Huicholes, there have been only two eras: the primal times and their consequence, the present. Ignorant of the lessons of history, isolated by geography and tribal wars, hemmed in by outsiders who have encroached on their lands, condemned to live in poverty, again and again they take up the quest for a lost time.

Of the deer-corn-peyote trinity, it is the cactus, a god in itself, that *makes visible*, in a series of dazzling epiphanies, its association with the other deities. It is the great accelerator of the magical process, the essential element of unity, the protagonist of a mythology and a ritual that are by no means free from sportive overtones. The important fact is that the practices of this cult obey "not *just any order*, but the true order of the universe; the order by which men live, and which dominates their vision of reality."[4]

Tatei Matinieri

Our little group headed back toward Valparaíso, retracing its steps. With baskets filled with peyote on their backs, the pilgrims moved quickly through the lunar landscape, which in the early hours of the morning looked like an etching. The sun glistened on the solitary expanse of gorges and mountain passes, and the white patches of caliche stood out in violent contrast to the mysterious, black silhouette of hills that were like motionless waves of lava.

The silence of the highlands was broken only by the sound of the mules' hoofs. Through a notch in the mountains the plains of San Luis Potosí appeared before us, with their sprinkling of white houses.

Beyond, in the luminous background of the sierras, lay the end of our journey.

We passed the crumbling walls and gutted hillsides of Real de Catorce, the overrun houses of Potrero, the barren desert, and the motionless multitude of *Opuntia.* At last we entered the narrow main street of Cedral, where we had left the bus.

A renewed passion for feathers and its amusing consequences provided the only diversion during the return trip on the bus. Whenever Hilario spied a turkey along the way he would set up a great shout, beat on the back of the driver's seat, and force him to stop. The farmers could not understand why these bizarre beings were bent on stripping their fowl of their feathers; but after their first astonishment had passed they began demanding astronomical prices, which hampered mercantile operations considerably. At the next stop, where we remained for two hours, things got even worse. A veritable black market was set up; by the time we left, a dozen villagers carrying turkeys of every shape and size were assaulting the bus, demanding fifty pesos for a handful of feathers.

We got rid of them by offering prices as ridiculously low as theirs were high. When all the haggling was over, only four or five of the pilgrims ended up with a few of the precious ornaments. The others would have to wait for their feathers until the magic hunting of the deer, the prescribed sequel to the journey to Wirikuta.

As the bus spun along the highway, we passed through a succession of villages of desert plants: the *Yucca carnerosana,* with their spiky crowns and imploring arms; the *Opuntia;* the slender clumps of *Dasylirion;* the low forests of mesquite (*Prosopis juliflora,* perhaps the most widespread plant in Mexico); the thorn bushes with their long, spiny branches; and various microphyllous shrubs.

Something seemed to be wrong. Hilario showed increasing signs of uneasiness. According to the best explanation Jerónimo ("Turtle Feet") could give us, the *gobernador* must now take us to Agua Linda, an especially sacred station on the journey. However, he could not say exactly where it was. Since venturing into unfamiliar territory could cause unpredictable complications and expense, I told the driver to take us as near Valparaíso as he could, or at least to Fresnillo.

Jerónimo, as Hilario's ambassador, came to talk with me several times, and the tension grew. The *gobernador* threatened to take his people off the bus and leave us right there, unless we agreed to take them to Agua Linda. After a long discussion, in which gestures played a more important part than either Spanish or Huichol, we concluded that Agua Linda was probably somewhere near Salinas. Exhausted, I put myself in the hands of Tamats Kauyumari, the benevolent god of the Burned Hill, and the bus turned off the main highway. It was after dark when we reached Salinas.

As usual, our arrival created quite a stir. Citizens of Salinas flocked around us in the little plaza, wanting to know where we were going. Hilario descended from the bus, his god-canes in their scarlet wrappings hanging on his back (luckily, none of the townspeople knew what a red flag symbolized). In his broken Spanish, the *gobernador* asked about Agua Linda. It was clear that no one had ever heard of it.

Some time later a farmer came by and listened to the discussion. "Maybe you mean Agua Hedionda," he said. "Some Huicholes usually show up there this time of year."

"Yes! Agua Hedionda!" Hilario agreed, excitedly. "Agua Linda, Agua Hedionda. That's it! That's where we're going!"[5]

Agua Hedionda turned out to be a hamlet thirty or forty kilometers from Salinas, in the middle of the most inaccessible region of the San Luis Potosí desert. Our bus would never make it. So we had to hire a truck to take us early the following morning. We would be going not to "La Hedionda," as the mestizos called it, but to Tatei Matinieri, one of the key stations in the pilgrimage. There lived Tatei Turikita and Xuturiwiyekame, the goddesses of fertility and of children, in a house of flowers surrounded by serpents of five colors who had assumed the form of water.[6]

The Place Where Children Are Born

We left Salinas at seven Friday morning, after Jerónimo and Gregorio had been carefully blindfolded. The pilgrims were shaking with cold under their faded serapes. Through the thin mist that lay over the desert rose the ghostly shapes of the yuccas; from time to time a coyote crossed the plain with his characteristic loping gait.

An hour later we came to the adobe houses of La Hedionda, from where paths led in various directions through the mesquite and grayish vegetation to other small settlements. In a little store the pilgrims bought candles, crackers, and chocolate—one could see that the proprietor was used to selling to Huicholes. Then, in Indian file, we set out for Tatei Matinieri, the entrance to Xirikitá, the huge natural temple that extends to Wirikuta.

The goddesses' house of flowers, "the place where children are born," was merely a small swamp; the colored serpents that guard the dwelling were an expanse of green, stagnant water with patches of grass and algae.

The pilgrims bared their heads. Eusebio, *muwieris* in hand, turned to face the four points of the compass, then delivered a long incantation. Everyone sat down by the water. For a moment the spot took on a sacred aspect. It was a tiny oasis in the middle of a desert of salt and limestone. The water shimmered in iridescent greens and blues, and the *jarales*, the yellow, fragrant flowers of the wormwood, emerged from the mist and gleamed as they were touched by the hand of Father Sun. Some goats and calves were grazing nearby.

Preparation of the offerings took some time. It was incredible how many things the shaman had in his knapsack: the *muwieris* in their wrappings; bottles of blood, *sotol*, and *tesgüino*; the indispensable arrows, to which were tied ears of corn, scraps of cloth, tufts of wool, and tiny huaraches; gourd bowls filled to the brim with peyote; dried deer meat; corn; *tostadas*; and another collection of empty bottles and gourds to carry water from the holy places back to Las Guayabas.

Tatei Matinieri was one of the essential stages in the pilgrimage dedicated to the Divine and Luminous. These miraculous waters were the wellspring of fertility and health.

In addition to the exacting task of preparing the offerings, Hilario had also to brush away, with his *muwieris*, any illness or evil spells the pilgrims may have been exposed to during the journey.

When the arrows were ready and the candles decorated, Eusebio touched them to the bowed heads of the *peyoteros*, then handed them to the *gobernador*. Arrows, embroidered *xuturis*, flowers, and candles tied with colored ribbons were offered to the gods by tossing them into the water.

Eusebio removed the blindfolds from the *matewames*, turned toward the water, and said: "These are two of our brothers who have come to Wirikuta for the first time. See them, Our Mother Matinieri, look at them carefully, so you may know them and never forget them. We have killed a deer and a bull for the journey, and we bring you an offering of their blood. We have kept our vow. Accept, too, our sons' arrows and our daughters' and wives' gourd bowls. Give them health and long life, and give us luck in the hunt."

Two hundred yards from this first pool was a grassy glen with two springs called Tsaurixita and Nariwame Makanieri, after the goddesses who inhabited them. Tsaurixita had special virtues. It was to her that the pilgrims who wanted to rise to the rank of *mara'akames* and medicine men addressed their pleas, along with farmers who prayed for a plentiful harvest.[7]

The shamans cut flowers from the wormwood and used them to sprinkle the spring water over the offerings, the heads of the pilgrims, their clothing, their baskets, and the violins and guitars. It was more a ritual cleansing than a bath,[8] completing a meticulous magical depuration.

Each pilgrim removed his shirt and squatted. Hilario blew on his *muwieris*, then swept away the illness, fatigue, and evil spirits of the road. Again and again he brushed them, touched them, squeezed them; finally he took a large mouthful of the sacred water and sprayed it noisily over their faces and naked torsos.

Once again offerings were thrown into the water: arrows, a crude cross with copper centavos nailed to it, and a color print of Saint Anthony blessing the animals.

The water trickled down their heavy locks, their faces, their backs. When it was Hilario's turn, he received his shower with terrible grimaces and a great deal of leaping about. A few seconds later, however, he was moved to tears as he leaned over the pool and drank reverently of the water of fertility from his cupped hands.

We got on the bus again in Salinas and reached Valparaíso late that night. There, the next morning, I left them. I would never forget our trip to the Land of the Divine and Luminous. That they had allowed an outsider to witness ceremonies and visit places that were strictly forbidden to strangers seemed to reveal an openness and a liberalism incompatible with their most deeply rooted customs and beliefs.

Hilario invited me to the peyote festival that was to take place in Las Guayabas as soon as they returned from the hunt that always concludes the pilgrimage to Wirikuta. Then, for the first time, he shook my hand. As I watched him walking away with his god-canes on his back, I reflected that this *gobernador*, shaman, medicine man, and patriarch who combined majesty and camaraderie, pontifical solemnity and playful good humor, deserved—like other great personalities among the Indians—a better fate.

Difficulties in San Andrés

I returned to San Andrés with a head filled with visions and new sensations. I had been luckier than Lumholtz and Zingg, for I had witnessed an archaic rite hitherto known only through fragmentary reports by my illustrious predecessors. Even so, as time passed I felt a growing uneasiness. Not only had the journey departed from the traditional itinerary, but also I still knew nothing about many of its religious and mythic associations. I had seen the ritual—the actions—but the incantations—the words—had escaped me.

The situation in San Andrés—considered to be one of the most important religious centers in the sierra—was the same as the one Lumholtz had had to face seventy years earlier. At first the many local shamans did not seem especially wary; but after a few days of working with me they vanished like phantoms, leaving vital information incomplete. They showed no hostility. They simply disappeared, after having received some mysterious message, or closed up completely. It was no use trying to change their minds. Their faces turned to stone or assumed expressions of utter contempt. Under these conditions, getting together with a shaman informant and an interpreter turned out to be harder than making the pilgrimage to Wirikuta. Sometimes I had interpreters—the teacher José Carrillo (Hilario's son) or another teacher, Ramón López Hernández, who came from San Sebastián to help me—but no shaman was available. On other occasions I had a willing *cantador* but no interpreter. I had before me an enormous treasure house of myths, and yet, in spite of all my hard work, I often had to be satisfied with a single coin or a jewel of little value.

Nevertheless, I was able to record a few myths and shamanic chants; I took notes, filled in the most obvious gaps, and succeeded in reconstructing the shattered mosaic of the pilgrimage.

The Festival of the New Corn and Squash

The pilgrimage begins not in Valparaíso but two weeks earlier at the time of the Festival of the New Corn and Squash. This celebration of joyful abundance has the dual purpose of clearing the first fruits of the harvest of their dangerous sacred nature, and of sending the children—the Huicholes' most precious and beloved possessions —on their symbolic journey to Reunar, led by the shamans.

Early in the morning the villagers gather in the courtyard of the *xiriki*, before an altar covered with candles, ears of new corn, squash, necklaces of dried deer meat and peyote, flowers, and heads of Tamats Kauyumari. This time it is the women who take the front-row seats, their larger children beside them on the benches and the smaller ones on their laps.

At seven the *mara'akame* begins chanting and playing the *tepu*, a drum decorated with *zempoalxochitl* wreaths. He is seated on his ceremonial chair, on the back of which he has hung three shoulder bags filled with crackers—"the children's peyote."[1] "We are preparing for our journey to the Burned Hill. I wish to tell you, Tamats Kauyumari, that we shall arrive at noon, and the children will greet you there. Their parents have kept the promise they made to you and have brought them to the festival. I shall guide them to the Burned Hill."

The shaman offers the gods *tesgüino* and chocolate with the five *muwieris* he holds in his hands. He "takes off." "We are coming to the Hill of the Lily, Reukanamaté, where Tamats left some stones in the shape of a deer."

(The deer, as Panchito explains it, whistles like this: *Reu, reu, reu.* "You can hear him best at night. Once when I was walking in a canyon a deer suddenly leaped out of the brush, whistling angrily: *Reu, reu, reu.* He stared at me with his glistening blue eyes, and my hair stood up. My grandfather had told me that when deer are angry they cast a spell over you.")

The shaman goes on: "From here, from Reukanamaté, we shall go to the Hill of the Eagle, Werikatukamate, where the great bird that always watches over the Huicholes is painted."

Before their arrival the *mara'akame* dips his *muwieris* in holy water and offers it to the gods of the four points of the compass. "I am flying like the eagle, leading all these children to the Burned Hill. Protect them, Tamats Kauyumari."

He spends ten minutes on the Hill of the Eagle, arranging the gifts for the gods; then he flies to the Hill of the Star, where he makes further offerings of gourd bowls, arrows, ears of corn, and squash before Xurawemuieka and the gods of the four directions. The next stop is Urumutiú, the spot where Tamats Kauyumari erected a blue pole he brought from the sea and nailed an arrow to it to show the way to the country of the peyote.

"From here we shall go to Tatei Matinieri. Hold on tight to my wings, little hummingbirds—*tupinaris*. We shall rest where Our Mother, Matinieri, awaits us."

As they approach the sacred lakes, the shaman asks the mothers to light candles, as is customary whenever they reach another stage in the journey. However, since this deity is Tatei Matinieri, the patron goddess of children, the women are careful to use new candles.

The parents rise and say: "Tatei Matinieri, accept our children's greetings. These are the ones you caused to fall ill last year because we were unable to celebrate your Festival of the New Corn. They are here with us now, and the *cantador* will speak for them. They are on their way to Reunar, the Burned Hill."

"All the children are here," chants the *mara'akame*. "I have brought them." He turns to the audience. "The children greet Our Mother, and she takes them in her arms. She says she is pleased to see them here. She will see that they do not fall ill, that they grow strong and healthy, so that one day they may come to visit her in her house of flowers. Our Mother blesses them. She embraces each one, and says farewell."

The *mara'akame* suspends his chanting for twenty minutes. Then he resumes the journey to Wirikuta, and the mothers light another new candle. "Here are the children," the *mara'akame* announces to Tuihapa, the Goddess of the Blue Water with Flowers, who dwells in a small spring. "And you, Wirikuta, who are very near us, be with us. I shall return this way, but I shall not be able to see you. I shall be flying high in the air."

The parents address Wirikuta: "You are Our Second Mother. We have kept our promise to the *cantador*, and here are the children. In five years they will come in person to greet you."

"Soon we shall come to the Burned Hill, where Tamats Kauyumari is waiting for us," the *mara'akame* announces. The Indians are overcome by emotion.[2] Each mother holds a lighted candle in one hand; with the other she shakes the ritual rattle her child is grasping.

Some of the men lament: "I was not able to pay my respects to you at Reunar last year, but my son is doing it for me. He will salute you. I am here praying for him. It is my hope that in two months I may be able to go myself to the Burned Hill with the offerings I owe you."

Meanwhile, the *cantador* is giving Tamats an account of their trip. "We visited the Hill of the Lily, the Hill of the Eagle, and the Hill of the Star. We paid homage to Tatei Matinieri and Tatei Tuihapa. Wirikuta was with us. At last we stood on Reunar, your home. I bring you the children. I have come to present them to you. When they are grown, they will come in person to greet you and bring their offerings. Now take the first taste of the *tesgüino* their parents are offering you. Bite into the first tender ears of corn and the first squash."

Since children cannot take part in the peyote hunt, the *mara'aka-*

me collects the cactus for them; while doing so, with the help of his *muwieris*, he leaves them in Tamats's care.[3]

At the beginning of the ceremony, the squash and ears of corn were lined up before the *cantador*. Each squash—Tsikokoame, the Man-Squash—represents a boy, and each ear of corn—Tsitaima, the Woman-Corn—represents a girl. They have been lying pointing toward the east; now that the *mara'akame* is about to begin the return trip, one of his assistants turns them toward the west. Everything else is turned around: the flowers, the offerings, and the *wikuxao* cord, to which the children are tied.

At one thirty the shaman says farewell to Tamats, promising to return the following year. He also takes leave of the other gods, still wielding his *muwieris*, and says: "I shall lead the little hummingbirds; the eagles [his assistants] shall protect them on my right and on my left."

He takes leave of Wirikuta, of Mukama the Eagle, and of Tatei Matinieri: "Until next year. If it is the gods' will that we are still alive, and they command us to come, we shall make the journey by land with the children's fathers. Each will come of his own free will." Thus the shaman emphasizes that there is no obligation in these religious acts.

When they are above Urumutiú, where the red-tailed hawk Kwixu has his throne of woven reeds (*uweni*), the shaman decides that it is time to take the peyote. One of his assistants hands out the crackers to the children and their parents. "We found a great deal of peyote," he says jokingly. "I hope we don't get too drunk."

When the "peyote" has been eaten, the *mara'akame* stops at Wakurikitenie, the Gate of the Clouds (there, too, is found a painted figure of the Deer); he opens the gate with his *muwieris* and distributes crackers again. "We have had a good journey, going and coming. We showed the gods their offerings, but we did not leave them there. We promise to deliver them without fail next year."

The *mara'akame* stands up, counts the children, closes the gate, and says: "Goodby. We can remain no longer on the Hill of the Star; I shall tell the goddess Xurawemuieka that we will return next year on the same date, come what may."

As he flies over the Hill of the Eagle, the *cantador* addresses Werika: "Here we are again, on our way back. Come with us for a little, that our road may be easier."

They arrive at the hill called Takuwari, where there is a water hole belonging to Tatei Matinieri. According to Panchito, it is the smallest one along the way, where the Huicholes stop for water. At Tatei Matinieri lives Xuturiwiyekame, the Goddess of Childbirth, while at Teakata is found Turikita, the Goddess of Children, to whom barren women address their pleas. The goddess answers their prayers, with the warning that they must not beat their children, or they will die and be taken back again to the house of their mother Turikita.

At five o'clock the *cantador* announces their return. "We are almost home. We have brought peyote. We met with good fortune on our journey. Are the parents well?"

The parents rise and answer: "Yes, we are well. You have guided our children to Reunar, and we thank you. We promise that they will take the journey with you again next year."

The *cantador* descends. Using his *muwieris*, he brings the children down to join their seated mothers. (According to Panchito, this is the "landing.") The drum is struck more softly. The assistants take the children's rattles, beat the drum with them, and leave them lying on the drumhead.

Everyone partakes of a broth made from the meat of the sacrificed bull, along with beans and tortillas. The first fruits—ears of corn and squash, still festooned with flowers—are left on the altar. No one is allowed to touch them. They belong to the gods. They have inaugurated a new order of things and thus are especially sacred.

At nine o'clock the *mara'akame* begins chanting and drumming again. On his chair and on those of his two assistants are now hung the *muwieris* and the children's rattles—whose function during the journey was to attract the gods' attention, so that the little people would not go unnoticed.

"We have performed our duty this day," chants the *mara'akame*. "Now we shall go to the north to tell Nariwame, Teakata, and Aitsarie that the children have journeyed to the Burned Hill; we shall also ask them not to let the rain stop, for the corn ears are still green and need the water. The gods have received their corn and squash, and next year we shall offer them the first fruits of the harvest again."[4]

After having visited the sea and the caves at Teakata, the shaman goes to Aitsarie. This is where they take the horns of bulls sacrificed when children are seriously ill. "We have been to Catorce. We have kept our vows," says the shaman, giving in careful detail the incidents of the journey. "We earnestly beg you, O Our Mother, to look after our children and not to withdraw your gift of rain. Now we must say goodby. We shall return next year without fail."

From Aitsarie the shaman flies to Xapawiyemetá, on Lake Chapala. It was there that the canoe of Watákame, the Huichol Noah, touched land for the first time; there, also, is found a *zalate* called Xapa, the magic fig tree that provides rain and paper. The deity who inhabits it is Xapa, the Goddess of Paper. Xapawiyemetá, the source of the great rains, is symbolized by the tree, surrounded by luminous and refreshing water that gushes from its foliage.

"I have been traveling all day," says the shaman. "All day I have been visiting sacred places, taking our children with me. I am weary, but I could not fail to come to see you, Our Mother, great goddess of the rains. You have given us abundant rain all year, and thanks to you the cornfields have flowered and been filled with corn, squash, beans, and *wave*. How could I have forgotten you? At the spring that is also your home we have offered the ears of corn and the squash that belong to you.[5] Eat of them, Our Mother, and continue to favor us with your rain. Our crops need it now more than ever.

"Listen! Listen, all of you!" says the shaman, turning to his audience. "Hear how Our Mother Xapa answered me: 'Yes, it will rain all month, and you will have a good crop. I shall see to it that you have a plentiful harvest.'

"In the name of the children and their parents, I thank you," the shaman answers. "I have brought your *tesgüino*. Drink, O Our Mother; drink first, and then we shall drink."

The shaman pours a libation and takes leave of the goddess. He then flies toward the Nayar mesa, the home of Tsakaimuka, the deity shared by the Huicholes with their neighbors the Coras; there he pleads for a prolongation of the rainy season.

This, like all Huichol festivals, goes on for three or four days. From planting time and throughout the rainy season, they try to ensure divine favor by means of a long series of sacrifices and ceremonies.

The goddesses are scattered about in distant places, and it is necessary to visit them all, bearing offerings of blood and bringing back their sacred waters. This means a continual carrying to and fro, a succession of journeys through the mystical region they call the Middle World. The Festival of the First Fruits ends the cycle of the rains, ruled by the goddesses of the water, and opens the solar cycle governed by Tamats Kauyumari, the deer-peyote.

The *tepu* is heard for many days in the cloud-capped sierra, calling people to the festival. This is the preparation for the long trip to Wirikuta. The shamans chant the myths of the Huichol Noah, and of the Birth of the Corn; their people listen, drinking *tesgüino* and eating the tender corn and squash that once again have been provided through the good offices of Aitsarie, Xapa the Rain Tree, Tsakaimuka, Nariwame, the earth goddess Yurianaka, and the fish goddess Utuanaka. In the east the gods of the dry season are approaching, with their retinue of golden colors and dazzling visions.

The Myth of the Huichol Noah

Once there was a man named Watákame who loved work. He spent the entire day in the fields, cutting down trees, planting, and harvesting. He wanted always to be working. Once, when he had cleared a large area, he returned the following day to find that the trees had all grown up again; the forest was just as thick and tall as before.

He cleared the field again; but on three successive occasions everything grew back overnight as though it had never been touched. On the fourth day Watákame asked himself: "Why is this? Who is making the trees grow as fast as I cut them down?"

After he had finished his work on the fifth day, Watákame hid behind a tree to see what was going on. After a time he saw a little old woman approaching from the south, a bamboo crook in her hand. She gestured with the crook toward the four points of the compass, and finally toward the center of the earth. At that moment the forest began to grow up again.

Watákame seized his axe and ran up to the old woman, shouting: "Stop! I have sweated and toiled for four days clearing this land, and every evening you have cast the same spell. I'm going to kill you."

"Look, don't be angry," she said. "I am Nakawé, the Mother of the Gods, and I tell you that you have been wasting your time. In five days it will begin to rain, the rivers will burst their banks, and the world will be covered with water. I have come to save you."

"Tell me what I must do."

"Over there is a *zalate* tree. Tomorrow cut it down and use the wood to make a boat with five holes on the right side and five on the left. When you have finished, find me five squash shoots, five grains of corn of each color, five beans, five *wave* seeds, five acorns, five pine nuts, and five *zalate* seeds. If you know where there's a little black bitch, get that, too."

Nakawé appeared again five days later and asked, "Did you get the things I wanted? Is the boat ready?"

"Everything is ready, just as you ordered," Watákame replied.

"Very good. Get into the boat quickly, because the water's coming. Listen to your friends and neighbors screaming. The animals are eating them."

"What animals?"

"The *metate*, the cooking pots, the griddles, and the *molcajete* have turned into wild beasts. They are eating your friends."[6]

Watákame hurriedly embarked with his seeds and his little black bitch, and shoved off. The goddess Nakawé rode on the roof.

After five days, Nakawé said: "I'll let you look out a little, so you can see what's happened to the world."

Watákame peered out through one of the holes, and saw a lake dyed red with the blood of his friends who had been killed by the *metates*, the cooking pots, and the griddles.

The boat drifted first to the west until it ran against Waxiewe, the White Hill that stands in the sea; then it headed eastward and struck the rock Tamana Tinika. It turned and went north until it touched the rock Xauramanaka, then drifted to the south and landed on the beach. Later it was transformed into the stone Mahakate, which can be seen there today. This place is called Xapawiyemetá, which means the place of Xapa.

When the boat had lain on the beach for five days, Nakawé said to the man: "You can set foot on land now without fear. The waters have receded."

Watákame stepped ashore, his feet sinking into the mud. His footprints can still be seen there, as can the squash shoot that had not been eaten during the voyage; it is in a cave nearby, turned to stone.

"You have done everything very well," Nakawé said. "Now all you have to do is plant the seeds at the four cardinal points and begin your life in the Middle World."

Watákame took five steps in each of the four directions—the equivalent of walking for five days—and planted the seeds. Then he returned to the Middle World, which lies on the coast between San Blas and Tepic. He built a house and moved into it with his little bitch. For four days he cultivated the earth, as had been his custom.

Now whenever Watákame came home in the evening he found fresh, hot tortillas. He ate them while the little dog watched, her tail wagging. "I wonder who makes these tortillas?" Watákame said. "This is very odd. I must find out."

On the fifth day he came home earlier than usual and hid near the doorway. He saw his little dog take off her skin, hang it up on a rafter, and go down to the river for a drink of water. Watákame took the skin and threw it into the fire; the moment it began to burn, he heard the dog let out a cry of pain down by the river. Watákame lost no time. He ground a little corn and mixed it with water. When the dog returned he washed her with the *atole* made from the raw corn, the blue corn called Ikuyuime. As soon as he had finished washing her, she changed into a woman before his eyes. He named her Taxiwa, which means "washed with corn water."

He said to Taxiwa, "Since you like making tortillas, from now on you can cook my meals and keep my house. You shall be my woman."

He went to bed with the dog-woman for four nights, and on the fifth they mated. Five days later twins were born. They were male and female, so that the earth that had been depopulated by the flood might soon be filled with people.

Tamats watched all this from the Burned Hill; from the Burned Hill he saw everything. The children of Watákame and Taxiwa were the first to make the pilgrimage to Reunar. From their union were born many other children who also went to Reunar, the Burned Hill.[7]

(A myth from Ocota, related by Panchito.)

The Corn Myth

In Tuakare the goddess Nakawé had a child named Tsikoakame. This child was always sick; he had diarrhea and was weak and skinny. Nakawé tried to get rid of him by abandoning him in a field behind her house.

The child went into a cave, came out along a creek bed, crossed Niwetari, and came to the place called Muddy Water.

He was playing in the sand when his brother Wakuri, the Corn Child, came to get him. "Hullo! What're you doing here? I came to take you home," said Wakuri. He tried to pick him up.

Tsikoakame changed into a snake and slithered into a hole in a boulder, where a stream of water poured out. Then he took a path across the mountains that led to Aitsarie, Aukuericatsie, the Hill of the Tree with White Flowers, Tekupatsie, Pedregal, and Hayukarita, the Damp Earth. Here his brother was finally able to catch up with him.

"Why do you keep following me? Why do you want to take me home? My mother tried to get rid of me; she threw me out and left me to die. You've hounded me for the last time," Tsikoakame said. He changed into a thunderbolt and struck his brother, who flew to pieces and became the white, yellow, blue, red, and black corn that scattered as far as the Blue Hill and turned into corn-children.

Tsikoakame crossed Wikatsie, the Hill of the Stake, and came to Tsakaimuta. When he was able to catch his breath he told Tsakaimuta: "I won't stay; I'm only passing through. I'm heading west."

He rested at Muxatsie, the Hill of the Lamb, and then struck out for Yoawimekatsie, the Blue Hill, where the dove Kukurú Uimari lived in a white house with her daughters the corn-girls, fathered by Wakuri. The boy became friendly with the girls, and they all played together in the streets and squares of the Blue Hill. This was risky, though, because of the leaf-cutter ants who kept trying to carry them off.

Once the ants caught Tsikoakame sleeping. They were unable to carry him away, but they chewed off his hair and eyelashes. When he awoke he found himself bald and nearly blind. He heard the dove on its branch singing in the south, but he could not see it. Then he heard it in the north and the west, still without seeing it. When it called from the east he at last spotted it, high in a treetop. He took aim with his bow and arrow.

Then the dove spoke to him: "You have been everywhere and know the world. Why should you try to kill me? If you're hungry, I'll give you something to eat. I am the mistress of all food. Here are some tortillas and a calabash of black *atole*. Eat until you are full."

Tsikoakame thought, "How can I eat until I am full when the tortillas and the calabash are so tiny? Kukurú Uimari is playing a trick on me."

He began to drink the *atole*. Although his stomach swelled and swelled, he could not empty the calabash. "Thank you," he said, handing back the gourd. "Thank you very much. I couldn't finish it."

"I bet you thought it wouldn't be enough," the dove said.

"I didn't say that."

"No, but that's what you were thinking. Tomorrow, whenever you're hungry, come and see me. I live in that house over there."

When Tsikoakame went to the house the following day, he was greeted by a woman instead of the dove. A very old man was sitting in the sun in a chair nearby.

"Good afternoon," said Tsikoakame.

"Good afternoon," replied the woman, who was Yoawimeka. "Sit down and rest."

"Give the boy something to eat," the old man said. "I think he's hungry."

The woman went to the kitchen and returned with a small gourd bowl and five tiny tortillas.

"That isn't much to eat, considering how hungry I am," Tsikoa-kame thought. But once again he found himself full without having finished the bowl of *atole*.

"Thank you very much, Señora. I've had plenty," he said, handing her the bowl.

"You thought it wouldn't be enough, but you couldn't drink it all."

Then Tsikoakame said to himself: "This woman talks just like the dove. She *is* the dove; no doubt about it. The food she gave me has made me grow and restored me to good health."

When Tsikoakame had rested, he turned to the old man. "Could you sell me a little corn? I must take some to my mother Yurianaka."

The Lord of the Corn did not answer, which saddened Tsikoa-kame. But after a while the old man got to his feet and took a few painful steps, leaning on his cane.

"I'm going to see if the girls want to go with you," he said. "I'm going to talk to them."[8]

The house was filled with girls. Tsikoakame could see them inside, sitting or walking about. He thought, "I didn't say I wanted girls; I just asked you for a little corn."

The old man turned to Yoawimeka. "The little boy wants some corn. What do you say? I think we ought to give it to him."

"All right. Let's see which one is willing. Let's ask them."

They summoned the corn-girls, who are called the Tsitaima. The old man asked Yauma, the black corn: "My child, would you like to go with this boy?"

"No," Yauma answered. "Nobody wants me because I'm so dark."

Then they asked Tasawime, the yellow corn, and she said: "No. Nobody wants me because I'm yellow and smell bad."

The woman turned to Taulawime, the red corn. "Do you feel like going with this boy?"

"No, nobody wants me because I'm red, and because I turn into blood."

Then Yoawimeka said to Túsame, the white corn: "My child, this boy wants to take you home with him."

"No, I'm too pale. My eyes are weak, and I can't see."

To Yoame, the blue corn, her mother said: "My child, you ought to go with the lad."

"Very well, I'll go."

The woman turned to Pitorax, the corn that is spotted and streaky. "And what about you, my child?"

"I'll go with my sister Yoame."

"I'll go, too," said Kupime, the pod corn.

"There! Three of my daughters are willing," the old man exclaimed.

Tsikoakame was frightened. "I didn't *ask* for the girls," he said. "How can I take them when I have no corn for them to eat?"

"We won't give them to you right now. First you will have to go to your mother's house and prepare a *xiriki* with an altar, an arrow, and a gourd bowl. Tell your mother that the bowl must be decorated with four bands of glass beads—two white and two blue—and four pictures of the cornfield worked in wool, one on each side of the bowl, facing north, south, east, and west. When that is done, you will build a *kaxaton* [a granary elevated on posts] and five *ikis* [cylindrical silos]. Come back in five days and we'll give you the girls. Now you may go. We hope you have no bad luck along the way."

Tsikoakame went to the house of Tatei Yurianaka, an aunt of his who had been kind to him when he was sick.

"You've been gone for a day and a night," she said. "And you look very happy. Where have you been?"

When the boy had told his story, they both set to work and in one day accomplished everything the old man had ordered. They worked fast, because those were hard times at Yurianaka's house: she had run out of corn, and they were both hungry.

When Tsikoakame called again at Yoawimeka's house, all eight sisters wanted to go back with him. And not only the girls, but the Mume, the bean-women; the ancient bean called Utsiema; the squashes; the *wave*; and the other plants. But the old man would allow only the blue corn Yoame, the eldest sister, to return with him.

"Here is my daughter," he said. "I give her to you on two conditions: you must not make her work, and you must respect her always. She must remain on the altar of the *xiriki*, seated on five branches. You must cut these at sunup—one at the center of the world, and the others in the four directions."

When they got home Tsikoakame placed the girl on the altar, in a gourd bowl resting on the boughs. At midnight his aunt came to the *calihuey* and lighted a candle. In a moment she heard a sound that warmed her heart: the rattle of kernels of corn pouring out and bouncing about on the floor of the *xiriki*. The astonished Yurianaka blew out the candle and left.

The following morning Tsikoakame said to the girl: "I'm off to work. You mustn't get down from the altar, even if my mother tells you to."[9]

At noon the corn-girls, the bean-women, and the squash-men arrived. They poured themselves into the granaries, which soon overflowed with corn, beans, and squash.

Yurianaka took the corn and boiled it. Then she ground the *nixtamal* on a *metate* placed flat on the ground; for in those days *metates* had no legs.

When the tortillas were ready she took them to the *xiriki*. Tsikoakame and his mother ate together; the girl had already had her *chinari* of *atole*.[10]

The boy worked in the field for four days. The fingers of both his hands turned into men, who moved about, bent over, and straightened up like fingers as they cut down trees, tore out grass by the roots, and piled brush in great heaps.

On the fourth day Yurianaka went out looking for Tsikoakame. She peered out from behind some rocks and saw the men working with her son. She was very surprised.

She thought: "I won't be able to feed all these people. Yoame is sitting there on the altar, doing nothing. I'll ask her to help me.

"My son has a lot of workers out there in the field," she said to Yoame, "and they must be fed. You're just sitting there resting. Come on, you lazy girl, help me grind this corn."

"Please don't ask me to do that," the girl answered. "I can't move from here."

The boy overheard them talking. He left his workers, the *watá-kame*, and went to the *xiriki*. "What did my mother say to you?"

"She wanted me to help her grind corn, but I'm doing my duty here on the altar. It isn't proper for me to do as she asks."

"Please pay no attention to her. Even if she asks you again, don't come down from the altar. You must remain in the *xiriki* for five years."

On the fifth day, while Tsikoakame was resting in the field, he heard thunder in the east. "What is that great noise I hear? What does it mean? The girl must know.

"I heard a voice thundering in the mountains," he told her. "Tell me what I should do."

"Take flint, tinder, and torch pine, and light five bonfires: one in each of the four directions, and one at the center of the world."

"And what will you do when the smoke comes?"

"You and I will crawl into one of the granaries my father told you to build. The smoke won't reach us there."

When Tsikoakame had set the fires, he took the girl into one of the *ikis*. The smoke shot up, leaped five times, and reached the sky, where it turned into a cloud. Then Kutsaraupa, He Who Thunders, said: "The smoke has reached my nostrils. The boy has done his work well; he has burned off the cornfield without leaving a single stump. Everything is ready. Soon it will rain."

The rain came down in torrents. The water soaked into the ashes and washed them from the cornfield into the rivers, and the rivers carried them to the sea.

When the first rains were over, Yoame said: "I can leave the *xiriki* now. Tomorrow we will go to the cornfield with your mother."

They left the house early in the morning. When they stood in the center of the cornfield, Yoame asked, "Where did you set the first fire?"

"Here, in the center," Tsikoakame replied.

Yoame touched the earth with her finger in the five places where the fires had burned, and the boy's mother lighted a candle.

"Ask the gods of the four directions to send rain," Tsikoakame said. "The cornfield needs the water."

"Ask them yourself," the girl said. "Tell them I have touched the earth with my finger. That's where the corn will come up."

She stood with bowed head as he invoked the gods. When he had finished, she raised her head and said, "Look here."

Tsikoakame saw corn sprouting at the center of the field.

"Now look to the east, the west, the north, and the south."

Corn stood in every direction; the entire clearing was green with growing plants.

"Now we shall go home to the *calihuey*," said Yoame. "Today corn has been born."

Soon the tassels appeared and the ears ripened. Then the three of them came back to the cornfield, and Tsikoakame began to harvest the ears. He cut the first one, which was white, in the south; the second, which was blue, in the north; the third, which was spotted, in the west, in the direction of the sea; and two more, red and yellow, in the east. The sixth, which was black, he cut at the center of the field. At the same time he harvested the barren stalks, the beans, and the *wave*, and tossed them all into the girl's skirt, which she held out before her. But when Tsikoakame had finished, he saw that Yoame's skirt was empty.

The girl took her place on the altar again, this time at one side of the gourd bowl; she had grown so large that it was obvious she could no longer fit inside. They stayed together in the *xiriki* until midnight, when Tsikoakame was awakened by the sound of pouring corn. He heard the endless rattling of the kernels and the hollow sound of squash falling into the granaries.

"Now give me the chocolate that has been prepared for me," the girl said.

Tsikoakame grasped his *muwieris* and handed her the cup. "Now you must rest," he told her. "The chocolate will help you sleep. You will remain here on the altar, and we will all come to the *xiriki* with our offerings."

The cornfield had been stripped. Nothing remained but dry, broken stalks. The silos were filled with corn; and yet Yurianaka was still scolding Yoame for her laziness and insisting that she help her with the cooking. She never stopped persecuting her.

Now we shall tell what came of all this. We shall tell what happened to the girl. One morning Yoame was so annoyed that she got down from the altar, took a cooking pot, and boiled the *nixtamal*. The lye irritated her eyes and made her weep. When the *nixtamal* had cooled a little, she began grinding it on the *metate*. Blood gushed from her bruised hands, staining the dough red as though it were her own flesh. When that happened, she stopped work and left the house without anyone seeing her.

When Tsikoakame came back from the fields and could not find her anywhere, he was angry. He called his aunt Yurianaka. "You have behaved badly. Yoame lost patience with you, and has left us. I'm going to bring her back."

Tsikoakame went straight to the house of the corn. The father and mother would hardly answer when he greeted them, for they were annoyed and offended.

"She left me," the boy told them, weeping. "It was my aunt's fault, not mine."

"We warned you. We told you that she must not do any work for five years. We're not going to give her back to you. If your aunt has anything to say, she can come and see us. We will not close our door to her."

As soon as Tsikoakame got home he cut a stick. Then he looked in the *calihuey* and the granaries, but there wasn't a single grain of corn anywhere. He called his aunt. "There is no corn, or squash, or beans. And it's all your fault."

His aunt fell on her knees, and Tsikoakame struck her three times with his stick.

"Stop, father!" she cried. "Listen to me!"[11]

"It's too late."

"I told her to work in the kitchen only because that is the custom."

"Come with me," said Tsikoakame. "Her father and mother want to see you."

"I won't go. If I do, they'll beat me, too. You go and ask them to forgive me."

Tsikoakame went sadly back to talk with Yoame's parents again.

"My aunt refuses to come. She says she merely asked her to grind *nixtamal*."

All the corn-girls were locked up in their room. Their mother, Yoawimeka, looked at Tsikoakame and shook her head.

"Since you didn't keep your word, we can't let you have her," she said. "If you have any money we'll sell you some corn, as you asked us to do the first day."

"I have a *cuartilla*."[12]

"We'll give you five kernels, one of each color, for planting, and five liters for eating. You must realize that things will be different now. You will have to work hard, clearing brush, burning, planting with a stick, and weeding the cornfield. That will be your life. Now take your corn and go home."

Tsikoakame put the corn into a small pouch and took it home. When he reached the *calihuey* he placed it on the altar.

"This is all Yoame's parents would give me," he told his aunt. "They said you must make your *nixtamal* with just two kernels of corn."

His aunt did so, and the *nixtamal* grew until it filled half the pot.

Later he laboriously cleared the brush for planting. When he was ready to burn it, the fire caught only in a few places; it did not catch fire all at once and burn completely, as it had the first time. The clouds were gathering, and he had to work fast. It took him five days to finish the job. Then it began to rain, and the two of them planted the corn; but they had to leave a large section unplanted. When weeding time came it took them another five days, even though it was a very small area. When September and October had passed, they harvested the ears and carried them home on their backs.

Tsikoakame remembered the sound of the corn and squash pouring into the *kaxaton*, and how happy he had been when Yoame was in her gourd bowl on the altar, helping them. He was terribly sad. Now he had to toil endlessly, with no help from anyone, just as the Huicholes do to this day.[13]

(A myth from Ocota, related by Panchito.)

A Concise Itinerary of the Pilgrimage

Preparations are begun for the trip to Wirikuta at the conclusion of the Festival of the New Corn. A supply of toasted tortillas (practically the only food carried by the peyote pilgrims) must be made ready, and a little money got together to buy candles, glass beads, paper, and woolen yarn for the offerings.

They select the pilgrims; appoint the old man who is to take care of the women in their absence; and prepare arrows, gourd bowls, flowers, *xuturis*, and the ropes to be used in the confession. Then, after nightfall, they gather in the *calihuey*.

When the pilgrims have formed a circle around the fire, Uruwakame Tatewarí, also known as the Man with the Arrows, who represents Grandfather Fire and who will march at the head of the procession, takes the *wikuxa* rope (in which have been tied thirty knots, one for each day of the journey) in his right hand. With his left hand he rolls it up and gives it to the Tekuamana or Uxatuki, the elder who is to be left in charge of the women.

"Take this rope and keep it with you," he says. "Every evening you will untie one knot. In this way you will keep track of the days;

you will know where we are and will be able to communicate with us. Don't forget that in five days you must hear the women's confessions. If we meet with no misfortune along the way, we shall see each other here again when we return."

They wash their heads and feet with *amole* and water, and sit down facing the fire. The women take their places a little behind their husbands, at a ritually prescribed distance, and the Mara'akame Tatewarí recites the myth of the birth of fire.

The Birth of Fire, the Moon, and the Sun

Once a long time ago there were no fire, no moon, no sun, and no people. In caves, crannies, and under rocks lived the nocturnal animals—the bat, the salamander, the owl, the badger, the rat, the wildcat, the opossum, the snake, and the scorpion: all those that still live in darkness today. They kept bumping into each other in the dark and devouring each other.

Darkness had reigned for ages in the Middle World when Tatei Yurianaka, Our Mother Earth, tried five times to rise from her subterranean dwelling. The first time she moved, a light appeared on the horizon, like the dying glow of a cigarette. The second time she rose a bit higher, and it was like the darkened sun during an eclipse. The third it was like the first rays of dawn. The animals looked at one another in astonishment, not knowing what to make of it. The fifth time a flame appeared in Teakata; this flame was Tatewarí, Grandfather Fire, the Old Fire we Huicholes call Tai.

Near him stood the deer Maxa, dazzled and frightened at what he saw. All at once Tai leaped upon Maxa, strangled him, cut him up in pieces, hung his body from a tree, and, sitting beneath him, began to cook him. The fat of the deer dripped into the Fire and fed him, until the Fire took the form of a man with a light in his breast. Tamats Kauyumari stood watching all this from Reunar, the Burned Hill.

The animals, attracted by the light, drew nearer. Tatewarí offered them the flesh of Maxa, but after tasting it they rejected it. This is why wild animals eat only raw meat today.

Tai stood erect. He threw the deer's carcass over his shoulder and walked through the canyons. When he had gone only a little way, Tsaurixikame appeared in the shape of the wind and asked the animals: "Why did you let him get away? You should have killed him right then with your arrows."

"We let him go," they replied, "because he is the Fire, the sign that soon there will be light in the world. But, if you want him to die, we will hunt him down with our bows and arrows."

It was Maye, the mountain lion, who shot him first, with an arrow made of straw; it glanced off Tatewarí's side, wounding him slightly. Then Tatei Ipau, a very fierce serpent, loosed an arrow made of *tsipuxa*. These were followed by arrows made of reeds, shot by the little rattlesnake called Xainú and the black boa called Haiki, who lives in the water. None of them found its mark.

The animals were furious, and appealed to Xurawe Temai, the New Star, who was looking on from a hilltop. "Kill Tatewarí!" they called. "Our arrows of reeds and straw are like children's toys. They are powerless against the Fire."

Xurawe Temai shot an arrow from his lookout. He hit Tatewarí, who came to earth in a whirlwind of blue sparks, like a flame that has been stamped out.

"You have brought down the Fire, and you shall remain here forever, guarding the Middle World," Tamats told Xurawe Temai. Because of this decision on the part of Our Elder Brother Deer Tail, the New Star still watches over the Middle World; and when the great serpents grow wings and threaten to come forth and devour the human race, Xurawe Temai shoots them in the water with his bow and arrow.

When Tai fell, he was extinguished and transformed into an old man.

"Go get him," Tamats Kauyumari ordered. "Lift him up and bring him here to me." The first to go was Xarei Wiwieri, the serpent with black and white stripes. He was followed by Muxeka, the gray snake, and finally by Wikaxao, another gray serpent who lives twined around the trunks of trees. All three spoke to Tatewarí and tried to get him to his feet, but in vain. He lay there motionless and silent, as though he were dead.

Then Watemukame, the deer with the tiny horns, approached, and this time Tatewarí raised his head. He recognized him. "Are you Watemukame, Tamats's brother?" he asked. "What do you want?"

"Yes, I am Watemukame. I have come for you. My brother wants to see you."

"Tell him I will speak with him; but first he must prepare a black gourd bowl decorated with red glass beads, a black arrow, and a cane (*haka itsú*) to help me rise to my feet. When these things are ready, Tamats himself must come to get me."

When the *xiriki* had been built and the offerings laid out, Tamats asked the animals for their *muwieris*. But, since these were made from the feathers of owls and vultures, they were not good enough. So Tamats took from his bag his *muwieris* made of eagle feathers, tied them to the cane, and went with his two brothers to get Grandfather Tatewarí.

"Here are the offerings and the cane you asked for," they said. "You fell in the Middle World, and we have come to lift you up and ask you to come with us."

They took him by the arms. With their help, and leaning on the cane, Tatewarí took five steps and stopped at the door of the *xiriki*. There he demanded: "How am I going to light myself, when you haven't prepared the things I need?"

"Tell us what you want, and we will get it at once," Tamats replied.

"Cut that oak and that pine tree into firewood," Tatewarí said. "And make a pair of forked poles, too."

They laid two oak logs on the ground, threw on some pine for kindling, and placed Tatewarí on top. Grandfather Fire took the two forked poles and gave them to the two young deer, saying: "You, Uxikwikame, who took my right arm, will guard me always on the right. You, Watemukame, who took my left arm, will guard me always on the left. And you, My Father Tamats Kauyumari, will be my heart, the heart of the Fire."

"Yes," Tamats answered, "and you will be Tatewarí Tamats. You will be with us always, giving us warmth and life."

Tai took out his flint and tinder and turned to address the others. "The time has come for all of you to say with me: 'The first spark from the flint will fall in the south, the second in the north, the third in the east, the fourth in the west, and the fifth in the center'—which is I myself, Tatewarí Tamats."

With this he set fire to the tinder, and the Old Man became a leaping flame. The animals were frightened. It was not only the first time they had seen fire, but also the first time they had seen each other. "We didn't know how our faces looked," they said. "We didn't know what the things in the world looked like. We were blind."

But Tatewarí gave off so much heat that they were driven back; and ever since that moment wild animals have feared the fire.

"Now," Tamats said to his brothers, "the fire is ours. Tatewarí has named you his guardians and assistants, and you must care for him and see that no one steals him from us. Be alert. Never take your eyes off him."

As Uxikwikame guarded the fire on the right and Watemukame did the same on the left, the hummingbird darted through so swiftly that before they could stop him he had carried off a burning ember in his beak. But he didn't get far. The ember burned his beak—it was originally twice as long as it is today—and he had to drop it.

A little later the opossum approached the fire. "Where did this bright thing come from?" she asked in her little shrill voice. "My, my! Even I, who live under the ground, am enjoying this nice, warm fire."

As she spoke she surreptitiously reached out with her tail and snatched a coal; but, as she ran off with it, it burned her severely. That is why there is no hair on her tail today. When the deer finally caught up with her, she had just enough time to stuff the coal into her pouch.

Uxikwikame and Watemukame looked for the coal in vain. They kicked the opossum, wrung her neck, and left her for dead. But, as soon as the deer had gone back to the fire, she pulled the coal from her pouch and offered it to the gods of the five cardinal directions. At once five huge bonfires leaped up.

"Our vigilance has been useless," the deer said when they saw the fires. "The opossum is still alive and has succeeded in stealing the fire from us."

Then the little old woman Takutsí Me'kima Erena appeared. She was so sleepy she kept falling down.

"Be careful, Granny," the guardians warned her. "You're dying from lack of sleep, and you might tumble into the fire."

The old woman didn't pay much attention to their warning. She stumbled, and before anyone could catch her she fell headfirst into the flames. No sooner had she been burned to ashes than the deer noticed a trembling in the east. Over the mountains rose the slender sickle moon, called Xewi (one) in our language. There was a second tremor, and the moon grew larger and brighter, reaching the phase known as Hota (two). At the third, it rose a little higher and became rounder: it was then Haraika, the half-moon. At the fourth it became Nauriaka. And, finally, after a fifth tremor, it was completely round and became Auxiwiriaka, the full moon.

"No, this is not what I wanted," said Tamats Kauyumari. "It's hard to see things; we need more light. We must think of something better."

Tamats ordered Teiwari Yukauna, Tukipa's assistant, to wield his eagle-feather *muwieris* and sacrifice a five-year-old boy by throwing him into the fire. But, to everyone's surprise, the bird Itayame, with his black, red, and white feathers, flew up out of the flames. Five days later (five years, in that time of the world) they sacrificed another child. This time the bird Xaukita, with its red breast and blue wings, appeared. At five-day periods they threw three more children into the fire, giving birth to the red-and-black bird called Tsukwai, the bird Tuamuxawi with its red wings and gray topknot, and Yaukukuy, the scarlet cardinal.

Seeing that all his schemes had come to nothing, Tamats was depressed. His eye wandered over the mountains and the plains, lit up by the bonfires and by the pale glow of the old lady Erena. Nearby were playing the serpent-man, the quail-man, the turkey-man, the macaw-man, and many other creatures that were half-human and half-animal. They were running after a disk of *pochota*, shooting arrows at it; the only one who was able to hit the target was a child. He was a terribly ugly boy with puffy eyes and a body covered with boils and pimples. He was known as the Pustulous Child.

Tamats Kauyumari noticed the Pustulous Child and was impressed by his marksmanship. He sent two *kakauyaris*, one after the other, to bring him into his presence. But the boy refused to go with them and went on shooting arrows at the *pochota*. Tamats then sent his two brothers, Watemukame and Uxikwikame. When the child saw them coming he hid in his house, but the deer followed him inside.

"Tamats has sent for you," they told him. "He wants to talk to you. It's urgent."

The boy did not answer.

"Say something! What are we going to tell Tamats? He's expecting you, and nobody can keep Tamats waiting."

At last, tired of pleading, Watemukame and Uxikwikame took him by the arms. But the Pustulous Child changed himself into the snake Haiku and crawled into a hole.

The deer, frightened, returned to Tamats. "He changed into a snake."

"Go back and get him. It doesn't matter whether he's a snake or not."

The deer went to the house again, but this time the Pustulous Child appeared in the form of a jaguar. Watemukame and Uxikwikame were really scared now. They ran back to Tamats. "Don't send us again," they pleaded. "He has changed into the jaguar Tuwe, and he tried to eat us."

"It doesn't matter if he's a jaguar or a snake. Go and bring him back by force."

The third time the jaguar was nowhere to be seen, and the boy was standing there.

"You won't get away this time," they said.

Watemukame took one of his arms, and Uxikwikame took one of his legs; but when they tried to pick him up, the arm and leg came off as though they had been stuck on with wax. This new magic frightened them even more than the jaguar and the serpent. The deer didn't know what to do. They stood there holding the arm and the leg, while the Pustulous Child regarded them with his puffy eyes and laughed.

"Don't be afraid," the boy said at last. "My mother Tatei Yurianaka and my father Tatewarí have given me permission to go with you. But first Tamats Kauyumari has to prepare a *xiriki*, a cane, a *nierika*, an arrow, and a gourd bowl."

When the *xiriki* was built and the offerings were ready, Tamats took his two brothers and went to get the Pustulous Child. "Here are the offerings you asked for," Tamats said, giving him the cane. "The *xiriki* is in the Middle World, where your father Tatewarí lives."

Watemukame and Uxikwikame led the boy reverently to the *xiriki*, which they reached in five steps. Behind them came the Pustulous Child's friends who had been playing with the disk of *pochota* on the mountain, as well as all the *kakauyaris*, members of an ancient generation who would later become rocks and plants.

"Have the gods and the *kakauyaris* reached an agreement?" the boy asked.

"Yes, we have," they answered.

"In that case, you, Tamats Kauyumari, will occupy the east; you, Uxikwikame, the south; you, Watemukame, the north; you, Tatei Nariwame, the west; and you, my father Tatewarí, will remain at the center of the world."

Then the Pustulous Child handed his cane to Itsú. "You will remain with Tatewarí in the Middle World and will be the *gobernador*." The boy picked up the captain's staff and gave it to another of the men. "You will be the captain and will go always at the *gobernador*'s right hand. And you," he said to another of those present, handing him another staff, "you will be the alcalde, and will be always at the *gobernador*'s left." He gave a third man a staff and told him, "You will be the *comisario*, and will walk behind the *gobernador*."

In addition, the Pustulous Child asked that a man and a woman light candles to help him ascend to the sky. This is why in our festivals today we Huicholes light candles when the sun appears in the east.

When he had appointed the authorities and seen all his orders carried out, the Pustulous Child called a small boy from among the bystanders. "Come, don't be afraid. Give me your hand."

He made a small cut in one of the lad's fingers and caught the blood on a piece of cotton, which he put into a hollow reed. Then he turned to his playmates. "Now you have all taken your places, my friends the turkey-man, the quail-man, the macaw-man, and the parrot-man. I want you to stand at the center of the world and tell me if you can hear my footsteps when I begin my long journey. Will you promise to do that?"

"Yes, we promise," the animals replied.

The Pustulous Child made his farewell speech: "The moment of sacrifice has come, the moment of dying. Tamats, Elder Brother Deer Tail, never take your eyes off me. Watch me always, my father." With these words he leaped into the fire.

A great whirlwind sprang up—no one had ever felt such a powerful wind—and caught up the Pustulous Child's diseases and flung them over the faces and bodies of the authorities. This is why the Huicholes have been subject to illness ever since. Itsú caught a cold; the captain developed a case of pinkeye; the alcalde got pneumonia; and the *comisario* was stricken with smallpox.

The Pustulous Child crossed Xewitemaká, the first sea, Hutariakamaká, the second sea, and Hairakamaká, the third sea; but none of the animals heard him.

Filled with fear, they ascended Reunar, the Burned Hill. When the Pustulous Child crossed Nauriakamaká, the fourth sea, at four o'clock in the morning, they heard his footsteps very clearly. The cock crowed and the birds burst into song, announcing that they had heard him. The man and the woman lighted their candles. At five in the morning the Pustulous Child crossed Auxuwiriaká, the fifth sea, which was swirling with foam. This time every bird and animal cried out in its own fashion. Flocks of green parrots, macaws, quail, and marine birds rose from the turbulent sea and flew toward the nascent sun, assisting him with their song.

But the sun had not been named yet. The deer, the ocelots, the squirrels, the rabbits, and the snakes turned to face the sun, but nobody knew what to call him. At this point the turkey cried, "*Wexi-coa, tao, tao!*" which in Huichol means "Our Father the Sun"; and Tao has been his name ever since.

In a few moments it became evident that Tao was unable to rise any higher above the earth, although his heat was unbearable. The *kakauyaris* melted and turned into stones. The lizards, the iguanas, and the scorpions crawled under rocks. The black snake slid into the water, and the ocelots ran to hide in caves.

Then Tamats Kauyumari said: "Our Father the Sun is too low. I will try to raise him."

He lifted him a little with his horns. "Is that enough?"

"No, no!" the animals cried. "We're suffocating. Raise him a little higher."

Tamats lifted the sun four times more, and at the fifth the heat diminished. After many disappointments, the Makers had at last seen their plans carried out.

(A myth related in Ocota by Bartolo Chibarras.)

A Journal of the Pilgrimage

The First Day. Next morning the pilgrims shoulder their bags and line up in the order they will scrupulously maintain during the trip. As noted above, at the head of the procession is the Mara'akame Tatewarí, supreme authority of the pilgrimage and representative of Grandfather Fire. It is he who carries the arrows and calabashes of wild tobacco and sets the pace. Next comes Tatari, the *cantador*. In third place is Tatutsí Tekuyuaneme, "he who moves about"; he is the Mara'akame Tatewarí's assistant and transmits his orders to the rest. The fourth is Tatewarí, the *mara'akame*'s representative, who accordingly bears his name. The rest follow in this order: Tawexika, the Sun; Maxa Kwaxí (Deer Tail), who lives in Reunar; Akatewari, the Principal Deer and God of the Wind; Xapawiyeme, the God of Lake Chapala; Itsúwauya, God of the Canes; Tatei Nariwame, the Mother of the Gods; Auxatemai, God of the Coastal Region; Tatei Utuanaka, the Fish Goddess; Yurianaka, Mother of the Deer; Kiewimuka, God of the Coras; and Parítsika, God of the Hunt and Lord of the Deer.

One by one they take leave of their wives, who are standing in their doorways. They touch the women on the shoulder and say: "The time has come for us to part. With the gods' help, we will return in thirty days. Don't forget to gather in the *calihuey* every evening and light the candles. We will be thinking of you always. Take care of the children, and obey the Tekuamana's orders."

Tears come to their eyes as they think of the long separation and the dangers awaiting them. The success of the pilgrimage depends upon the conduct of both the men and the women at this time—as does, in the last analysis, the very stability of their lives.

On the first day they visit the waterfall Aitekua; Turikie Tsamurawemakúxaure, "where the mothers of the wolves live"; and Muichimayaku, "where the mountain chives grow." They spend the night at Mu'túa, "the head on the ground"; there are found the scattered heads of the five Hewis—the supernatural beings who founded an earlier race and were changed into stones. Before lying down to sleep they cut firewood and light the fire Tatewarí, with the help of Akatewari, Parítsika, and Kiewimuka. They address Grandfather Fire: "You have been with us and watched over us this first day. Rest now, Tatewarí, our Father and Grandfather."

The Second Day. After taking a turn around the fire and asking Tatewarí to protect and guide them, they visit Chimompa, "the stone shaped like a shoe"; Makuriuya, "the place of the oak trees"; Makatuxa, "white earth"; Harakuna, "the lake"; Hayemaanyehane, "where the path leads"; Kuxurimayewe, "where the cross is"; Umukasari, "the place of the *tasuyate*" (a palm whose fibers are used to make hats); and Harituá, "where the *kakauyaris* are" (the beings Nakawé changed into stones). There they rub themselves with grass to relieve their fatigue, for they have traveled without rest or food for twelve hours.

"It has been a long day's journey, Tatewarí, Our Father. Give us rest," they intone.

The Third Day. They pass Atsiyapa, "the outskirts of San Andrés"; Torillo; Zapote; Itúparitusá, "the white door"; Harakunamautaname, "the lake behind the dam"; Teumakakarutsitúa, "the stony place under the squash" (there lie the *kakauyaris* turned to stone); the

Tenaire River; Kuwari, "the twisting of the serpent Kuwari" (another *kakauyari* turned to stone); Zapota; Muwamemayenena, "where the grindstones are"; and, finally, Riktekie, "the house of the bees." There they rub themselves again with grass to relieve their weariness and to rid themselves of any evil that invisible demons may have done them along the way.

Tatewarí faces the fire and announces: "We are approaching the Hill of the Star. There we shall have to confess our sins and be cleansed. We must think of these things. We must prepare ourselves."

The Fourth Day. The pilgrims arrive in Hapúripa, as they call the town of Huejuquilla. Here they buy candles. Then they proceed to Maunyaxawa, "where the hole is"; Nakarimuyau, "where the so-called nopals are"; and Makuriuyakitenie, "the gate of the oaks," from where they can see Xurawemuieka, the Hill of the Star.

"We are now passing through the gate of the gods," announces the *mara'akame*, opening it with his *muwieris*. This time they use candles to brush away the devils encountered along the road. They leave a large five-peso candle adorned with ribbons—one for each pilgrim—which is dedicated to the sun; other candles, similarly decorated, are offered with prayers for "a long life." The *mara'akame* brushes the pilgrims with his *muwieris*, saying, "May the gods in Wirikuta grant us long life."

They proceed toward Muwierihaituakamemanatiwe, "beyond are found the *muwieris*." This is a white hill where dwells Haituakame, a demon who stole the gods' *muwieris* as they were returning from Wirikuta; as a result the gods went mad and were transformed into stone *kakauyaris*. They leave the demon an offering of arrows, gourd bowls, and a container of *tsinarimayama* (sour *atole*). Then they visit the place called Tehohanu, "where the maguey grows." (It was here we met them at the beginning of our trip.) Near Valparaíso they stop to rest and prepare the *kaunari* ropes with which they tie the pilgrims and record their sins.

The Fifth Day. This is a day of fasting, purification, and entry into holy territory. When the pilgrims reach the Mesa of Mexatsie, the great ceremony of confession takes place. Then, after passing through the rural settlement of Yermita, they come to Xurawemuieka, the Hill of the Star. There they light the bonfire and perform the ritual we witnessed on the outskirts of Valparaíso.

Meanwhile, back home in Las Guayabas the pilgrims' wives, who have observed a strict fast, gather that night with the Tekuamana about the fire blazing in the *calihuey*. The old guardian addresses them: "Now that the pilgrims have gone hunting, and are gathered at the Hill of the Star, the time has come to confess your sins."

He turns to the wife of Eusebio, the Mara'akame Tatewarí. "You shall be the first to confess."

"Very well. I am ready," she replies.

"Have you done anything bad?" the Uxatuki asks. The woman confesses aloud the most imponderable lapses from marital fidelity. As in the case of the men, of all the capital sins it is only those of the flesh that count. The old man records each transgression by making a knot in the rope. When she has finished he says, "You have done as I commanded. Only Tatewarí, Grandfather Fire, knows whether you have told the truth or concealed any of your sins."

He then throws the rope into the fire. When the general confession has been completed, the women shake themselves before the fire to complete the act of purification. They declare, with a certain laconic irony: "Very well. We have obeyed the law. It remains to be seen whether those who are absent have complied as conscientiously. It remains to be seen how matters stand with those who are now at the Hill of the Star."

(Up to this point I have related what Eusebio, the Mara'akame Tatewarí who headed the pilgrimage to Wirikuta, told me. It was much against his will that he agreed to give me this detailed information, and his good intentions ran dry when he reached the fifth day. That evening he got savagely drunk, and I had to promise a great many things before his father, Hilario, consented to go on with the account. The Carrillo family was in an awkward situation. The fact that they had accepted our friendship and allowed us to accompany them had caused them many difficulties. The isolationists in San Andrés, set against any sort of peaceful coexistence, charged them openly with negotiating the sale of tribal lands—an accusation that Hilario and his three sons resented deeply. The airstrip built by the Indian Institute, the school, the store, the free medical service, the veterinary assistance—all these had alarmed the isolationists. The old shamans predicted that this invasion of their privacy would sooner or later destroy the world they lived in. They were making a last stand: small acts of vengeance, slanderous rumors, refusal to cooperate with the Institute, simply pretending that we did not exist. On the other hand, they were tolerant toward those who actually were trying to take over their lands—undoubtedly because these "neighbors" were armed, so that resistance would mean a civil war. Caught between intertribal hatred, distrust, and opposing forces, I accepted the inevitable. I had to content myself with salvaging what I could of a culture inexorably doomed to extinction.)

The Sixth Day. In the morning they offer an arrow to the star Xurawe, "the guardian of the arrows we see in the sky." They pass through Teaparimatimane, "where the stones for grinding *uxa* are," and end the day at "the big trees."

The Seventh Day. They visit Naranjal, the Sheep Ranch (in Hilario's Spanish, "Porcacosi"), and Xunurinukaka, which means something like "land of the maguey." At nightfall they light a bonfire and address Grandfather Fire: "Thank you for delivering us from the serpents, the scorpions, and the demons along the road. You must be as tired as we; rest, then, Our Grandfather, and sleep well."

The Eighth Day. The pilgrims arrive at Harahuerta, "where the holes are." This is an orchard and a lake inhabited by the goddess Tatei Nariwame; here they leave offerings of an arrow and a candle. They enter Zacatecas. Nearby is the spring where Tamatsiska, the Lord of Wine, resides in the form of a *sotol* plant. They offer an arrow decorated with a *sotol* blossom, and pour *tuch* (an alcoholic drink made from palm) into the water.

"Drink this liquor," the *mara'akame* says, "and accept this arrow. Protect us in Wirikuta and keep us from going mad. We Huicholes always think of you with love and reverence."

They come to Tawekame, on the edge of Makuipa, the home of the Mad God Xiskatemai; he is a Hewi accompanied by several *kakauyaris* as crazy and brutish as animals. The pilgrims pay them a tribute in coins and arrows for the privilege of entering Makuipa. They cross Kiakamuyewe, "where the ivy grows," pass through the village of Guadalupe, and spend the night in Haxuretumáyama, "the place of the red water." Here lives a *kakauyari* who is the guardian deity of the ears.

The Ninth Day. Before their departure, they offer the *kakauyari* an arrow, a candle, and a gourd bowl dedicated to the goddess Utuanaka, so that they may be free of diseases of the ear. (The *kakauyari* failed to pay his tribute to the gods, and in punishment they caused his eardrums to burst.) They move on to Takuatsitisie, the Hill of the Mara'akame's Shoulder Bag, where the *kakauyaris* dropped their pouches. They pass Puxekotsi or Parturillo (according to Hilario, "the sheep" or "the little shepherd"); Mayatepurikiya, "the ant hill"; Tupinatsie, "the place where children go in the form of hummingbirds"; Wicherkatúa, "the big hill"; and Teanuipa, "the place of the *kakauyari.*" They visit the home of Kurukuxa Mutiwu, the God of the Squash, "where there are many stones shaped like squash," and leave an offering in his cave. After stopping at Zacatón they proceed to Ramura, "the branches," where they spend the night.

The Tenth Day. At Kiaraka, named for the god who lay in wait for the rat who untied the deer Watemukame, the pilgrims leave a bowl with coins in it; failure to do this may mean death. They make another offering to Niwetarikitenie, the deity of the gate called Niwetari; and they leave a third for the three deer that guard it: Maxatawekame, the crazy deer; Maxatame, the white deer; and Maxayawime, the black deer. When the gods and the *kakauyaris* made their first journey to Wirikuta, they tried to pass through the gate without paying any attention to the deer or asking their permission. As a result, they found themselves helplessly drunk. Then the black deer said, "You didn't even speak to us. Now you are in our power. We demand an offering of peyote, arrows, and gourd bowls. You must set them out in the north, the south, the east, and the west, so that others who come to Wirikuta will know to do the same." The gods obeyed and soon recovered. The first to pass through was the sun. He was followed by Tseriakame, the god of the left hand; Tekuyuaneme, the god of motion; Witseteiwari, the black eagle; Tunuwame, the god-*cantador* of the *calihuey*; and all the other gods of the *calihuey*.

They cross La Noria. At Ritupa, the next stop, the pilgrims urinate. Should they do so before reaching that point, the many gods who dwell in Tatei Matinieri might see them and inflict some disease upon them for their lack of respect. When they reach the house of Tatei Matinieri they remove the *matewames'* blindfolds and introduce them to the goddess.

"These are your sons, Our Mother. They have come to see you for the first time, so that you may know them. During the Festival of the New Corn we promised to come, and here we are. We have killed a bull and a deer in your honor. We offer you their blood and flesh, the harvest ears, our daughters' bowls, and our sons' arrows. In exchange, please do not forget us. Give our children good health, and grant us plentiful harvests. See that our cows conceive and give us many calves."

After making these offerings they move on to some nearby springs called Tsauxirita; here the peyote pilgrims ask Nariwame Makanieri to help them become *mara'akames*. These little pools are peopled by Xuturiwiyekame, the God of Lightning; Haramara; and the gods of all the *calihueys*, who have gathered here with their offerings. Then they go to the Hill of Parítsika, where live the God of the Hunt and the goddesses Utuanaka and Waxawimari. There the pilgrims make further offerings, including the head of the deer that was sacrificed before the journey began.

"O gods, receive your sacrifices. We made our promises, and we have kept them. You, Parítsika, allowed us to kill a deer. It has rained plentifully. We have had good crops, and we thank you for them. Do not forget your children, the Huicholes."

The day ends at Narkatua Mamatúa, "the place of the ashes," where there is a large lake. Tatewarí, Grandfather Fire, rested his hand there, and the rocks were burned to ashes. The ashes rose to the sky and became the clouds that hang over Reunar and the other hills near Catorce.

The Eleventh Day. The pilgrims come to Uxataremekamaku'u, "the place where the gods painted themselves yellow." When the gods painted themselves, they turned cold and became stones. From these stones grew the tree called Uxa, whose root provides the yellow pigment for the pilgrims' faces. They pass through Horqueta and arrive at Tuimayen, a grassy place with a spring. This spring is called "the water of Itsú appeared." Its water is used to bless Itsú, the God-Cane, and is also taken to the church, since it is sacred to Saint Andrew.

The Twelfth Day. This day's journey comprises Baldosara (the Salt Ranch); Mateikarita, "the place where the gods left their hand-prints"; and Wakurikitenie, the gate where stand the deer Wakuri, Akatewari (God of the Wind), and Tsamurawi (the God of the Wolves), who led the wolf-gods to Wirikuta. When the sun was born the wolf-gods melted and were transformed into stones.

The Thirteenth Day. The travelers cross the desert and spend the night on the outskirts of Santa Gertrudis. The arid Catorce range lies before them, dominated by the enormous bulk of Reunar, the sacred dwelling of Tamats Kauyumari. The pilgrims must prepare themselves spiritually and contemplate the ordeals and revelations awaiting them in Wirikuta.

The Fourteenth Day. On entering Wirikuta they make an offering to Tiskatemai or Tatewarítawekame (the Neighbor or the Drunken Man). This being, angered because he had received no tribute from the gods when they went hunting, took his revenge by making them drunk.

"Accept this sacrifice," the pilgrims say. "And do not let us suffer the same fate. We are on our way to collect Nierika, the peyote. It will guide us home, and will enable us to shoot a deer."

When the Huicholes find the first peyote, they see it as a deer. "We have cornered him," they exclaim. The gods who took part in the first hunt heard the cactus cry out like a deer and saw it take the deer's shape. At the first touch of their arrows, peyote plants burst from his body. But the gods failed to save the first peyote and thus were unable to hunt the actual deer from that time on. This is why the Huicholes keep their first peyote in a bowl: it guides them home again and leads them to the deer's hiding place.

The Return
of the Peyote Pilgrims

Two weeks after we had left them in Valparaíso, our friends the peyote pilgrims had still not returned from the sacred hunting of the deer, and alarming and conflicting rumors were beginning to circulate. Some said that they were in the mountains near Mexquitic; others reported that Hilario's younger brother Antonio was seriously ill; still others swore that they had seen them near San Andrés, loaded down with deer.

While waiting at the ceremonial center in San Andrés, I went every afternoon to the edge of the mesa; there I climbed up on the rocks overlooking the Las Guayabas ravine and tried to see some signs of life at the distant and almost invisible *calihuey*. There was no one there: a sure sign that the pilgrims had not yet returned.

At the end of the third week it was confirmed that Antonio had been stricken with pneumonia near Chapalangana. It seemed that his illness had been brought about by some deviation from the ritual, incurring the wrath of some as yet unidentified god. This provoked a series of conjectures and sinister observations inspired not only by theological considerations but also by tribal rancor over the unorthodox aspects of our trip to Wirikuta.

By the time Hilario's son José, the schoolteacher who was my principal informant in San Andrés, told me one morning that the pilgrims had returned, these speculations had created a great deal of tension in the air. The mystery was to be cleared up five months later, when I visited the area again. In the meantime, Marino Benzi and I, tired of waiting, mounted our mules and left San Andrés and its bitter theological disputes.

The *calihuey* at Las Guayabas, in the shade of a luxuriant *zalate,* is smaller than that at San Andrés. As is traditional, there is a cleared area in front, reminiscent of the courtyard found before the ancient Mexican temples. Here the old ceremonies are still performed. At one side are two old thatched roofs resting on poles.

The temple and its courtyard were silent and deserted. Determined to be on hand when the pilgrims' envoy—Nauxari, "he who recounts"—arrived, I laid out my sleeping bag and sat down to wait.

At four o'clock in the afternoon the Nauxari suddenly materialized in the cornfield. He took two turns around the courtyard and entered the *calihuey,* where a fire had been burning since morning. He appeared and disappeared so swiftly that, although Marino leaped for his camera with the agility of a cat, he was unable to get a picture.

Under the sumptuous regalia of the Nauxari, our friend was unrecognizable. His hat was covered with long turkey feathers painted yellow, and his half-hidden face was marked with yellow stripes and dots. In one hand he carried two forked sticks from the bonfire. From his shoulders hung calabashes of tobacco, a stuffed squirrel, two bags loaded with peyote, and—Surprise!—the two plastic canteens we had bought in Catorce. He seemed distant and mysterious. His ritual purity, the trials he had undergone, and his contact with the gods in Wirikuta lent him an air of holiness. In spite of his filthy clothing and his automobile-tire huaraches, he made me think of the priests in the ancient Mexican ceremonial centers who suddenly sprang into view before the worshipping multitudes, dramatically announcing the presence of the gods.

Inside the *calihuey,* he laid the offerings on the *itari,* cleansed his feet by brushing them with the forked poles, which he then threw on the fire, turned around once, and plunged his arrow into the ground before the *itari*. After placing the shoulder bags of peyote on the altar, he set the stuffed squirrel upright on a stone as though it were an important personage and sat down facing the fire. His immobility was total. We drew near, hoping for some sign of friendship from our traveling companion; but the Nauxari, dazed with peyote, had shut out the exterior world.

He was performing his office. He was giving Grandfather Fire an account of even the most insignificant details of the journey. From time to time he put out his hand, took a peyote button, and slowly ate it. In the silence of the *calihuey*, broken only by the crackling of the fire, the Nauxari was experiencing things that our senses were incapable of perceiving. According to the description given me by a famous *mara'akame*,[1] the Nauxari *hears* the sun dropping in the west, marking the passing of time as though it were a clock, while the sound is repeated in the fire. This certainly accounts for his strange absorption.

We left the envoy with his peyote visions and went with José to look for the rest of the pilgrims, who, by ritual imperative, were waiting a kilometer from the *calihuey*. They were busy with preparations for the great peyote festival. Antonio Bautista, with the shattered expression and melancholy eyes of a man who had looked death in the face, was cutting up a black lamb with a long knife. Hilario looked on with bleary eyes; one leg was bruised, and one foot so swollen that he could not wear his sandal. The other pilgrims, faces drawn with fatigue and hunger, were using a straw to paint the yellow symbols of the peyote on their guitars, their violins, and the feathers in their hats.

Beneath the pink granite cliffs of the San Andrés mesa, the ravine was warm and pleasant. In the light of the setting sun the tall grass, the fields of ripe corn, and the leaves of the oak trees glowed yellow and gold under an autumn sky, where rounded summer clouds still floated. In the midst of this peace, this timeless mountain landscape, the peyote pilgrims were engaged in religious rites they had been observing for three thousand years.

Even without talking with them, one could feel that they were happy to be back, to have come home; home meant not simply the hut or windowless adobe room where they slept and died, but something far greater and more complex: the landscape, the cattle, the corn, the immortal spirits. Now I understood a little better the suffering and ordeals to which they subjected themselves during these annual pilgrimages far from the sierra. Today they were no longer the trapped, uneasy, defenseless, miserable men they had been in Cedral, San Luis Potosí, and Real de Catorce. The mountains were their natural refuge, the maternal breast; the joy of winning back to them was so obvious that I wondered if it would not be better to give up the idea of providing them with schools, doctors, stores, and landing strips, and leave them immersed in their mystical dreams and the abject poverty that is the ineluctable concomitant of those dreams.

At this point, however, the return to their own world was still more symbolic than actual. Their very sanctity kept them at a distance from their homes and wives. They were, in fact, in a kind of quarantine. Only their children, being ritually pure, could approach them and bring food without the risk of contamination. Little Gregorio, in his hat covered with turkey feathers and his new huaraches, appeared bearing tortillas in a napkin for his grandfather, the *gobernador*. Eusebio, the one-eyed *mara'akame* who had been lucky enough to obtain some macaw feathers near Chapalangana, held one of his children in his arms. Every few minutes there was a movement in the grass, and other children emerged with tortillas or messages for their fathers.

As he painted his swollen foot with iodine, Hilario told me of their misfortunes. Antonio Bautista had been at death's door for two nights, and no one had expected him to get back to Las Guayabas alive. The rain had soaked the peyote collected in Wirikuta, and half of it had rotted. They had run out of *tostadas*, and for several days had had nothing to eat. He related all this in a doleful tone, from time to time scratching his head under its thick, long hair and spitting. The others nodded in agreement, moaning: "Aah, aah, aah, aaah!"

Dreams of Wealth

The altar of the *calihuey* was crowded with burning candles, bags of peyote, gourd bowls, and votive arrows. The fire was blazing, and the smoke that could not escape through the chinks in the roof gradually filled the large temple. The pilgrims' wives, with yellow suns painted on their cheeks, began to arrive. The Nauxari sat with his back against a pillar, his feathered hat on his knees. He did not move or speak.

By eleven o'clock the *calihuey* was filled with women, children, and the men who had not gone to Wirikuta. The Nauxari roused himself from his visions (he had been required to eat one peyote button for each pilgrim who had made the trip to Reunar) and gave each woman the peyote brought back by her husband, following the hierarchic order established during the journey.

The women sat on the ground, heads bowed, slowly and gravely peeling the buttons and eating them. After half an hour they began to feel the effects.

However, the ritual of the festival calls for a kind of struggle against the trance, so that they may be alert enough to take part in the game, which goes on all night. Even so, they know that the sacred cactus will overcome them in the end.

The game is based on the misunderstandings arising from the ritual changing of the names of things. The stuffed squirrel represents the pilgrims and speaks to the women in their name, through the *tsikuaki.*

The *tsikuaki* is the clown of the Indian festivals. He wears a wooden mask—the face of the oldest man, called Tapuri—and swings in one hand the Tekuamana's rope, with its knots recording the days.

"I have brought you some hard-working men," the *tsikuaki* announced to the women. "Would you like them?"[2]

"I should say not," the women exclaimed. "They are here only because they want to take our land away from us."

"What foolish women! You don't know what you're missing. These men are very rich. They don't care for money; they throw it away by the handful."

"We don't want them! They're cheaters and thieves," one woman called out, laughing uncontrollably.

"You crazy women, how can you talk that way? They have goats and cattle the way we have termites. And they wear shoes."

"What a lie! They wear huaraches, not shoes."

"You're very bad, you women. You ought to write them a letter."

"All right, we'll write to them," one woman said. She got up, seized a piece of charcoal, and scrawled a couple of lines on a scrap of newspaper. "Let the squirrel's secretary send them this."

"What did you say in your letter?"

"That they can stay home and scratch their lice. That's what it says."

"What language did you write it in?"

"In Huichol. I don't know any other language."

The *tsikuaki* laughed, his voice muffled behind the mask. "They can't read Huichol. They're Spaniards."

"Spaniards? Then how are we going to understand each other? If they were Coras, or Tepehuanes, at least . . ."

"They're foreigners, but they're here to buy land. The squirrel's secretary and his surveyor have sold them a lot of land. Here are the deeds," the *tsikuaki* said, showing them a roll of newspapers.

"Papers don't mean anything. Papers tell lies."

"These men know how to make automobiles, trousers, and railroads, so people can be happy and not wear themselves out walking over the mountains."

"Yes, we've seen their railroad trains. They're nothing but worms."[3]

"Women, women, why are you so suspicious?"

"Because men are always trying to deceive us. We don't believe a word they say."

"These men can dance and sing."

"Show us how they dance and sing."

The *tsikuaki* waved his rope in the air and began an insane dance around the fire. The stuffed squirrel, solemnly sitting on his rock, seemed to come to life in the flickering firelight. The *tsikuaki's* mask, with its hooked nose, floated in a ghostly way through the smoke.

The *tsikuaki* displayed an inexhaustible vitality. When he had finished his dance he seized a turkey-feather *muwieri* and a bladder (sometimes he fills this with bull's urine and employs it in a series of scatological games that are very popular). He leaped about, calling out numbers in Spanish: "Five, two, three, six, two, zero, two, three, zero, one, two, zero, two. Five pesos, two pesos, ten pesos. That's enough."

This reciting of numbers, taken up again and again, has a purpose: it breaks up the sequence of the game, introducing an esoteric element that accentuates the irrational qualities of the peyote trance. The figures hang in the air like long ribbons, resounding in a mysterious way, and are cut off abruptly at the *tsikuaki's* peremptory command: "That's enough!"

Sometimes he tells endless stories:

A fox-boy and a fox-girl were fighting on the road, when a man came along. The foxes took fright and ran away. The man followed the fox-girl and caught her by the tail.

"Let me go," she said. "I'm not a fox; I'm a person like you. Why did you grab my tail?"

"If you're a person," the man replied, "tell me what happened back there on the road."

"Well, you see, I was fighting with this fox-boy, and then you came along, and we ran away. Then you grabbed me by the tail and I told you I wasn't a fox, but a person like yourself."

"Yes, I know. But what happened back there on the road?"

"Well, you see, I was fighting . . ."

The *calihuey* had now become a stage, and the building rocked with laughter. The men threw back their heads and laughed with open mouths, showing their beautiful teeth. The women hid their faces in their hands, trying to suppress their spasms of giggling.

The hilarious stage of the peyote trance is well known. When he is free from the spells of suspicion and naked terror the sacred cactus can produce, the subject responds readily to outside stimuli and tends to follow the pattern presented. We can imagine the reactions of an audience at a comedy of Aristophanes or Ionesco if before the performance they had taken some relaxing and mirth-inducing drug. The scene would be very much like this one in Las Guayabas. But here the spectators were the actors; they were playing their own comedy. They exaggerated each situation according to their own feelings, adding some monstrous distortion, even changing the lines of the dialogue in accord with their irrational state of mind. In these practices of an archaic shamanism there may be a glimpse of the theater of the future, where the spectators become actors and present their dreams—the dream of riches, the dream of freedom, the dream of love—following a skeleton script and responding to the stimuli of some extraneous element: a drug or a *tsikuaki*.

The struggle between the peyote and its worshipers went on. Some of the Indians had already succumbed; they were stretched out on the ground, sleeping peacefully. Most of the audience, however, was still attentive to the comedy and its religious duties. At midnight the women wiped away their tears of laughter, assumed a more serious expression, and distributed little balls of tortilla dough for feeding the fire.

The Nauxari stood and addressed Tatewarí: "You are back in your *calihuey*, where you can rest among your own people, among those who love you. Thanks to your help, our trip to Wirikuta was successful. Thanks to you, Grandfather Fire, we have returned. Receive your sustenance, your corn, your chocolate, your crackers. Eat now, and rest. You are home."

I was given some of the balls of dough. They were moist and slightly sticky in my hand. When the Nauxari picked up a bowl and emptied its contents into the fire, we all tossed in the Grandfather's nourishment and watched as the little balls gave off red, yellow, and blue flames among the coals.

Two Religious Ceremonies

At sunrise the women offered calabashes of broth and deer meat to Tawexika Xirikieya, the sun, and to Tatutsí Xirikieya Tekuyuaneme, the god of motion and of the Las Guayabas *calihuey*. The indefatigable *tsikuaki* was still making everyone laugh.

In the light of dawn everything looked awful. The *calihuey* was strewn with corn husks, cobs, and other trash. The Indians' tattered clothing was filthy and repulsive. Half-naked infants were crawling about in the Huichol fashion—on all fours, but without touching the ground with their knees. A few people were asleep, but most were sitting on the log benches against the walls of the temple. Outside, a small black bull wearing a paper flower stood waiting resignedly for the moment of sacrifice.

It was nearly noon when the sound of horns, guitars, and violins heralded the arrival of the pilgrims, still hidden from view as they advanced through the tall corn. Hilario stepped forth with a princely air, despite his limp, with his flags and god-canes slung on his back. The resplendent feathers in his hat and the suns painted on his dusky cheeks added to his dignity. Like the other *mara'akames*, he carried his *muwieris* in his hand; with them, and an herb called *toy*, he cleansed the women's and children's heads, after blowing on them to drive off the evil spirits.

The pilgrims handed over the bowls, the water, and the candles from Wirikuta and distributed the sacred cactus. The women lighted their candles. They all took the ritual turn around the courtyard and took their places by the bull. Over the animal's head Eusebio held the antlers of a deer they had killed during the hunt, while Hilario did the same with his canes. The officiant slowly sank his knife into the bull's throat. The shamans dipped their candles in the stream of blood and touched them to the gourd bowls, the arrows, the ears of corn, and the bottles, thus sanctifying them.

At the sight of blood they were seized by an ancient frenzy. The incantations, the sounds of the horns, violins, and guitars, the howling of the excited dogs, the lowing of the dying bull—all blended in a barbaric accompaniment to the ceremony. For the first time their faces betrayed their secret, smoldering madness.

This outburst of a passion that contradicts our notions of the order and structure of the universe—for they believe that it is man who tends and feeds the sun—brought to mind, by way of contrast, a religious scene I had witnessed aboard the *Himalaya*, a transatlantic vessel of the P & O Lines.

It was the first Sunday out, somewhere between Curaçao and Trinidad. The stewards had set up several hundred chairs in the ballroom—on each chair a prayer book, courtesy of the company—

and had installed a long table on the bandstand, near the organ. By these simple modifications the room was transformed into a Protestant church. The faithful began arriving at 11:30. The women, most of whom were nearer sixty than fifty, wore light summer dresses, straw hats, and white gloves. Their husbands, either rentiers or retired, came in blue jackets with gold buttons, silk ascots, and freshly pressed white trousers. They were solid citizens, exuding health (if a little withered), security, wealth, and good breeding. Through the open windows we could see the deep blue of the Caribbean, and the smell of the sea mingled with eau de Cologne and French perfume.

For me, citizen of a nation whose love for the dramatic not only reveals itself in the realm of religion but also distorts and lends grotesque meaning to even profane manifestations, this was an absolutely obscene spectacle. Although these worthy old ladies would soon be called before the judgment bench, they watched the service with one eye and, like chameleons, examined their neighbors' attire with the other, now and then lifting a gloved hand to their dyed hair, protected from the wind by plenty of hair spray. The Austrian musical director attempted a selection by Bach; but he had had too much to drink the night before and was badly out of tune. No one seemed to notice. Then the members of the congregation rose, smoothed their wrinkled clothing, and sang hymns in their slightly cracked, neuter voices.

They took the prescribed stroll on the promenade deck, and by 12:30 they were in the bars. Their expressions had not changed throughout all the carefully programmed activities from breakfast time until the noonday cocktail. Although they could say, like the Huicholes, "it has been consummated," their rites lacked passion and grandeur. Theirs was a society washed with detergents, bleached and dried by machines, so that there remained not the slightest smell or taste of the human being. Not one was capable of an act of bad taste, or even any departure from good manners. Neither in their religious world nor in their social world was any excess permissible.

Our pilgrims were now beginning their return to the realm of the profane. They emptied their shoulder bags and sat down with their backs against the walls of the *calihuey*. Their wives came to join them, after first purifying themselves before the fire. Hilario's wife wept convulsively. Everyone gave way to the joy of homecoming.

The women had their husbands back, but there had been a change in them. They were the same, and yet they were not. Their sacred aspect as half-men, half-gods lent them a dignity that discouraged intimacy.

The pilgrims gathered in a double row around the fire, and the shamans welcomed them by tapping their heads and shoulders with their *muwieris*; it was still not permissible to touch them with one's hands.

"We have had a good journey," Hilario said. "Again we thank you, Grandfather Fire, for guiding us to Wirikuta and allowing us to return home. We are all here with you. Together we went to Reunar, and together we have returned."

"Welcome to your village," the women chanted. "We thank you. You have brought back peyote, the blood of the deer, and the holy water of Tatei Matinieri. You have brought health for our children and nourishment for Yurianaka, the earth. Thanks to you, the gods have looked upon us with favor."

They made a turban for Hilario's wife and adorned her with crow feathers, for she was the Mother of the Corn. Then they turned to the dead bull. On the carcass rested the papers Hilario had written with his *muwieris*, the stuffed squirrel, and the candles. After touching the animal's genitals with their arrows, they joined in a long incantation.

The dogs were lapping up the spilled blood. The pilgrims, standing in their torn, dirty clothing and their hats bristling with feathers, were like some strange birds whipped by the storm. The odor of blood and wood smoke hung over that scene of religious fervor with its overtones of revelry. It was all disgusting and yet extremely beautiful.

The great festival of the peyote began. Inside the *calihuey* Grandfather Fire was resting; with a thousand luminous eyes he watched as his children slowly immersed themselves in the peyote delirium.

Games, Worship, and Fiestas

Even in Valparaíso, when I first had the opportunity to penetrate into the very center of their religious thought, I had been surprised to see how easily the Huicholes passed from tears to laughter, from the most solemn ceremonies to the most frivolous kind of play, from the sacred to the profane. I had heard them sobbing and groaning as they confessed their sins; and then, a few minutes later, I had found them laughing uproariously at the naming of things, at the grotesque incidents attending the appointment of the authorities, and at Hilario's jokes.

The trip to Wirikuta as described by Lumholtz and Zingg appears to be an interminable *via crucis*, an exceedingly painful ordeal; but in actual fact that *via crucis* is neither paved with thorns nor beset with unbearable hardships. Perhaps something of the kind could be said of the impressive ritual of ceremony and sacrifice that occupied a large part of the lives of the ancient American Indians. Seen from the outside and from such a great distance, that life seems to us atrociously harsh, no doubt because we have underestimated the complexity of the Middle American civilizations and the part that game elements played in them.[4]

If play, as Huizinga first defines it, represents "a certain kind of activity differing from that of ordinary life,"[5] our journey can surely be said to fall in that category. It is essentially a slow process of sanctification in which the pilgrims make an effort to do something different, something outside the activities of everyday life.

But play is also activity that is "free" and "superfluous," a "let's pretend"; however, as Huizinga observes, this does not mean that play cannot be pursued with the utmost seriousness and even with a dedication leading to exaltation. The jokes accompanying the confessions, the pervading festive air, and even the absurd pantomimes and comic episodes introduced into the ceremonies by other Huichol groups give the impression of spontaneous activity, a game that absorbs the player and fills him with genuine enthusiasm.

The problem arises when we try to determine the precise moment

when play—which Huizinga believes to be the primary element—
leaves off and religion begins. The boundaries are nearly imperceptible.

We cannot tell when the spiritual element appears, for the Huicholes seem to be crossing these frontiers constantly; they can apparently move with equal ease on quite different planes. At the end
of the eight months that make up the peyote cycle, the play, cult, and
festival seem to have fused into a uniform and coherent whole.

In any case, the trip to Wirikuta presents two essential play elements: the struggle for something and the acting out of something;
and "the practices of the cult can be described in terms of these
components."[6] In other words, the Huicholes act out, faithfully and
within a clearly determined time and space, the magical hunting of
the deer-peyote. This creative feat, like all those recorded in their
myths, is remarkable for its festive spirit. One has the impression
that the gods were in fact playing when they performed it. The theft
of the sacred fire, the sexual exploits of Nuipaxikuri (who was entrusted with the task of destroying the teeth with which the gods
had studded women's vaginas in an attempt to solve the problem of
overpopulation), the birth of corn, the dramatic episodes during the
flood, and the hunting of the deer are events in which the destiny
of the world is at stake. And yet they are permeated with sportive
elements, and their humorous aspects, like those found in the *Popul
Vuh*, lend them an unmistakably playful air.

While in the peyote cycle the element of play is clearly a secondary one, something obviously added, we are not concerned here
with the question of its priority in time. What we can affirm, perhaps,
is that the polarity of the sacred turns out to be much less extreme
than is generally believed. It awakens not only feelings of terror and
awe, but joy and exaltation as well. It inhibits and it liberates. It
discourages familiarity and yet glorifies it, giving it a new dimension.
It is something dangerous, something that must be handled with
caution; at the same time, it is a common patrimony to which everyone has access if he observes certain rules.

Regardless of how different the infrastructures of ancient cultures
and their frames of reference may have been from ours, we can ob-

serve that primitive man's religion was not conceived as a series of superhuman penances and torments. He knew how to relieve the sacred by tempering it with a feeling of humanity, a sense of play, and an unfettered imagination, thus reconciling its two antagonistic aspects: love and terror.

The lengthy ceremonies performed in the ancient ceremonial centers and the fasting and ordeals to which priests and worshipers alike subjected themselves must have been endured in a spirit not very different from that seen today in the pilgrimage to Wirikuta. They spared themselves no suffering and never lost sight of the ultimate object of the cult: the blood sacrifice; but neither did they neglect the game component, with its violent emotions. The mere recounting of their myths, so filled with playful episodes, was vitally stimulating because they re-created, with incomparable plasticity and dramatic force, the events at the beginning of time. Their gods appeared as animals, as men, or as monstrous beings; they had great magical powers and in addition were endlessly cruel and sensual. Capable of killing themselves, they demanded outrageous sacrifices, since all created things owed their existence to their own sacrifice. Worship reduced itself to pantomime and dazzling theatrical spectacles. There were priests disguised as gods or birds or animals; misshapen cripples; clowns; musicians and dancers; singers and tellers of fantastic tales; young men and virgins representing divinities, marching to their own immolation; hearts torn from living bodies; ears and lips pierced by thorns; and wailing and savage laughter.

In recapturing that primal time when nothing had taken on a precise form and when any metamorphosis or feat of magic was possible, the Indians make use again and again of the techniques of play. The Huichol makes believe that he is a god, that the fire is Grandfather Tatewarí, that the deer is both peyote and corn, that the shaman opens a nonexistent door with his eagle-feather scepter, that things must be named all over again, that the deer sings to him and turns into a cloud, and that the cloud becomes rain that falls on his fields and makes them fruitful. What is most important in this game is that the playing follows a certain order, and that an actual object— cactus, deer, corn—has given birth to a higher reality.[7]

Primitive man knows no golden mean. His virgin strength demands nourishment to suit his barbaric appetite. He reveals the same thirst for religion as for comedy and fiestas. He knows that when he plays the game of divinity it loses something of its original essence; it becomes desanctified. He then tries to restore its sacred nature by means of another game, another denial of the everyday world. Thus, without any mitigation of the supreme design he is able to re-create that morning of the world when the gods transformed their enemies into howling monkeys, flattened whole mountain ranges, chopped men into pieces and then brought them to life again, and burned palaces and made them rise again from the ashes.

It is possible that the "hope of salvation" and a desire for protection and security on the part of a people who are miserably poor, oppressed, and hemmed in have deformed and blurred the original religious feeling, and that the pilgrimage to Wirikuta may today include many elements that were absent in the past. Even so, the Huichol peyote cult has retained nearly all the basic features of the traditional culture, unlike the peyote movement among the Indians of the United States, where Christian elements have predominated. This "peyotism" dates from the end of the nineteenth century, as a reaction against the triumph and domination of the white man; the worship of the deer-peyote-corn trinity, on the other hand, has served to maintain a way of life in the face of the expulsion, segregation, and genocide that began with the Spanish conquest. The importance of religion in the lives of the ancient peoples of Middle America has not been thoroughly investigated, but it is evident that many of the changes that have taken place are owing to their acceptance of the fact of defeat and to their will to survive.

The great civilizations of Central Mexico accepted Christianity only after an active struggle of more than a century. They finally became semi-Catholics, distorting and nationalizing the new religion, mixing it (as did the Sioux and Apaches) with what the seventeenth-century Spaniards called idolatry and superstition. At the same time they strengthened tribal unity—their protective shell—and gave up their language, religion, magic, and customs almost to the point of confining them to the home. The impact of the conquest can be gauged above all by the terrible despair that drove them, even in early colonial days, to suicide and especially to alcoholism. "Let us not forget," writes Vittorio Lanternari, "that alcoholism, one of the most active factors in the social and cultural decline of the colonial society, was one of the products of European culture that made its evil effects felt particularly among the Indians."[8]

The people who lived in the mountains and the far desert, and those who were able to flee from the colonial domination by retiring to inaccessible places, were able to retain a large part of their cultural heritage, although it was constantly threatened. Curiously enough, the Indians who have been most successful in maintaining their independence and their mythic traditions are the Huicholes, worshipers of the Divine and Luminous, and the Mazatecas, who revere the Sacred Mushroom.

If, in the process whereby religion, play, and festival fuse into a single entity and become indistinguishable, the use of drugs helps to maintain an extraordinary social cohesion, it may also introduce a degenerative element, as Mircea Eliade has observed. We have seen that the peyote is one of the few ritual objects that do not receive their divine investiture from the outside, but are sacred in themselves: the Huichol has only to ingest it to feel that he is communing with a god. The cactus frees him from the conventions and rules of existence, allowing him to come in contact with divinity, converse with the dead without dying himself, pull aside the veil that conceals the future, and make visible the deer-peyote-corn association that governs his life. Its powers to heal and lay bare the soul are of secondary importance. The Huichol knows its aphrodisiac properties; but, unlike Leary, he does not make those properties the subject of propaganda. On the contrary, he devotes all his strength to fighting off that tendency, to attaining the state of immaculacy without which he cannot undertake the mystical ascension that is the ultimate object of shamanism.

The Festival
of the Parched Corn

The peyote cycle begins with the Festival of the New Corn and Squash; it ends with the Festival of the Parched Corn, which takes place in the middle of May, at the burning height of the dry season.

The landscape around Las Guayabas had changed remarkably since November, when our friends had returned from their ill-starred trip to Wirikuta. The cornfield surrounding the *calihuey*, where the pilgrims' envoy had suddenly materialized, was gone; now there were only hard, ashy furrows, covered with stubble. Some new leaves on the oak trees were the only spots of green in that yellow, ruined land awaiting the first rains.

The Huicholes were busy with preparations for the fiesta. Both men and women were painting their faces—in dots and stripes, mostly—with *uxa* and preparing pots of *tesgüino*, tamales, and *atole*. Everyone was drinking ground peyote mixed with water. Many families had come in from the surrounding settlements and settled themselves with their bottles of *sotol* and tequila near the *calihuey*.

In the courtyard several small areas had been closed off with partitions made of woven branches; some of these were occupied by the women who were in charge of the cooking, while others were reserved for the peyote pilgrims who had been invited from nearby villages. Las Guayabas had no ceremonial center comparable to that in San Andrés and could offer the guests no better lodging; but the branches provided a little privacy, and, after all, the Huicholes do not mind sleeping in the open air.

With the approach of nightfall the men who had gone to cut firewood announced their return by sounding their horns. The activity was still centered in the yard outside the *calihuey*; inside, the firepit was dark. One by one, small fires were lighted behind the rude partitions. The first stars appeared, and darkness fell on the high San Andrés mesa. Soon the warm night came alive with children playing games, whispering, and coughing, while men and women moved to and fro in front of the fires, with dogs at their heels. They were alternately bathed in the golden firelight and lost in the shadows.

A little later we heard the sound of horns in the distance, heralding the arrival of the first guests: the pilgrims from Santa Bárbara. Hilario, his brother Antonio, his son Daniel (who had replaced him as *gobernador*), his other son Eusebio, and the men who bore the gourd bowls came forward to welcome them with candles and violin and guitar music. The leader of the pilgrims was Tatewarí Mara'akame, a tall *cantador* wearing a hat with a high crown bristling with feathers. As gifts he carried a stuffed deer's head and a bowl of peyote. The guests were received with all the courtesy accorded a foreign ambassador. They, too, had made the pilgrimage to Wirikuta and, like their hosts, had been sanctified. They were a little like gods and were received with the grave dignity and respectful affection befitting their rank. Their hosts touched them delicately on the shoulder. "This house is your house," they said. "You must be tired and in need of rest. Welcome!"

After guests and hosts had shared the bowl of peyote, the newcomers were taken to the shelter that had been prepared for them. The same reception was given in turn to the pilgrims from San Andrés, San José, and Cohamita.

When the bonfires had been lighted, the *mara'akames* took their places in the ceremonial chairs, surrounded by their assistants. About midnight they began the long chant that tells how the gods and the sacred animals of Tukipa hunted the deer Tamats in the beginning of the world.

The Magic Hunting of Elder Brother Deer Tail

The Earth, Our Mother Tatei Yurianaka, stood listening to the gods. They wanted to go to Reunar, the place we now call the Burned Hill, and she agreed to let them undertake the long journey.

Maxa Kwaxí, accompanied by his wife, set out from the center of the world. After traveling for a week, they reached the sacred lakes of Tatei Matinieri, where they found the gods already gathered at the edge of the water. "Did you bring the offerings Tatei Yurianaka asked for?" they asked.

They found that he had forgotten to bring the *awakame* (wild tobacco), the two parrots—one large and green, the other small with a red crest—and the yellow-and-black *wainu* bird that lives on the wooded banks of the Lerma.

Maxa Kwaxí left his wife with the gods and returned to the center of the world, to the region of the Great Sea, where Tatei Narema has her home. The goddess gave him the seeds he needed and a cage.

Maxa Kwaxí planted the seeds, caught the parrots, and waited. At that time plants grew very fast, so that the wild tobacco bloomed in three days. But, in that short time, Maxa Kwaxí sinned. This is how it happened.

As he sat waiting, he saw a girl bathing in the river and was moved by her beauty. He forgot his wife and the offerings and ran after her.

When he came back to his plants, Maxa Kwaxí found that the ants had devoured the tobacco, leaving only a few crumbs. He hastened to gather up what remained, put it in his calabash, and started back to the sacred lakes of Tatei Matinieri.

When he reached the fourth altar, the one called Nairaka Niwetari, his wife was there to meet him. "Where have you been all this time?" she asked. "I came looking for you."

Maxa Kwaxí tried to embrace her, but his wife's flesh melted in his arms. Her body collapsed, and she turned into a fly.

Maxa Kwaxí realized that his wife had died. He put down the cage and ran after the fly, heading west.

The fly begged Tatei Narema to protect her, and Maxa Kwaxí was unable to catch her. The goddess would not let him approach. Instead, she cut a section of reed, put the fly inside, and stopped the end with a piece of cotton. She handed it to Maxa Kwaxí. "Take this reed," she said, "and go to Wirikuta. But be more careful."

On the first day he reached the first altar, Xeini Niwetari; on the second he arrived at the second altar, Hutariaka Niwetari; and on the third he came to the third altar, Hairaka Niwetari. He spent the night at each of the three altars, and every morning when he awoke he saw his beautiful wife lying next to him. But he could not touch her; at his slightest movement the woman turned back into a fly and crawled into her reed.

Thus they reached the fourth altar, Nairaka Niwetari, where she had come to meet him earlier. There he was no longer able to control himself and threw himself upon her. This time the fly did not crawl into her reed, but flew away into the air. Maxa Kwaxí resumed his journey with sadness in his heart.

Soon he came to the spot where he had left the cage. It was empty. The birds had escaped, each leaving only a feather. And this is why we Huicholes take only three feathers to Wirikuta: two green ones from parrots and a black-and-yellow one from the *wainu* bird.

At the Hill of the Star the goddess Xurawe Muyaka, who guards the gate, came out to meet him. "Now you must confess all your sins," she told him. "Otherwise you will go mad at the Burned Hill."

Maxa Kwaxí confessed before the goddess and passed through the blue gates of Xirikitá, where the *calihuey* begins. When he came to Haikitenie, the second gate of the *xiriki*, whose name means "gate of the clouds," he carefully cleansed his entire body with a green feather, which he left hanging on the *maturaxno* bush. For that is where that small desert plant first appears.

He went on to the place known today as the Eagle's Throne, where he purified himself with the second green feather; that one, too, he hung on the *maturaxno* bush. From Haikitenie he had been able to see the eagle seated on his throne on a rock; but, when he moved on, that marvelous creature disappeared. The spot will bear that name forever.

The gods were still sitting by the water where Tatei Matinieri dwells, and there Maxa Kwaxí reverently presented his offerings.

"You have grown during your journey," the gods told him. "And you have suffered. From this moment on your name will be Tamats Maxa Kwaxí [He Who Has Brought Everything] and also Tamats Tsaurixikame [He Who at Last Understands]. You are now free to go on to Tatei Tuihapa."

At Wakurikitenie, the third gate, he asked Tatei Tuihapa for permission to enter. The goddess said as she opened the gate: "You may enter Wirikuta and climb to the Burned Hill. I know who you are. The gods have named you Tamats Maxa Kwaxí and Tamats Tsaurixikame."

As he entered Wirikuta he cleansed himself with the last feather, the black-and-yellow one, and offered to the gods his arrows and gourd bowls richly adorned with beads.

"You have obeyed, and we are content," they said. "Those who come after you will walk in your footsteps and do as you have done."

Maxa Kwaxí rested at Warley and then began the ascent of Umumui, the divine stairway. It has five steps. The first is Xeiwitari, at the foot of the hill; the second is Hutariaka Niwetari, on the slope; the third is Hairaka Niwetari, halfway up the hillside; the fourth is Nairaka Niwetari, between the midpoint and the summit; and the fifth is Auxuwirieka, at the very top. From there you can see almost all of Xirikitá.

The gods were waiting for him, sitting around the hole made when the new-born sun shot up and burned the surrounding trees to ashes. Said Maxa Kwaxí, "My fathers, I have come a long way to bring your offerings. Here they are. I give them with all my heart."

"That is as we wished," they replied. "Make your offerings of arrows, bowls, *tesgüino*, crackers, and chocolate. Then return to the west, where your mother Yurimáwika and your father Yukáwima are waiting for you."

Accompanied by the gods, Tamats rushed down the side of the

Burned Hill in the form of a wind, flattening the grass and snapping the branches of the trees. That is why there are whirlwinds on Reunar today.

Yurimáwika had set out two lighted candles on the sierra: one to welcome her son Tamats and the other for her two daughters, who were also coming from afar. The elder daughter was named Hacaibi, and the younger was Hamaibi.

After that Tamats lived with his mother in Turánita, a place hidden in high grass. Every day he stood on a mesa called Xautarietakúa and spied on his sisters as they grazed in the valley below. Sometimes they took the shape of women, sometimes that of does. Tamats watched them, filled with desire to make love to them and to hunt them.

It was then that Yurimáwika made Tamats his bow and arrows. Thus armed, he went out the next day toward the south and killed Xaurikue, the black eagle with white tail feathers. He took the trophy home to his mother.

"You are a great hunter, and I am proud of you," she told him.

The second day he went north and shot the eagle Piwame, small and gray with black stripes on his tail. The third day he hunted in the west and brought down the gray eagle Hapuri, who has red markings on his neck. The fourth day he went to the east and shot Kwixutaxa, the eagle with a white breast, black wings, and a yellow tail. While hunting on the mountain the fifth day he spied Werika, the great eagle, the fiercest of all, who can kill men and deer.

"Come down," Tamats called to him. "I want to talk to you." But Werika was afraid, and refused.

Then Maxa Kwaxí was angry. He cut an armful of straw—the grass we Huicholes call *kimai*—and set fire to it, making a great cloud of smoke. Out of the smoke flew Tuxa, the white eagle with black wing tips, and Maxa Kwaxí shot him in flight. This is why eagles take fright and fly about in confusion through the smoke when we burn brush today.

On the sixth day Maxa Kwaxí saw two eagles perched in a tree. One was Werika himself, and the other was Xarú, the great black one with gray feathers and white stripes on his tail. Xarú took flight and Maxa Kwaxí's well-aimed arrow caught him on the wing. Then Werika flew up, and a second arrow plunged into his heart.

On the seventh day Maxa Kwaxí, being thirsty, went to his spring. This was a secret spring, where no one else but he could drink. When he arrived he found a handful of freshly picked flowers—the white ones called *tseuye*—floating on the water; and there were footprints on the bank.

"Who has been drinking my water?" he asked. "Who has dared to muddy my spring?" His eyes flashed with fury, and he bellowed, "*Reu, reu, reu!*" as deer in the woods do when they are angry.

He followed the footprints. All at once Hacaibi and her younger sister Hamaibi sprang out of the brush; and, although they vanished among the trees with the speed of lightning, he had time to fire an arrow at Hacaibi, striking her under the foreleg. Maxa Kwaxí tried to head them off, but in vain.

"Where could they have gone? Where are they hiding?" he was asking himself, when two girls came walking by. "Excuse me," he said. "Have you seen a pair of does? One of them has my arrow in her."

"No, we haven't," they replied, and walked on.

When they had gone a little way Maxa Kwaxí saw that Hacaibi was carrying his arrow under her arm. He ran to catch up with them. "That's my arrow. Where did you find it?"

"It's our arrow," they answered. "It was a gift from our mother Yurimáwika."

Before Maxa Kwaxí knew what was happening Hacaibi had seized his right hand and Hamaibi his left, and they had begun pulling him about. He pulled back, and the sisters pulled him forward; he lurched forward, and they jerked him backward.

"Let me go," said Tamats. "I don't like people putting their hands on me."

But they dragged him to Xautarietakúa—also known as Reuta-teakú—the mesa where he had stood to spy on them. "Why did you call out to us from the mesa?" they demanded. "Why do you bother us? If you don't like people putting their hands on you, then why are you always following us around?"

"The gods gave me this arrow and this *nierika*," he said. "They also named me Tamats Maxa Kwaxí and Tamats Tsaurixikame. That's why no one must touch me."

When the girls heard this, they relaxed their hold. Maxa Kwaxí plunged his arrow into the ground and left his *nierika* in a bowl as an offering to the gods.

They took five steps forward, which in that time meant five days. At the first step they came to a place where the *amole* grows.

"You must be hungry," the girls said. "Have some of this."

All three ate a little, but the *amole*, which we call *kariuki*, was too bitter for Parítsika.[1]

At the second step they found the grass known as *haukuxa*. At the third they came to the *otuxa* tree that grows at the bottom of ravines. Maxa Kwaxí had to eat some of it because he was so hungry; but he was very unhappy.

At the fourth step they found the *pochota* tree, whose leaves were so bitter that Maxa Kwaxí could hardly eat them. He grew even more depressed. At the fifth step they entered the dense forest and came upon the *utsí* (pitch pine), the tree whose great branches deer love to eat.

"I have offered my arrow, my bowl, and my *nierika*," Maxa Kwaxí said to himself. "These little does drag me from one place to another and give me no peace. They are both beautiful, they both love me, and I am beginning to love them. I'd better take up with them."

That night Parítsika slept with the does. The next morning the sisters said, "We must talk to our mother Yurimáwika and see if she will let you come to live with us."

When her daughters approached, Yurimáwika was lying down. She got to her feet. "What has happened to you?" she asked. "You look different. Where is the one who slept with you? Where did you leave him?"

"He's not far away. We've come to ask you to accept him as one of our family."

"Go get him," Yurimáwika said. "If he's a hard worker he can stay with us."

Parítsika had gone back into the woods and was eating *utsí* branches. "Come with us," the does said. "Our mother Yurimáwika is expecting you."

They set out, with Hacaibi leading the way, Parítsika in the middle, and Hamaibi bringing up the rear. When the mother saw him, she merely said, "So here you are."

"Here I am," answered Parítsika.

Yurimáwika made him sit down in an *equipal*. She spread an *itari* before him and laid out the kind of food deer like, which is called *hatumare*. There were five thick corn tortillas and two little cups of *atole* and chocolate.

"I know the right food for you," she said. "I know what you like."

"Yes," Parítsika replied, "this is the food I like. This is what my mother used to give me in the woods."

"Eat, then, my son, and rest. This is your home. You are now a *cantador*. You have brought the feathers from the eagles you shot in the five cardinal directions, and you will make your *muwieris* with them. The *muwieris* will give you great powers. But you must be careful. Not far from here is Tukipa, the *calihuey* of the wild animals of the night. It is the home of the vulture, the owls, the rattlesnake and other venomous serpents, the ocelot, the mountain lion, the opossum, and the beasts of the caves. They will all come with their *cantador*, the snake Tekarau, and his assistant the evil serpent Teiwari Yakuana. They will invite you to Tukipa. The *cantador* will offer you his *muwieris* made of owl and vulture feathers. But his *muwieris* are bewitched, and, if you accept them and agree to return to Tukipa with him, you will be lost and all of us will be in serious trouble."

"Don't worry, mother," Parítsika said. "I have my *muwieris* made of eagle feathers. I can defend myself."

As Yurimáwika had foretold, the *cantador* and his assistant soon arrived, followed by the animals from Tukipa. They danced as they came, making a terrible racket. Tekarau was a great wizard. He knew the secrets of witchcraft, could explain mysteries, and was very eloquent. He begged Parítsika to go back to Tukipa with him, promising to make him its *cantador*. With sweet words he offered him his bewitched *muwieris* and Parítsika, seduced, accepted them.

At once the animals surrounded him and took him prisoner. Yurimáwika wept and cried out: "I told you not to take Tekarau's *muwieris*. Now they will carry you off to Tukipa and kill you."

Before they took him away, Parítsika was able to whisper to Yurimáwika: "Don't lose heart. All three of you go to the spring, and as soon as I can escape from Tukipa I'll join you there."

The animals led him to the *calihuey* and tied him to an *equipal*. It was very dark in Tukipa. A glowing coal hung from the ceiling on a string; this coal, which was called *tu'mari*, gave off only a very dim light. Parítsika called Naika the rat—who was also known as Tuamurats—and said: "Naika, my friend, climb up to the ceiling and gnaw the string with your teeth. When the coal falls to the ground and goes out, come and untie me."

When Naika had set about his task, Parítsika prayed to the gods for help. "O Nariwame, O Xapawiyeme, O Kutsaraupa, O Tatei Matinieri, let loose the wind, let loose the rain, so that Naika can cut the string without anyone noticing and set me free."

There was lightning and thunder, clouds gathered from the south, the north, the east, and the west, and a great tornado came down from the sky. The rain poured in, and the wind shook the walls and pillars of the *calihuey* until they groaned.

"Oh, oh!" the terrified animals cried. "The water is washing us away! Oh, oh! We'll all be drowned!"

In the confusion Naika was able to gnaw the string until it parted, and the coal fell to the ground and went out.

"Our light is gone," the animals moaned. "We're blind!"

Then came the voice of Tekarau: "Kill Parítsika! This is his doing. If he leaves Tukipa alive, we're done for!"

In the darkness the animals threw themselves upon each other, striking out with tooth and claw. The serpents stabbed with their venomous fangs, and the nocturnal birds slashed with their sharp beaks. It was a confused medley of howls, croaks, and snarls.

"I've got him!" the rattlesnake screamed. "He can't get away now!"

"Let me go!" roared the mountain lion. "This is me, Maye the lion!"

"Over here!" called the bear. "I've got Parítsika by the tail!"

"That's *my* tail!" the opossum cried. "Ouch! You're biting me!"

The animals fought in the dark for a long time before they realized what had happened. At last they understood that Parítsika had got away. Cut, bruised, mangled, blinded, crippled, they gathered around the *cantador* and said, "Tekarau must use his magic to tell us where to find Parítsika."

Tekarau seized his bewitched *muwieris* and announced: "He is not far from Tukipa. I can see him. He is at Yanukuáripa with his two wives and his mother-in-law, Yukáwima, Mother of the Does. If we work out a plan of attack and surround them, we can soon finish him off. Who will station himself in the east?"

"I'll take the east," said the vulture Komatemai.

"All right. Who will stand guard in the south?"

"I'll take the south," said Maye.

"And the north?"

"I'll keep watch in the north," said Maxaka Tewiyare, the snake who eats chickens.

"And who will guard the west?"

"We will," answered the yellow-and-black wasps; the scorpions; the serpents Xainiu Tewiyare, Raye Tewiyare, and Mare Tewiyare; and all the nocturnal animals from the caves, known as the Kakau-yaris Neniakate Yuwikate.

Off they flew, hopped, and slithered to hunt down Parítsika. It was Maxaka Tewiyare who saw him first. "There he is! There he is!" he hissed.

"Do you have to hiss so loud?" the other animals said, annoyed. "Don't you realize he can hear you? Just stay at your post and be quiet."

"I said 'There he is!' because there he is: lying there with Hamaibi and Hacaibi," Maxaka Tewiyare retorted.

When they heard Maxaka hissing, the elder sister Hacaibi, who was lying at Parítsika's right, leaped up and ran; she was followed by her younger sister, who had been lying at his left. The animals from Tukipa shot at them but missed. Then the rattlesnake let fly an arrow and hit Parítsika in the side.

"I've wounded him," Raye Tewiyare called out. "Now all we have to do is finish him off."

All the animals shot their arrows, but not one reached its mark. Even so, after a few steps Parítsika's legs doubled under him; he began to bleed and was about to fall. Then he heard the vulture Komatemai calling to him: "Don't give up. Come over here."

"Do you mean you're not trying to kill me?" asked Parítsika. "You're my enemy, aren't you?"

"No, I've come to save you," Komatemai said. He pulled out one of his own feathers with his beak and used it to stanch Parítsika's wound. When he saw that the deer was recovering his strength, the vulture said: "Look, this is what you must do. Take this arrow of mine, moisten it with your blood, and shoot it as far as you can. The animals of Tukipa will think I have wounded you. Go quickly! I hear them coming."

When the hunters appeared, shouting and leaping about as though they were crazy, Komatemai went to meet them. "Friends, I have good news," he told them. "I, too, have hit Parítsika. Now he has two arrows in him: Maxaka's and mine. He can't get far."

The fly Xaipi, the bloodhound of Tukipa, followed the scent to a clump of tall, thick grass. Xaipi began flying in circles over it.

"There he is! Xaipi has found him!" the animals cried. They sniffed about for a long time; but all they found was Komatemai's arrow, still wet with blood.

"That's my arrow. Look, Parítsika is still bleeding."

"You did well, Komatemai. You're a great hunter," they said. "We still have to find the deer, though. Xaipi, our bloodhound, has lost the scent."

Then the *cantador* Tekarau picked up the arrow and examined it carefully. After a few moments he rose and called out: "Seize Komatemai! The traitor has tricked us. He didn't shoot this arrow. He gave it to Parítsika to make us think he had wounded him."

"Now I'm in a fix," Komatemai said to himself.

"What shall we do with him?" the animals wanted to know.

"There's only one thing to do with a traitor. He must be killed."

So they wrung his neck and pulled out all the feathers from his head and throat. They took his own arrow and ran it through his beak. Thus our friend Komatemai is partly naked today and has two large holes in his bill.

Then Raye Tewiyare threw him over a cliff. The vulture had enough strength to fly to the red rock called Auxurita, where he wrenched the arrow from his beak.

In the meantime Parítsika had gone to join his elder brother Wakuri at Reunar. "I've been wounded," he said. "The animals of Tukipa hunted me down and almost killed me. And Tekarau's bewitched *muwieris* that are fastened to my head are very heavy. See if you can get them off."

Wakuri used his magic to remove the antlers, and Parítsika became the hornless deer.

"Now eat some of your horns," Wakuri told him. "It will make you feel better."

Parítsika did as his brother suggested. When there was only a small piece of horn left, he dropped it on the ground. From it sprang up seven peyote cactuses. The velvet from his antlers, which he had previously set aside, became the outer shell of the peyote.

After a time Wakuri passed his hand over Parítsika's face. From the tip of his left horn sprang the *nierika*, by which we mean Parítsika's mirror and shield; from the right tip came the votive gourd called *xukuri*. The other points of his antlers gave birth to the *cantador's muwieris* and the Great Candle, which lends its name to Hauriyapa, "the place where stood the great candle of Tamats."

In this way we Huicholes were given the peyote, the *cantador's* eagle-feather *muwieris*, the Sacred Candle, and the offerings we take every year to Reunar, the Burned Hill.

(This version is by Bartolo Chibarras, the shaman from Ocota.)

The Blood Sacrifice

I arrived in Las Guayabas with a case of bronchitis; the fantastic
and rather ghostly aspects of what I saw that first night were height-
ened by fever. I laid out my sleeping bag a short distance from the
calihuey and watched the Huicholes going in and out of the temple.
In the flickering firelight that came from behind the screens of oak
branches, the Indians, with their hair cut in the medieval fashion
and their long blouses, were like some strange angels. They hardly
seemed to walk on the ground; they glided soundlessly from place
to place, always busy with some magical task I knew nothing of. In
the distance I could hear the monotonous chanting of the shamans,
seated in their elaborate ceremonial chairs in the midst of relatives
and neighbors. Whenever one of the fires flared up for a moment,
some extremely beautiful face appeared before me and then suddenly
vanished in the shadows. A girl from a neighboring village sat in one
of the shelters facing me. She had finished her laborious duties of
carrying water, making tortillas, and tending to her younger sisters
and brothers. Her face was painted with red and yellow designs, and

on it was an expression of deep and serious concentration. She sat in the same position for two or three hours. One would have thought she was asleep, if the firelight had not glinted in her eyes and she had not scratched her head from time to time.

Occasionally I came out of my doze to hear the soft chanting of the shamans and the high voices of the acolytes as they took up and concluded the recitations. When I looked up from the bottom of our cleft in the mountains, the sky framed by the surrounding cliffs glittered with stars.

The peyote dance began at dawn. The dancers carried gourds filled with holy water, stuffed deer heads and hides, rifles, arrows, ropes, and, of course, the squirrel—which they would bury near the end of the festival. Men, women, and children danced in a ring before the *calihuey*, raising a great cloud of dust. Following the beat of the music, they leaped forward, took one long step, brought their feet together, and stamped on the ground so that the gods in their homes under the earth could hear them.

Their leader was a young man with muscular legs and a thick neck; it was he who kept the beat and directed the dancers' movements. He wore a silk handkerchief over his face to keep out the dust. Although he danced and whirled as furiously as the rest, he gave an impression not of frenzy, but of restraint.

The tempo increased. At a sign from the leader, the dancers wheeled and raced toward the *calihuey*, retreated when they reached the entrance, then rushed toward the bonfires. This maneuver was repeated five or six times.

At 7:25 the glowing crescent of the sun appeared above the San Andrés mesa. This was the supreme moment, the age-old punctual return of Father Sun—which we who live in the smoke and smog of big cities never notice. Here there still existed a living relationship, a sense of joy and gratitude, an awareness that the reawakening of life depends upon this magic event. One had returned to an age when the power of the sun was not merely the result of complex thermonuclear processes, but a holy miracle. It was a gift from the gods, but not a gratuitous one: it called for sacrifice and collaboration on the part of man.

Life was reborn. The sunlight gilded the dry grass, transforming the stubble field, the furrows, the rocks, and the leaves on the trees into virgin matter. It was like a vast vision; it was "what Adam saw in the morning of creation, the miracle of naked existence."

The time had come to sacrifice the bull, who had been tethered near the *calihuey* all night. It was his blood, together with the thick juice of the peyote, that would nourish the sun. The *mara'akames* dipped arrows and tortillas into the bowls of blood and peyote and turned to face the east; like priests performing the Asperges, they sprinkled the sun, the ears of corn from the *calihuey*, the tamales, and the heads and clothing of the crowd. When the offering and the sanctification had been completed, the Indians extinguished the fires with consecrated water and resumed the Dance of the Peyote.

Sanctification of the Earth

The men of Las Guayabas who had made the pilgrimage to Catorce had finished clearing their fields in anticipation of the coming rains; now it was time to sanctify the communal land belonging to the *calihuey*. Here they would grow the corn for *tesgüino*, which would be made from the kernels parched on the griddle at the conclusion of the festival.

At nine in the morning the Indians set out for the cornfield on a hillside half a kilometer away, accompanied by the music of guitars and violins. With them were Hilario and his son Daniel, the new *gobernador*. Daniel carried a shoulder bag filled with large candles and his scepters of authority in their wrappings of cloth and ribbons. One of the party, in a red paper skirt and wearing two bandannas over his long hair, looked like a woman; but he was called "the Cowboy." He was leading the "bull" by a ribbon; this was a twelve-year-old boy who wore the horns of the sacrificed bull strapped to his head and a tail made of small tamales twisted together.

The *calihuey*'s land was a stony hillside with a few spindly trees, partly cleared of brush. There could not have been more than fifty square meters of usable soil, by the most generous estimate; but for the Huicholes, living as they do amid boulders and sterile rubble, it was a real treasure.

As soon as they reached the cornfield the men began felling the remaining trees. Hilario urged them on with cries of enthusiasm, but they really needed no encouragement. They handled their curved machetes with great skill and precision, and the slender, leafless trees were soon lying on the ground. In a clearing nearby the musicians were still playing, and Hilario kept shouting and cracking jokes, making everyone laugh, as usual.

Then they dug a hole at the center of the field. Hilario grasped his *muwieris*, addressed the gods of the four directions, and turned toward the hole. With the water they had brought from Wirikuta they consecrated their offerings—votive bowls, two rifles, deer's ears tied to small pouches, arrows, candles, kernels of corn, paper flowers, deer meat—and dropped them in. As an additional consecration they touched each of the objects with three large peyote buttons. Everything within reach, including their own bodies, had to be sanctified. They covered the offerings with tree trunks and branches and sprinkled them with blood as Hilario intoned: "Mother Earth, Tatei Yurianaka, here are your food, your drink, and our offerings, as the gods have ordered. O our mother, we beg you to continue giving us good crops and rain, so that your children the Huicholes may go on living on the earth. Now that you have eaten and drunk, we shall do the same."

At the conclusion of the ceremony they went back down the hill to Las Guayabas.

Hilario's son José Carrillo summed up the offering in this way: "The earth eats and gives us to eat; she demands nourishment in order to be able to nourish us in turn."

Meanwhile the dancing was still going on. Eusebio and his two assistants were seated on a couple of logs in the center of the courtyard, surrounded by the dancers who turned tirelessly about them. We could hear the chants and the music, but the participants were hidden in the clouds of dust raised by their pounding feet. From time to time some of the dancers would drop out and others would take their places. A few held rifles in their hands, while others wore hides or carried deer heads and horns.

Inside the *calihuey* three girls, arms about each other's waists, were dancing on a hollow tree trunk. The wood resounded like a drum, adding to the din of violins, guitars, and chanting *mara'akames*.

The visitors and their wives sat in the shade of a spacious shelter made of branches and were treated with endless courtesy and attention. At least twice a day their hosts sent delegations with gifts: bowls hung with garlands of flowers and filled with *tesgüino*, loaves of bread, onions, bananas, tamales, and cigarettes. These things were tendered in a way that was half gentle and affectionate, half solemn and courtly. There was an extraordinary incongruity in this exquisite courtesy and their torn and stained attire, in their princely personal beauty and dignity and their miserable, slovenly trappings. Accustomed as they were to the contempt and abuse of their fellow Mexicans, to being regarded as pariahs, this homage moved them deeply. The entire group of visitors, and especially the Man with the Arrows, dissolved in tears several times. They buried their faces in their hands and sobbed, embarrassed by this excess of emotion. When they recovered their composure they all shook hands with the *mara-'akame*, and everybody drank great quantities of *sotol* and *tesgüino*.

By the time a special delegation came with gifts for the Man with the Arrows' wife and children, the great *mara'akame* had succumbed. Overcome by presents and libations, he lay on the ground with his long, black hair covering his face, his hat at his side.

The Return to the World

On Friday night the Indians built a bonfire of reeds—not in the courtyard, which was still filled with dancers, but a little way off. With the usual chanting, music, and ceremonies they burned Eusebio's hat with its ornament of Elder Brother Tamats Kauyumari's tail, the feathers from the other hats, the arrows from Wirikuta, and the *matewames'* wands with their ribbons. This meant that they were now free of the obligations contracted during the peyote pilgrimage. The fire had consumed the symbols of their sanctification, and now they could safely take up their worldly existence again. The flames that had purified them had stripped them of their sacred investiture. The peyote symbols were wiped from their faces, and their hats re-covered their everyday appearance.

The transition from the sacred to the profane was marked and facilitated by a period of debauchery, making the return to normal existence less traumatic. After two days of dissipation the men were weeping, falling into each other's arms, fighting, and eating and drinking like madmen. The *calihuey* echoed with the frenzied drumming of dancing feet on the hollow log. The dances grew faster. The musicians did their best to keep a reasonable tempo, but in the mounting tide of excitement their feeble sounds were all but inaudible. Even Tekuamana himself, the old man who had taken charge of the pilgrims' wives during their absence and kept count of the days, was drunk now, dancing with all the abandon of a youngster. Another ancient, who was recovering from a scorpion sting suffered the night before, came up to me with glittering eyes and revealed the *mara'akames'* secrets: "When the chant is good, good clouds come. When *cantadores* do not chant right, no rain falls on cornfields. That is true."

Another old man, who was 107 and had been in two fights that day, put his toothless mouth to my ear and confided in halting Spanish: "Mestizo does not live like us. He says Paternoster, Ave María, prayers for dead, and amen. That's all. Huichol religion is *hard work.*"

The expert on comparative religion was caught up in the whirlwind of dancers and disappeared in the crowd.

Eusebio's frenzy was just the opposite of the religious asceticism he had demonstrated so fully during the trip to Wirikuta. When the feathers on his hat were consumed in the fire, it was as though he had torn off a mask, revealing his true personality. His long, tangled hair, littered with bits of trash, framed a ferocious face in which his good eye, in contrast to the dead white sphere of the other, gleamed diabolically. He emerged from the dust like a ghost and threw himself into the dance with leaps and howls. Whenever he stopped to rest he consumed prodigious quantities of *tesgüino* and *sotol* and occasionally tried to pick a fight. But the Huicholes are extremely patient and kind with drunks. They can listen to them for hours with no sign of fatigue, and they have an emergency police organization whose job it is to pick them up when they fall and drag them out of harm's way. Eusebio never fell, however. Alcohol and lack of sleep seemed only to multiply his strength while others were dropping, exhausted. Even more incredible was the fact that he showed no loss of coherence. When a ceremony demanded his presence, he performed his duties impeccably.

The Monster We Have Awakened

Saturday, the penultimate day of the festival, was devoted to preparing additional gifts for the visitors and presenting them with great ceremony. A small tree had been erected before the Man with the Arrows, who still sat in his chair, surrounded by his assistants. Each new present provoked an emotional crisis, during which he was racked with sobs. His agitation infected the other members of his party and even the local ambassadors; they regarded each other in an embarrassed way through their tears, at a loss to know how to conclude a diplomatic ceremony that invariably resulted in such a violent explosion of sentimentality.

At noon the guests from Santa Bárbara responded by entertaining their hosts with a piece of slapstick comedy. The actors presented a scene in which a woman fought and vanquished several men; even though her opponents were all quite drunk, it was still an astonishing display of strength. She seized the men by the hair or clothing and after a brief struggle threw them to the ground. With each victory her energy increased, until in the heat of battle she seemed to be avenging her entire sex rather than taking part in a farce. After disposing of the rest of the contestants, she turned to face the Man with the Arrows. Before this giant she was like a David who in some ridiculous way had turned into a woman. She was no mean adversary. Her breasts jutted out under her short Huichol blouse, and her muscular legs showed in outline through her full yellow skirt; her resolute posture was that of the fighting princesses seen in the codices. In the face of such fury, the *mara'akame* pretended to be drunker than he was; with every blow he whirled like a top without quite losing his balance. At last he came down with a crash—much as Goliath must have done—and allowed himself to be dragged along the ground for some distance. Suddenly he gathered his strength, sprang to his feet, and escaped, leaving his trousers in the hands of his triumphant foe. This unexpected closing scene, in which the half-naked man tried to cover himself as he fled, was greeted with gales of insane laughter, especially from the women.

That afternoon Hilario gave me a large bowl of peyote. Over a period of time, Marino and I each drank half of it. My sleeping bag was still spread out under a shelter of branches not far from the *calihuey*; two hundred meters beyond, the ground fell away in a series of deep ravines. In half an hour I began to be nauseated. The dust, lack of food, and loss of sleep had made my bronchitis worse, and the past three days had been exhausting. Wishing not to make a disagreeable spectacle of myself, I withdrew to the edge of the Las Guayabas mesa, beyond which the mountains rose abruptly like the background in an Italian Renaissance painting. There I found Marino, in a state of indescribable misery. I vomited and went back to my shelter, still not seeing any connection between my illness and the peyote I had drunk.

I was worried about Marino and went to ask José to look after him. Knowing that any specific preoccupation can help to counteract the flood of irrational ideas that make the peyote delirium so dangerous, I was consciously inventing an unnecessary concern for my companion.

Suddenly THE THING was there: the fearful and mysterious force I had deliberately invoked. "I have summoned the monster," I told myself. He was crouching somewhere out there in the ravine, and I had no idea of what he was going to demand of me.

The conviction that one is in the presence of an invisible and all-powerful force is terrifying. This is the fear Michaux felt, and one the Huicholes know. It is the fear of going mad—or, rather, the fear of the fear of going mad. The brain defends itself from violation by secreting horror. One does not realize, of course, that this instinctive reaction is an attempt to defend the ego; he is aware only that there is a terrible thing somewhere. It is either a great god or a formidable and evil power; we know nothing of its nature. It sees and knows everything. It is everywhere. Between it and ourselves there exists some mysterious relationship. We have no idea why it is judging us, threatening us. If only we were not so terrified, we might be able to comprehend this revelation and learn the mystery of life.

My "I" spread out over the trees, the boulders, the canyons, the men, the blue deer, the eagles, the nocturnal birds, and the temples of the wizards with their enchanted *muwieris*. It had been given oneness. An immense ear listened to the rustle of the wind in the new green leaves on the oak trees, the rhythmic steps of the dancers pounding the earth so that the gods in their subterranean dwellings might hear them, the children coughing, Hilario's stories, the gentle wailing of the violins, and the sounds of the mountain. The sensation of being part of a great whole, of melting and diffusing into this fragment of existence and embracing it totally, brought with it a tremendous sense of relief. The terror had gone.

Green sparks. As I regarded the pole supporting the branches of the roof, green sparks danced about it. They ran along the pole and vanished in the air. A small marvel, bringing the terror again.

Green and red sparks. Blinking on and off. A chain of green triangles, red ones, transparent ones. Someone must be moving them. No. It was I who created them and controlled them. It had taken me some time to realize it, but now I saw that I had this unheard-of talent. I was made of radiant matter. I radiated spheres, triangles, rhombuses. They issued from some part of my body—or perhaps from my entire body—and lined up in rows, ran about, disappeared. I had not known that I was a radiant being; the discovery was part of my sanctification. The Luminous and Divine had made *me* divine. I was a god . . .

A god who could not keep from retching. I realized that my apotheosis was a slow one, for I was writhing and vomiting, trying not to befoul my sleeping bag in the process. The spasms left me sweating and exhausted.

It was revealed to me that I was a disciple of Spinoza. It was about time I admitted it. I had never been anything else, in fact. I myself was the proof of his pantheism. The infinite substance intuited by that "man drunk with God," as Novalis had called him, could be sensed lying at the bottom of the ravine. The Huicholes, too, were drunk with God. Because of that drunkenness, we all participated in His plenitude, His love, His wisdom, His transcendence. He held us all in His lap of flowing, flaming granite.

The teacher José was standing over me, looking worried. "How are you feeling? Better?"

"Yes, José, I'm better. Have you seen Marino? Is someone taking care of him?"

"We're keeping an eye on him. Don't worry."

Spinoza and Marino were the two things I grasped at in my attempt to free myself from the oppressive atmosphere of the Indians and their festival. This dense, strange environment had made a prisoner of me. My legs were in the stocks. I yearned for someone to protect me. What had become of my courage? My pantheism? My sanctification? They were gone, and in their place were loneliness, desolation, and the inevitability of old age. In some stealthy manner this last thought had crept into my mind. How could *I* ever grow old? How could such a horrendous metamorphosis happen to me? Far better to be an insect than an old man. Old age creates monsters. It changes us from men to monsters.

I must have cried out in terror when I opened my eyes and saw the *mara'akame* Eusebio leaning over my sleeping bag. The wild shock of tangled hair, the bulging sightless eye, the contorted features were nearly against my face. It was the demon Tukákame. It was an evil spirit, come for my soul. My scream frightened him off.

Beneath the fear, beneath the metamorphosis, deep down beneath everything, an old idea that until now had seemed to have no very profound meaning was emerging. Sanctity was a *mysterio fascinosum* and a *mysterio tremendum*: the first lesson of the peyote.

Everything was as important as anything else, everything had a meaning, and everything attained a higher nature in the vast primitive oneness, in the Yesterday, the Today, the Tomorrow, the Never. That barking dog had been barking since the beginning of the world and would still be barking at the consummation of the centuries: the second lesson of the peyote.

The world is nothing but one great metamorphosis: the third lesson of the peyote.

Someone had lighted a fire behind one of the partitions of oak branches nearby, transforming the shelter into a golden lantern, a heraldic banner of unimaginable splendor. Every wizened leaf, with its faded colors and varied texture, was like something from another world; together they made up a whole where nothing was too much or too little. I discovered the hidden marvels of organic matter. That bower held the beauty of the world. It was not a static beauty, but a vibrant and fluid one, partaking of the spirit and movement of the fire; and yet it was somehow fixed and complete, totally achieved. A shelter of boughs could easily become a god. I was face to face with the beauty of the world and was powerless to describe it. I wrote laboriously in my notebook "the burning bush"; but the next day the words meant nothing to me. They were empty, totally stupid. I must have stood by the shelter for two or three hours, lost in contemplation. As the fire burned down, the structure became a monster made of mother-of-pearl. Each leaf was a cold, opalescent scale, holding some undecipherable secret. That had been our history: we were forever on the point of learning the secret of the world, and it always escaped us. The lantern, the banner, the baroque branch, the magic forest—it was all a sphinx in the night. I slowly repeated my incantation: *Mysterio fascinosum, mysterio tremendum.*

Thanks to his abundant vitality, Marino had recovered from the effects of the peyote. He had spent most of his long and arduous "trip" in the *calihuey*, near Grandfather Fire, as both participant and spectator in the collective diabolical frenzy. I, on the other hand, had been left to my own devices, ignorant of those techniques of ecstasy taught by María Sabina, the great female shaman of the Mazateca range. I wanted desperately to come back to earth and could think of no better way than asking Marino to recite something from the *Divine Comedy*. With his recent delirium in mind, he chose this passage from the "Inferno":

> *La bocca sollevò dal fiero pasto*
> *quel peccator, forbendola a'capelli*
> *del capo ch'elli avea di retro guasto.*
> *Poi cominciò: "Tu vuo'ch'io rinovelli*
> *disperato dolor che 'l cor mi preme*
> *già pur pensando, pria ch'io ne favelli.*
> *Ma se le mie parole esser dien seme*
> *che frutti infamia al traditor ch'i' rodo,*
> *parlare e lagrimar vedrai inseme."*[1]

No. I really couldn't bear it. That head feeding on another head, that picture of hellish cannibalism, seemed grotesque and laughable. It offered me no way out—only a too concrete image of a hatred I could not share. "That's enough, Marino! Enough!" I cried. "Give me something cheerful. The *canzone* of Lorenzo the Magnificent, for example."

Marino had studied in the seminary and knew classical Italian literature thoroughly. He began obediently:

> *Quant'è bella giovinezza,*
> *che si fugge tuttavia!*
> *Chi vuol esser lieto, sia:*
> *di doman non c'è certezza.*
>
> . . . .
> *Questi lieti satiretti,*
> *delle ninfe innamorate,*
> *per caverne e per boschetti*
> *han lor posto cento agguati:*
> *or da Bacco riscaldati,*
> *ballon, salton tuttavia.*
> *Chi vuol esser lieto, sia:*
> *di doman non c'è certezza.*[2]

Again I had to beg him to stop. I was in torment. I wanted to free myself from these Indian phantoms, but Lorenzo's *canzone*, worked as exquisitely as a Renaissance cameo, had made me even more miserable than had Dante's poetry. In my present state, where a dead oak leaf offered in itself all the glory of paradise, becoming an astonishing visual delight, the Italian language seemed unbearably comic. It was all a ridiculous imposture. Calling satyrs *satiretti*, lovers *innamorate*, and little groves of trees *boschetti* was more than I could stand. It was like hearing an operetta, or some maudlin Neapolitan song accompanied by mandolins. The poetry had profaned the majesty and religious mystery of my experience in some way, scattering the embers, the dead ashes that had given birth to my mother-of-pearl monster and its fascinating enigma. The comic opera had drowned out the music, had demolished the unity of the world. Lorenzo the Magnificent had wrenched me from the beginning of time and hurled me back into this night in Las Guayabas. I had come down to earth, there in my sleeping bag, and I was disconcerted and furious.

Primitive Man and Civilization

My first concern Sunday morning was to examine the screen of oak branches that had filled me with such ecstasy the night before. It was no more than a meter from my sleeping bag. I could see nothing remarkable about the leaves, which were withered and partly eaten away by insects. That pile of trash had been desanctified; the spirits of the previous night had abandoned it, and it had lost its magic. The festival, too, had lost its magic. All of us looked indescribably dirty and forlorn. The feathers, the flags, the gourd bowls, and the clothing were all damaged and stained. The sacred paraphernalia were spotted with dried blood, and the *calihuey* and its courtyard were carpeted with rubbish. It looked like a battleground. Indians were lying about everywhere; they had simply toppled over and remained where they fell until the *topiles* had dragged them into the shade of the trees.

The parched-corn ceremony began at one in the afternoon. Eusebio's wife, who held an important position in the community because of her husband's rank, was in charge of the operation. She wore a *muwieri* tied to her head and held a whisk made of straw. First the kernels were stripped from some ears of corn of various colors that had been tied in a bundle with a deer's tail; the kernels were then toasted on an earthenware griddle over the fire. Eusebio consecrated the corn by sprinkling it with a few drops of the water brought from Wirikuta, and his wife stirred it with her whisk. Once again we witnessed the metamorphosis that with repetition had become such a familiar sight. This woman's dignified bearing, her devoted concentration, the importance she took on because of her task—all served to remind us that she was now engaged in a sacred ritual and had assumed sanctity herself. The kernels flew about on the griddle like the dancers who had acted out the magic hunting of the Deer-Peyote; thus was completed the eternal trinity that governs the lives of the Huicholes.

As far as I was concerned, the Festival of the Parched Corn was over. Accompanied by one of the villagers, I took the path leading to the San Andrés mesa, that miniature sun that had fallen among the barrancas. The landscape of the sierra unfolded slowly and majestically before us: the banana trees on the banks of the stream, the little patches of sugar cane and guava groves, the forests of oak and pine. Far above us hung a fantastic city of crags, pinnacles, and stone cliffs. These were the heights where "the air is still, arrayed in rare beauty and light." In the distance a veil of mist was falling, and a symphony of golds, blues, and pinks was beginning to play about us.

I reined my mule at a turn in the path and looked back up the mountain. I could barely make out the clearing with its cleft, and the tiny *calihuey*. The Festival of the Parched Corn and its celebrants were no longer distinguishable. Almost at the very edge of the mesa stood the ruined hut where the Huicholes leave food and drink for the dead, so that they will not come to claim their share of the banquet and disrupt the ceremonies. The pleading and menacing voices of supernatural beings rose from the *kieri* plants, demanding their offerings. The spirits were laying their traps.

The time of magic transfigurations was over. Soon the Indians would wait for the clouds attracted by the smoke from their burning cornfields and by the *mara'akames'* mirrors. Once again they would be obliged to seek the approval of the gods and to begin their long pilgrimages. To dream again, to play at creation again. The magic, the dream, the return to the beginning of time, the ritual of the blood sacrifice, the myths recited by the shamans—all served to strengthen the profound relationship between "the invisible universe and the visible one," between the past, the present, and the future, between the word and its primeval symbol.

I thought of one of Johann Paul's characters and the dream he recounted:

Like the Chaos, the invisible world was trying to give birth to all things at once; shapes were appearing incessantly; flowers were changing into trees and then into pillars of clouds, from which emerged flowers and faces. I saw a vast, desolate sea, with the world floating on it: a tiny, gray, mottled egg tossed this way and that by the waves. In my dream I was told the name of all things, but I could not understand what it was. Then a river crossed the sea, bearing the corpse of Venus. It snowed luminous stars, and the sky emptied; but in the place where the sun stands at noon the flush of dawn appeared. Directly beneath that spot the sea sank, and the horizon heaped up upon itself to form enormous spirals of lead-colored serpents that blotted out the vault of the heavens. From the depths of the sea sorrowing men floated up like cadavers to be born . . .[3]

Why should we now evoke the spirit of German romanticism? Why reject the interpretations of the ethnologists? Because in the world of the Huicholes and in that of German romanticism—and of every romanticism—there is a way of looking at things and a life style that are intimately related.

"The world must be romanticized," Novalis argued. "Whenever we attach some higher meaning to the commonplace, lend an air of mystery to the banal, concede the dignity of the unknown to what is known, or surround the finite with the halo of the infinite, we are romanticizing . . ." All our troubles, he showed, are the result of conscious thought, too sure of its own power; it denies us access to all those untapped forces that are revealed to us only in dreams.

It may be that our recourse to hallucinogenic drugs, the rebellion of millions of young people, and the creation of a new mythos are all doomed to failure; for we have forgotten how to use the hidden powers of the mind to sweep aside the barriers between the conscious and the subconscious, between the visible and the invisible. Today, when man lives under the constant threat of violent death, devoting his ingenuity both to inventing ways of destroying himself and to learning how to defend himself against his own devices, the time of the Word has come. It is time for the exorcism by poetry, heralding not so much the arrival of tomorrow as the eternal return of tomorrow, the return to that age of creation in which sacrifice—the blood of the innocent spilled by his own hand, rather than by paid assassins and world police forces—once created a brotherhood of man and a magic world that made the misery of the real world bearable. That sacrifice meant the renewal of life, the renewal of the poetry of existence, as well as man's reconciliation with himself, with his universe, and with the war of time.

We must romanticize the world. Perhaps we might even say that we must return to the savage state, to the primitive condition.

GLOSSARY

aguamiel: a liquid extracted from the heart of the maguey plant; fermented, it becomes pulque.

amole: any one of several plants yielding a soaplike substance (from the Aztec *amulli*, soap).

atole: a drink made of ground corn.

biznaga: a spiny, barrel-shaped cactus.

calihuey: in Huichol communities, a rude structure used as a temple and ceremonial center. The term derives from the Aztec *huey calli*, big house; in Huichol, the native temple is called *tuki* or *tukipa* (q.v.).

cantador: a "chanter"; a Huichol shaman.

castillo: a towerlike framework of bamboo, on which an elaborate fireworks display is mounted.

clavellina: a cactus (*Opuntia tunicata*).

coamil: a plot of ground cleared for planting.

comisario: a peace officer, chief of police.

cordón de San Francisco: a strip of flannel worn around the neck to ward off respiratory diseases.

corrido: a traditional type of Mexican narrative song.

ejido: land held in common by an *ejido* community, whose members have the right to use it but not to sell it. These communities were set up at the time of the Agrarian Reform.

encomendero: a holder of an *encomienda*, a tract of land that, with the Indians living on it, was granted by the Spanish crown to favored individuals.

equipal: a chair with seat and back made of woven palm, used by shamans and in miniature by the gods. The Huichol term is *uweni*.

gobernador: the headman of a Huichol community; in Huichol *tatuan*.

gobernadora: the creosote bush (*Laurea mexicana*).

guapilla: a maguey (*Agave falcata*).

Hewi: a mythical pre-Huichol people who perished in the universal flood and now appear as stones.

hojasé: a desert shrub.

iki: in Huichol, a cylindrical granary.

itari: in Huichol, a straw mat.

ixtle: a fiber made from the agave; also known as Tampico fiber.

kakauyari: a supernatural being who, according to the Huicholes, was changed into a stone or plant at the time of the creation of the world. The plural, *kakauyaris*, is also used for the divine ancestors who dwell in Wirikuta.

kaxaton: in Huichol, a granary elevated on posts.

kieri: a plant inhabited by a *kakauyari* (q.v.); may be either a species of *Datura* or, according to recent information from Timothy Knab, of *Solanum*.

lechuguilla: a variety of maguey.

macuche: the potent Indian tobacco (*Nicotiana rustica*) the Huicholes call *yé*; the distinctive tobacco gourd, *yé'kwé*, is the mark of the peyote pilgrim, as it was once that of the Aztec priest.

mara'akame: in Huichol, a shaman.

matewame: in Huichol, one who is making the peyote pilgrimage for the first time.

metate: a rectangular stone mortar for grinding corn.

milpa: a cornfield.

molcajete: a small, round stone or pottery mortar for grinding chili, spices, and the like.

muwieri: in Huichol, a shaman's scepter, made of arrows with eagle, hawk, turkey, and other feathers.

nierika: in Huichol, divine face, image; also a large peyote with three smaller ones growing on top. It is known as "the face of god," and "the emblem of Parítsika."

nixtamal: the Aztec word, used everywhere in Mexico today, for corn processed for making tortillas.

palma: one of the many varieties of maguey.

peyotero: a peyote pilgrim. In Huichol, peyote is called *hikuri*, a peyote pilgrim *hikuritame*.

pinole: a drink made with ground parched corn and water.

pochota: a Bombay tree.

quiote: the tall, flowering central stalk of the maguey; it is eaten boiled or roasted.

rebozo: a long narrow stole.

Reunar: in Huichol, also called *'unaxu*, Burned Hill (Sp. Cerro quemado);

dominant peak of the Wirikuta, or Real de Catorce, mountain range and birthplace of the Sun Father in Huichol mythology.

sotol: an intoxicating drink made from the desert plant of the same name.

tepu: a three-legged upright Huichol drum made from a hollowed-out log with a deerskin head. Curiously, the word is closely related to the Aztec *teponaztli*, which, however, is a hollowed-out log perforated by slits in the shape of an ʾH, played horizontally with rubber-tipped drumsticks. The upright Aztec equivalent to the Huichol drum was called *huehuetl*.

tesgüino: an intoxicating drink made from toasted corn, sugar, and water. It produces a cardiac acceleration (from the Aztec *tecuini*, to have palpitations of the heart). The native Huichol word for the drink is *nawá*.

topil: a constable.

tostada: a toasted tortilla.

tsikuaki: a Huichol festival clown.

tsompantli: among the ancient Aztecs, the rack where skulls of sacrificial victims were displayed on wooden stakes.

tuki or *tukipa*: a large circular Huichol community temple with a hearth representing Grandfather Fire and an emergence hole of the gods.

urukame: from *uru*, arrow; Huichol name applied to souls of deceased shamans, which, in the form of rock crystals, are attached to arrows and are regarded as personal guardians of Huichol farmsteads.

uxa: a yellow face paint made from a plant growing in the desert.

wainu: in Huichol, a black-and-yellow bird, probably of the American oriole family.

wave: in Huichol, amaranth or *chia*.

xiriki: in Huichol, a shrine, domestic temple hut.

xuturi: a flower, especially a paper flower.

zalate: a large tree of the genus *Ficus*.

zempoalxochitl: a marigold; yellow flower of Day of the Dead ceremonies throughout Mexico; also used for other ceremonial occasions.

NOTES

Prologue

1. Robert Mowry Zingg, *The Huicholes: Primitive Artists* (New York, 1938).
2. I made the mistake of taking Mr. Marino Benzi to the mountains with me as photographer, and of allowing him to make use of my notes for a book of photographs he told me he was preparing on the Indians of Mexico. Not long afterward, Mr. Benzi published several shamanic chants and a fragment of the myth of the Birth of Fire in two Mexican literary magazines. Naturally, it was not his publishing these that annoyed me; it was the fact that he claimed to have gathered and translated the material himself. The truth is that the translations had been made by the Indian teachers at the National Indian Institute (Benzi does not know Huichol, and neither do I), and that the information had been provided by shamans whose services I contracted and paid for in the course of two expeditions.

The Huicholes are in fashion today—yesterday it was the Mazatecas—and this extremely rich ethnographic vein is presently being worked by North American and European specialists. Thus it would not be surprising if they were to complete the research that was begun more than sixty years ago by a Norwegian (Lumholtz), a German (Preuss), an American (Zingg), and a Frenchman (Rouhier).

3. Jean Cazeneuve, *L'etnologie* (Paris: Ed. Larousse, 1967).

Why Do We Study Indians?

1. Alexander Humboldt, *Ansichten der Natur* (Stuttgart and Tübingen, 1808).
2. Claude Lévi-Strauss, *Tristes tropiques* (Paris: Union Générale d'Editions Col. 10/18, 1962).
3. Title given to shamans in the Huichol mountains.
4. *Tratado de las supersticiones y costumbres gentilicias que hoy viven entre los indios naturales desta Nueva España, escrito en México por el Br. Bernardo Ruiz de Alarcón* (Mexico City: Ediciones Fuente Cultural, 1953).

5. The fact that sections of automobile tire are now used for the soles of huaraches, thus modifying the ancient characteristics of the sandals, has been taken into account. If when a Huichol dies his family is too poor to replace his sandals with leather ones, he is buried without them. They believe that the rubber will grow heavy and round "like the wheels of a truck," so that he will be unable to walk in the underworld.

6. This is not as meaningless as it seems. Two years earlier a venturesome Huichol had gone to Cuba; the fact that one of their people had been able to visit an island in the boiling waters of the Fifth Sea so astounded them that they incorporated it into the ritual. This shows not only what lively imaginations they have, but also the way in which their myths and ceremonies undergo modification.

7. Carl Lumholtz, *Unknown Mexico* (New York: Charles Scribner's Sons, 1904).

Scenes of the Desert

1. The essential data upon which this chapter is based are taken from Dr. Helia Bravo H.'s invaluable study *Las cactáceas de México* (Mexico City: Universidad Nacional de México, 1937), as well as from conversations with its author.

2. Elio Baldacci, *Vida privada de las plantas* (Buenos Aires: Ed. Sud-americana, 1943).

3. Alexander Humboldt, *Essai politique sur le royaume de la Nouvelle Espagne* (Paris, 1811).

4. Baldacci, *Vida privada.*

5. Oscar Lewis, *Los hijos de Sánchez* (Mexico City: Fondo de Cultura Económica, 1964).

Other Religions, Other Inquisitions

1. Substances with the same chemical composition but different molecular structures.

2. Sidney Cohen, *The Beyond Within* (New York: Atheneum, 1964).

3. Ibid.

4. Dr. Cohen is director of a Los Angeles neuropsychiatric hospital.

5. Jean Cau, "A Visit to Hell," *Crapouillot* (Paris), no. 71.

The Pilgrims

1. Shamanic chants by Antonio Bautista Carrillo, of Las Guayabas.

In the Beginning Was the Deer

1. Ad. E. Jensen, *Mito y culto en los pueblos primitivos* (Mexico City: Fondo de Cultura Económica, 1966).

2. The fact that the various Huichol communities have different names for the deer adds to the confusion.

3. Jensen, *Mito y culto.*

4. Ibid.

5. Agua Linda means "Beautiful Water," while Agua Hedionda means "Stinking Water." This is an example of the ritual reversal of meanings that is an integral part of the peyote pilgrimage.—P. F.

6. Robert Mowry Zingg, *The Huicholes.* Zingg adds that "there are also glass beads surrounding the house, for the peyote hunters leave them as offerings to Sturiviakame as they pass by. Stepping on one of these means the death of a child. Thus the Indians have to walk with great care near the swamp. They must also cross the creek [*sic*] in five leaps. Failure to do this also means the death of a child."

7. There is actually no agreement about the names of these pools and springs, or about the gods who live there. The pilgrims from Ocota believe that the large pool is sacred to Tatei Matinieri, and the rest to Tatei Yurianaka, Tatei Haramara, and Tatei Tsakaimuka. These last are the deities of the earth, the sea, and the Coras, respectively. It also seems that the entire area belongs to Tatei Kutsaraupa, the god of clouds and rain.

8. Zingg, *The Huicholes.*

Difficulties in San Andrés

1. Unfortunately, the conditions in San Andrés at the time made it impossible for me to obtain an account of the festival from the shamans, and here I have had to depend upon a version provided by Panchito López, who is from Ocota. This undoubtedly differs from what Hilario or Eusebio might have told me, since myths and ceremonies vary according to the personal preferences of each *cantador.*

2. The grandparents pick the child up in their arms and offer it to the sun, to the gods, and finally to Tamats Kauyumari, saying: "We present our child Muwiertemai [New *Muwieri*]" or "Maiweme [The God Descended]"—or whatever name the grandfather happened to dream of the night before the ceremony.

3. Since the children are small and must fly during their journey, they are allowed to bring back only five peyotes.

4. When the squash and the ears of corn are very small, the Huicholes hasten to take them to the gods of the various regions. This means five or six additional arduous trips.

5. As a rule, the Huicholes do not go to the distant Xapawiyemetá, but leave their offerings at a spring on a hilltop near one of Xapa's houses.

6. Since historians and ethnologists have not as yet concerned themselves with assembling the ancient myths to be found scattered here and there in books and preserved orally among indigenous peoples, let alone making a systematic study of them, we are still lacking the overall view of mythology that is so necessary to an understanding of Middle American cultures. The

revenge taken by the *metates* and cooking pots for having been pounded and burned by their owners appears in the *Popul Vuh*; it is one of the many common episodes in various myths encountered today.

7. The Mazateca Indians of the plains have a similar myth. They believe they are descended from a small black dog.

8. The Indians who speak Spanish rarely conjugate their verbs in the conventional way. Instead of saying *veré* (I shall see) or *iré* (I shall go), for example, they will say *voy a ver* (I'm going to see) or *voy a ir* (I'm going to go), and the like. This makes for a lack of precision in their speech. They never quite affirm or deny anything. They are rather uneasy and uncertain in the language imposed upon them by their conquerors.

9. In Huichol the word *netey* means both ritual "mother" and "aunt." Thus Tsikoakame refers to Yurianaka as "my mother," literally "my aunt."

10. The people of Ocota use the word *chinari* for a receptacle made from a certain kind of gourd.

11. She addresses him as "father" because it is only the father who punishes a child by striking it.

12. An ancient coin with a value of three centavos.

13. These versions are not definitive. Huichol religious chants embrace a vast and complex mythology, handed down orally from one generation to the next. They are intoned during the ceremonies by the shaman. He is seated before a straw mat—the *itari*—upon which he has arranged his paraphernalia and which lies between him and Tatewarí, Grandfather Fire. These chants go on all night and sometimes into the following morning. The shaman's two assistants sit beside him, repeating the last lines of each strophe.

The shaman is both a skillful chanter and a consummate actor. His voice may range from the deepest bass to the highest falsetto, so that at times he can sound like a woman. Often he is carried away by emotion and bursts into tears; and just as often he may have his audience in gales of laughter.

This custodian of mythic treasures speaks only Huichol, of course; and the Indian teachers and village officials speak the Spanish of the poorest and most ignorant mestizo. When the shaman acts as informant he gives a summary, and the interpreter necessarily abridges the material even further. Since he is incapable of giving a word-for-word translation (which would be preferable), the interpreter merely conveys a general idea of what he hears. The investigator, with no notion of the original syntax and sentence structure, must thus be content with an approximate version.

Even so, the translations given here, the result of many hours of laborious effort, are the only detailed versions existing in either Spanish or English. Those made by Robert Mowry Zingg are too condensed and give a wholly false idea of the structure and sense of the myths.

I have resisted the temptation of giving them a "literary treatment." On the contrary, I have tried to be faithful to the interpreter's style, even to the point of retaining some of his "Mexicanisms."

Such considerations aside, I have observed that Zingg's versions—he worked exclusively in Tuxpan—are quite different from mine collected in Ocota, San Andrés, and Las Guayabas. There are several possible reasons for this. In the first place, there is the geographical isolation in which the various Huichol groups live; this seclusion is aggravated by intertribal conflicts. The personal element, too, must be kept in mind: each shaman is an artist, and he puts his individual stamp on every myth. Differences in daily life, as well as the degree to which each audience demands humorous episodes in the narratives, also introduce appreciable modifications. One might say that there exists a common mythic background upon which all these circumstances are constantly at work.

What is needed, then, is to collect chants from several different areas, find a satisfactory translator, and compare them. I have not as yet been able to do this; but someone should. Huichol mythology, one of the best preserved in all Mexican Indian folklore, constitutes not only a priceless literary heritage but also a fund of information that would help us understand the religious mechanisms of ancient cultures.

Other important aspects are the different names used to designate the same gods and the same objects of worship, the various phonetic changes, and the problem of spelling; these are technical matters belonging to a highly specialized field. It is in these areas that my work has been most deficient. I have not succeeded in normalizing the spelling of Huichol words, nor am I sure that the forms and meanings I have given are the correct ones.

There remains only to add that a fourth expedition, made after these notes were in print, has given me access to new material of great ethnographic value, which I shall publish in the second volume of *The Indians of Mexico*.

The Return of the Peyote Pilgrims

1. Pedro Haro, from Ocota.

2. A version from Ocota, supplied by Pedro Haro.

3. Trains make them think of worms because of the way they crawl over the earth. From this point to the end I have given the ceremony as I took it down in Las Guayabas.

4. Of course this mixture of the sacred and the profane, of religion and play, of spirituality and practical good sense, of the most barbaric superstitions and the most exalted mystical ideas is to be found not only among the Aztecs and the Huicholes. André Bonnard has pointed out that in the century of Sophocles, Hippocrates, and the Parthenon, the Athenians indulged in "superstitions and customs that were so grotesque, so 'Polynesian,' at times so atrociously cruel, that one would have thought he was a thousand leagues from any civilization" (*Civilisation Grecque*).

5. Johan Huizinga, *Homo Ludens* (Boston: Beacon Press, 1955).

6. Ad. E. Jensen, *Mito y culto en los pueblos primitivos*.

7. Ibid.

8. Vittorio Lanternari, *Movimenti religiosi di libertà e di salvezza dei popoli oppressi* (Milan: Ed. Feltrinelli, 1960).

The Festival of the Parched Corn

1. From this point on the shaman calls the deer either Maxa Kwaxí or Parí-tsika, the god of the hunt.

The Blood Sacrifice

1. "Then lifting his face from that bloody meal,
    He wiped his mouth with the hair
    Of the human head he fed on,
And spoke: 'Mere thought of my frightful tale
    Weighs this heart with grief enough;
    Yet you would hear it told again.
But if my words, like seeds, bear fruit
    Of infamy for the traitor I torment,
    Then hear me speak, and speaking, weep.' "

—Dante Alighieri, "Inferno," Canto XXXIII.
[My translation.—J. U.]

2. "How lovely to be young,
    Though youth is ever fleeing!
    Take pleasure while you may;
    Tomorrow may never come.

.   .   .   .

Satyrs, young and joyous,
    In pursuit of loving nymphs,
    Have set a hundred snares
    In every cave and wood;
    And now, inflamed by Bacchus,
    They dance, they dance and leap.
    Take pleasure while you may;
    Tomorrow may never come."

—Lorenzo de' Medici, "Trionfo di Bacco e Arianna."
[My translation.—J. U.]

3. Johann Paul Richter, German writer (1763–1825).—J. U.

INDEX

acculturative pressure, xiv–xv
Agua Hedionda, 95
Aitekua, 129
Akatewari, 128, 135
alcalde, 126
animals: in Huichol mythology, 76–
81, 120–128, 142, 160–164. *See also*
deer
aphrodisiac, 64
arrows: decoration of, for peyote hunt,
46; as offerings, 44, 47, 91; ritual
use of, 45, 97; in the songs of the
peyote, 76, 77–78, 79–80
authorities, appointment of, 15–16
Auxamanaka, 77, 78
Auxatemai: order of, in pilgrimage,
128; in the songs of the peyote, 80
Auxiwiriaka, 124
Auxuwiriaká, 127
Aztecs, 34

Baldosara, 135
Bautista, Antonio: illness of, 136,
138, 139; renaming of, 22; ritual
chanting by, 74; wife of, 22, 23, 24
Benítez, Fernando: experience of,
with peyote, 172–175; native distrust
of, 43
Benzi, Marino: and peyote ritual,
172, 174, 175, 176; on pilgrimage,
9, 12, 13, 137; renaming of, 22
birds: in Huichol mythology, 90, 93–

94, 102, 124, 127, 154, 155, 157–
158
black magic, 82–83
blood: ritual use of, 44, 45, 48, 97;
sacred nature of, 167; use of, in
consecration, 47, 92, 144
Blue Deer: birth of, 80; as singer, 51;
song of, 74; in the songs of the
peyote, 76, 78, 79. *See also* Elder
Brother Deer Tail; Tamats Kauyumari
Bolaños, 6, 7
bull: sacrifice of, 144, 167
Burned Hill: in the songs of the
peyote, 77. *See also* Reunar

cabeceras municipales: definition of,
6; role of, in Indian life, 7
cactus: reproduction of, 33; varieties
of, in desert, 29–32. *See also* peyote
calihuey: composition of, xiv; sanctification of land belonging to, 167–
169; in the songs of the peyote, 79,
81
candles: as offerings, 44, 47, 101, 102;
origin of ritual use of, 126; in the
songs of the peyote, 80
cantadores: influence of, on rain, 170;
mythic origins of, 160; procedure
for becoming, 85; ritual functions
of, 79. *See also mara'akame*;
shamans